COMMON CORE CODE X™

STUDENT EDITION
[COURSE I]

Further credits and acknowledgments appear on pages 318–319, which constitute an extension of this copyright page.

Copyright © 2014 by Scholastic Inc. All rights reserved.

Published by Scholastic Inc.   Printed in the U.S.A.

ISBN-13: 978-0-545-62351-3

ISBN-10: 0-545-62351-0

(meets NASTA specifications)

SCHOLASTIC, COMMON CORE CODE X, and associated logos are trademarks and/or registered trademarks of Scholastic Inc.

LEXILE and LEXILE FRAMEWORK are registered trademarks of MetaMetrics, Inc.

Other company names, brand names, and product names are the property and/or trademarks of their respective owners. Scholastic does not endorse any product or business entity mentioned herein.

Scholastic is constantly working to lessen the environmental impact of our manufacturing processes.

To view our industry-leading paper procurement policy, visit www.scholastic.com/paperpolicy.

1 2 3 4 5 6 7 8 9 10   123   22 21 20 19 18 17 16 15 14 13

Text pages printed on 20% PCW recycled paper.

[Welcome!]

Dear Reader,

Do you ever ask yourself big questions like, "Can one person make a difference?" or "What do my dreams reveal about who I am?" These are some of the questions you will explore together as you read Code X.

Here's another question: "So, what is a codex, anyway?" To find the answer, we have to go back almost 2,000 years to ancient Rome. People wrote on long rolls of paper called scrolls. These scrolls were very long and very heavy. The Romans realized there was a better way. They started stacking sheets of paper on top of each other and binding them together to make books. Soon, the whole world was using them!

The ancient codex revolutionized how people wrote and read. The Common Core Code X provides you with a whole new way to access texts. You'll ask questions to analyze and understand different kinds of texts from *The New York Times* and *Smithsonian*. You will write about new discoveries happening in ancient Egypt and create your own short story.

There's a lot to learn and investigate in Code X, so it's time to get started. Let us know what you think! Email us at CodeX@scholastic.com.

Sincerely,

The Editors

The Editors

COURSE I | Table of Contents

UNIT 1

STORIES OF SURVIVAL

UNIT 2

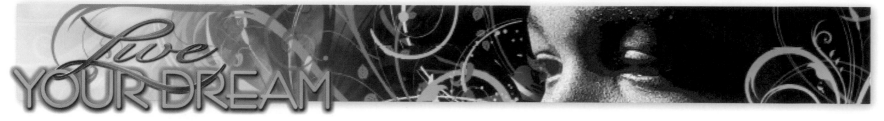

Live YOUR DREAM

UNIT 3

WORLD WONDERS

UNIT 4

Coming to America

UNIT 5

Cities of GOLD

UNIT 6

History Lost and Found

UNIT 7

THE BIG GIVE

NOVEL STUDIES

Throughout the course of the year you will read two novels. You will read some sections with your teacher and peers and some sections on your own.

- In *Tuck Everlasting*, Natalie Babbitt tells a story about a young girl who encounters a family who are doomed to—or blessed with—eternal life.

- In *I Thought My Soul Would Rise and Fly*, Joyce Hansen tells the story of Patsy, a freed slave who teaches others to read.

Tuck Everlasting
by Natalie Babbitt

I Thought My Soul Would Rise and Fly
by Joyce Hansen

CONTENT AREA ICON KEY

As you read the texts, you will learn about science, economics, history and the arts. The more you read the more you learn about the world around you.

 US History

 Economics

 Civics and Government

Science

 Math and Statistics

 Technology

Individual and Society

 Fine Art

 Environment

World History and Geography

 Earth and Weather

 Literature

STORIES OF SURVIVAL

How are people shaped by the challenges they face?

Unit Introduction

Witness how difficult situations affect and shape two different narrators.

In the short story "Tuesday of the Other June," author Norma Fox Mazer describes the ordeal of the young narrator, June, who is the target of a bully.

The speaker in Maya Angelou's poem "Life Doesn't Frighten Me" declares her inner strength in the face of terrors, both real and imaginary.

WRITING PERFORMANCE TASK

Write a short story in which a character from one of the Unit texts faces another challenging experience.

⬛ SHORT STORY/POEM _____

"Tuesday of the Other June" by Norma Fox Mazer

Language
- Academic Vocabulary
- Word Study: Context Clues

Reading Literary Text
- Identify Evidence
- Key Ideas & Details
- Craft & Structure

"Life Doesn't Frighten Me" by Maya Angelou

Language
- Academic Vocabulary
- Word Study: Suffixes

Reading Literary Text
- Identify Evidence
- Key Ideas & Details
- Craft & Structure

⬛ SPEAKING AND LISTENING _____

Present a Speech
- Collaborate and Present

Checklist: Speech
- Scoring Guide

⬛ WRITING _____

Writing: Fictional Narrative
- Student Model
- Analyze the Model
- Generate Ideas
- Organize Ideas

- Language Study: Character Development
- Conventions Study: Pronouns
- Revise, Edit, and Publish
- Performance Task Rubric

⬛ EXTENDED READING _____

Memoir
"Dirk the Protector"
from *My Life in Dog Years* by
Gary Paulsen

Academic Vocabulary

"Tuesday of the Other June" by Norma Fox Mazer

Rate your understanding of each word. Then read its meaning and write an example sentence.

Word	Meaning	Example
recite (v.) p. 11 ① ② ③ ④	to say aloud or repeat from memory	*For our final project, we each recited a poem in front of the class.*
rigid (adj.) p. 12 ① ② ③ ④	stiff; not bending	*I was very uncomfortable sitting in the rigid chair.*
torment (v.) p. 15 ① ② ③ ④	make someone suffer, especially mentally	
adjust (v.) p. 20 ① ② ③ ④	gradually get used to a new situation	
mocked (v.) p. 20 ① ② ③ ④	made fun of someone or something by copying them or making them look stupid	
devoted (adj.) p. 22 ① ② ③ ④	strongly committed or loyal to someone or something because you admire them	

Rating Scale | ① I don't know the word. ② I've seen it or heard it.
③ I know its meaning. ④ I know it and use it.

Word Study

Context Clues

Context Clues are words or phrases in a text that help you figure out the meaning of an unfamiliar word.

Make inferences to determine the meaning of the bold words in the sentences below:

1. "She was **sprawled** on the stoop of a pink house, lounging back on her elbows, legs outspread, her jaws working on a wad of gum."

2. "The Other June followed me around during recess that day, **droning** in my ear, 'You are my slave, you must do everything I say, I am your master, say it, say, "Yes, master, you are my master.""'"

Tuesday of the Other June

by Norma Fox Mazer

¶1 "Be good, be good, be good, be good, my Junie," my mother sang as she combed my hair; a song, a story, a croon, a plea. "It's just you and me, two women alone in the world, June darling of my heart; we have enough troubles getting by, we surely don't need a single one more, so you keep your sweet self out of fighting and all that bad stuff. People can be little-hearted, but turn the other cheek, smile at the world, and the world'll surely smile back."

We stood in front of the mirror as she combed my hair, combed and brushed and smoothed. Her head came just above mine; she said when I grew another inch, she'd stand on a stool to brush my hair. "I'm not giving up this pleasure!" And she laughed her long honey laugh.

¶3 My mother was April, my grandmother had been May, I was June. "And someday," said my mother, "you'll have a daughter of your own. What will you name her?"

"January!" I'd yell when I was little. "February! November!" My mother laughed her honey laugh. She had little emerald eyes that warmed me like the sun.

¶5 Every day when I went to school, she went to work. "Sometimes I stop what I'm doing," she said, "lay down my tools, and stop everything, because all I can think about is you. Wondering what you're doing and if you need me. Now, Junie, if anyone ever bothers you—"

"—I walk away, run away, come on home as fast as my feet will take me," I recited.

Close Reading

Words and Phrases in Context

1. Explain what June's mother means when she begs her daughter in **paragraph 1** to "turn the other cheek."

Writing

2. How does Mazer depict June's relationship with her mother?

   Mazer depicts June's relationship with her mother as ____, which she demonstrates using phrases such as ____ and ____.

Close Reading

Writing

3. Describe how the narrative point of view of this short story adds to your understanding of the characters.

This story is told from the point of view of ____. This helps me understand ____, because ____.

Point of View

Point of view is the lens through which the reader sees the events of a story.

Text Structure

4. How are **paragraphs 8 and 9** different from the surrounding paragraphs?

Text Structure

5. What can you infer about June based on what she says about these "robbers, thieves, and murderers" in **paragraphs 8 and 9**?

¶7 "Yes. You come to me. You just bring me your trouble, because I'm here on this earth to love you and take care of you."

I was safe with her. Still, sometimes I woke up at night and heard footsteps slowly creeping up the stairs. It wasn't my mother, she was asleep in the bed across the room, so it was robbers, thieves, and murderers, creeping slowly . . . slowly . . . slowly toward my bed.

¶9 I stuffed my hand into my mouth. If I screamed and woke her, she'd be tired at work tomorrow. The robbers and thieves filled the warm darkness and slipped across the floor more quietly than cats. **Rigid** under the covers, I stared at the shifting dark and bit my knuckles and never knew when I fell asleep again.

In the morning we sang in the kitchen. "Bill Grogan's goat! Was feelin' fine! Ate three red shirts, right off the line!" I made sandwiches for our lunches, she made pancakes for breakfast, but all she ate was one pancake and a cup of coffee. "Gotta fly, can't be late."

¶11 I wanted to be rich and take care of her. She worked too hard; her pretty hair had gray in it that she joked about. "Someday," I said, "I'll buy you a real house, and you'll never work in a pot factory again."

"Such delicious plans," she said. She checked the windows to see if they were locked. "Do you have your key?"

¶13 I lifted it from the chain around my neck. "And you'll come right home from school and—"

"—I won't light fires or let strangers into the house, and I won't tell anyone on the phone that I'm here alone," I finished for her.

¶15 "I know, I'm just your old <u>worrywart</u> mother." She kissed me twice, once on each cheek. "But you are my June, my only June, the only June."

Words to Know

<u>worrywart</u>: *(n.)* someone who worries a lot

She was wrong; there was another June. I met her when we stood next to each other at the edge of the pool the first day of swimming class in the Community Center.

¶17 "What's your name?" She had a deep growly voice.

"June. What's yours?"

¶19 She stared at me. "June."

"We have the same name."

¶21 "No we don't. June is my name, and I don't give you permission to use it. Your name is Fish Eyes." She pinched me hard. "Got it, Fish Eyes?"

The next Tuesday, the Other June again stood next to me at the edge of the pool. "What's your name?"

¶23 "June."

"Wrong. Your—name—is—Fish—Eyes."

¶25 "June."

"Fish Eyes, you are really stupid." She shoved me into the pool.

¶27 The swimming teacher looked up, frowning, from her little chart. "No one in the water yet."

Later, in the locker room, I dressed quickly and wrapped my wet suit in the towel. The Other June pulled on her jeans. "You guys see that bathing suit Fish Eyes was wearing? Her mother found it in a trash can."

¶29 "She did not!"

Close Reading

Words and Phrases in Context

6. What is the first detail Mazer uses to describe the Other June in **paragraph 17**? What is the effect of this word choice?

Text Structure

7. What is the effect of putting dashes between each of the words in the sentence "Your—name—is—Fish—Eyes" in **paragraph 24**?

Close Reading

Literary Analysis

8. What specific words and phrases describe the Other June as a bully?

Words and Phrases in Context

9. What does June mean when she uses a simile to say that the Other June was "training me like a dog" in **paragraph 34**?

Simile

A **simile** is a comparison of two things that uses *like*, *as*, or *as if*. For example, "a smile like sunshine," or "a smile as warm as the sun"

Writing

10. Why does June try to "slow down time," as she describes in **paragraphs 35–36**?

June's experiences with the Other June during the week make her feel ____, so she ____.

When June says, "I tried to slow down time," she means that she ____.

The Other June grabbed my fingers and twisted. "Where'd she find your bathing suit?"

¶31 "She bought it, let me go."

"Poor little stupid Fish Eyes is crying. Oh, boo hoo hoo, poor little Fish Eyes."

¶33 After that, everyone called me Fish Eyes. And every Tuesday, wherever I was, there was also the Other June—at the edge of the pool, in the pool, in the locker room. In the water, she swam alongside me, blowing and huffing, knocking into me. In the locker room, she stepped on my feet, pinched my arms, hid my blouse, and knotted my braids together. She had large square teeth; she was shorter than I was, but heavier, with bigger bones and square hands. If I met her outside on the street, carrying her bathing suit and towel, she'd walk toward me, smiling a square, friendly smile. "Oh well, if it isn't Fish Eyes." Then she'd punch me, blam! her whole solid weight hitting me.

I didn't know what to do about her. She was training me like a dog. After a few weeks of this, she only had to look at me, only had to growl, "I'm going to get you, Fish Eyes," for my heart to slink like a whipped dog down into my stomach. My arms were covered with bruises. When my mother noticed, I made up a story about tripping on the sidewalk.

¶35 My weeks were no longer Tuesday, Wednesday, Thursday, and so on. Tuesday was Awfulday. Wednesday was Badday. (The Tuesday bad feelings were still there.) Thursday was Betterday, and Friday was Safeday. Saturday was Goodday, but Sunday was Toosoonday, and Monday—Monday was nothing but the day before Awfulday.

I tried to slow down time. Especially on the weekends, I stayed close by my mother, doing everything with her, shopping, cooking, cleaning, going to the Laundromat. "Aw, sweetie, go play with your friends."

¶**37** "No, I'd rather be with you." I wouldn't look at the clock or listen to the radio (they were always telling you the date and the time). I did special magic things to keep the day from going away, rapping my knuckles six times on the bathroom door six times a day and never, ever touching the chipped place on my <u>bureau</u>. But always I woke up to the day before Tuesday, and always, no matter how many times I circled the worn spot in the living-room rug or counted twenty-five cracks in the ceiling, Monday disappeared and once again it was Tuesday.

The Other June got bored with calling me Fish Eyes. Buffalo Brain came next, but as soon as everyone knew that, she renamed me Turkey Nose.

¶**39** Now at night it wasn't robbers creeping up the stairs, but the Other June, coming to **torment** me. When I finally fell asleep, I dreamed of kicking her, punching, biting, pinching. In the morning I remembered my dreams and felt brave and strong. And then I remembered all the things my mother had taught me and told me.

Be good, be good, be good; it's just us two women alone in the world. . . . Oh, but if it weren't, if my father wasn't long gone, if we'd had someone else to fall back on, if my mother's mother and daddy weren't dead all these years, if my father's daddy wanted to know us instead of being glad to forget us—oh, then I would have punched the Other June with a <u>frisky</u> heart, I would have grabbed her arm at poolside and bitten her like the dog she had made of me.

¶**41** One night, when my mother came home from work, she said, "Junie, listen to this. We're moving!"

Alaska, I thought. Florida. Arizona. Someplace far away and wonderful, someplace without the Other June.

Close Reading

Text Structure

11. What details does Mazer include to show that the conflict between June and the Other June is ongoing?

Academic Vocabulary

12. What is the effect of using the word "torment" in **paragraph 39**? What does this word tell you about how June is dealing with the bullying at swimming class?

Words to Know

<u>bureau</u>: *(n.)* a piece of furniture that has many drawers for storing clothes

<u>frisky</u>: *(adj.)* full of energy and fun

Close Reading

Word and Phrases in Context

13. Use text clues in **paragraph 43** to determine the meaning of *trouble-shooters*.

Text Structure

14. How does Mazer show that April and June are getting closer to the date of their move in **paragraph 46**?

¶**43** "Wait till you hear this deal. We are going to be caretakers, trouble-shooters for an eight-family apartment building. Fifty-six Blue Hill Street. Not janitors; we don't do any of the heavy work. April and June, Trouble-shooters, Incorporated. If a <u>tenant</u> has a **complaint** or a problem, she comes to us and we either take care of it or call the janitor for service. And for that little bit of work, we get to live rent free!" She swept me around in a dance. "Okay? You like it? I do!"

So. Not anywhere else, really. All the same, maybe too far to go to swimming class? "Can we move right away? Today?"

¶**45** "Gimme a break, sweetie. We've got to pack, do a thousand things. I've got to line up someone with a truck to help us. Six weeks, Saturday the fifteenth." She circled it on the calendar. It was the Saturday after the last day of swimming class.

Soon, we had boxes lying everywhere, filled with clothes and towels and glasses wrapped in newspaper. Bit by bit, we cleared the rooms, leaving only what we needed right now. The dining-room table staggered on a bunched-up rug, our bureaus inched toward the front door like patient cows. On the calendar in the kitchen, my mother marked off the days until we moved, but the only days I thought about were Tuesdays—Awfuldays. Nothing else was real except the too fast passing of time, moving toward each Tuesday . . . away from Tuesday . . . toward Tuesday. . . .

¶**47** And it seemed to me that this would go on forever, that Tuesdays would come forever and I would be forever trapped by the side of the pool, the Other June whispering Buffalo Brain Fish Eyes Turkey Nose into my ear, while she ground her elbow into my side and smiled her square smile at the swimming teacher.

Words to Know

<u>tenant:</u> *(n.)* someone who lives in a house or apartment and pays money to the building's owner in order to live there

And then it ended. It was the last day of swimming class. The last Tuesday. We had all passed our tests, and, as if in celebration, the Other June only pinched me twice. "And now," our swimming teacher said, "all of you are ready for the Advanced Class, which starts in just one month. I have a sign-up slip here. Please put your name down before you leave." Everyone but me crowded around. I went to the locker room and pulled on my clothes as fast as possible. The Other June burst through the door just as I was leaving. "Goodbye," I yelled, "good riddance to bad trash!" Before she could pinch me again, I ran past her and then ran all the way home, singing, "Goodbye . . . goodbye . . . goodbye, good riddance to bad trash!"

¶**49** Later, my mother carefully untied the blue ribbon around my swimming class <u>diploma</u>. "Look at this! Well, isn't this wonderful! You are on your way, you might turn into an Olympic swimmer, you never know what life will bring."

"I don't want to take more lessons."

¶**51** "Oh, sweetie, it's great to be a good swimmer." But then, looking into my face, she said, "No, no, no, don't worry, you don't have to."

The next morning, I woke up hungry for the first time in weeks. No more swimming class. No more Baddays and Awfuldays. No more Tuesdays of the Other June. In the kitchen, I made hot cocoa to go with my mother's corn muffins. "It's Wednesday, Mom," I said, stirring the cocoa. "My favorite day."

¶**53** "Since when?"

"Since this morning." I turned on the radio so I could hear the announcer tell the time, the temperature, and the day.

Close Reading

Word and Phrases in Context

15. What is the meaning of the phrase "good riddance" in **paragraph 48**? What context clues helped you determine its meaning?

Writing

16. Synthesize the details in **paragraphs 52–54** and describe how June changes once swimming classes are over.

Although June ____ while she was taking swimming classes, now ____.

Words to Know

<u>diploma</u>: *(n.)* certificate stating you successfully completed a class

Close Reading

Text Structure

17. Explain what April means in **paragraph 57** when she says that the "flowered Mexican tray" is "as close to foreign travel" as she and June will ever get.

Writing

18. As they leave their old home, June says in **paragraph 58**, "it was only then that I understood we were truly going to live somewhere else, in another apartment, in another place mysteriously called Blue Hill Street." What can you infer about June's feelings in this moment?

Based on ____, I can infer that June ____.

Although June is ____, she realizes ____.

¶**55** Thursday for breakfast I made cinnamon toast, Friday my mother made pancakes, and on Saturday, before we moved, we ate the last slices of bread and cleaned out the peanut butter jar.

"Some breakfast," Tilly said. "Hello, you must be June." She shook my hand. She was a friend of my mother's from work; she wore big hoop earrings, sandals, and a skirt as dazzling as a rainbow. She came in a truck with John to help us move our things.

¶**57** John shouted cheerfully at me, "So you're moving." An **enormous** man with a face covered with little brown bumps. Was he afraid his voice wouldn't travel the distance from his mouth to my ear? "You looking at my moles?" he shouted, and he heaved our big green flowered chair down the stairs. "Don't worry, they don't bite. Ha, ha, ha!" Behind him came my mother and Tilly balancing a bureau between them, and behind them I carried a lamp and the round, flowered Mexican tray that was my mother's favorite. She had found it at a garage sale and said it was as close to <u>foreign</u> travel as we would ever get.

The night before, we had loaded our car, stuffing in bags and boxes until there was barely room for the two of us. But it was only when we were in the car, when we drove past Abdo's Grocery where they always gave us credit, when I turned for a last look at our street—it was only then that I understood we were truly going to live somewhere else, in another apartment, in another place mysteriously called Blue Hill Street.

¶**59** Tilly's truck followed our car.

"Oh, I'm so excited," my mother said. She laughed. "You'd think we were going across the country."

Words to Know

<u>foreign</u>: *(adj.)* related to a country other than your own

¶61 Our old car <u>wheezed</u> up along, steep hill. Blue Hill Street. I looked from one side to the other, trying to see everything.

My mother drove over the crest of the hill. "And now—ta da!—our new home!"

¶63 "Which house? Which one?" I looked out the window and what I saw was the Other June. She was sprawled on the stoop of a pink house, lounging back on her elbows, legs outspread, her jaws working on a wad of gum. I slid down into the seat, but it was too late. I was sure she had seen me.

My mother turned into a driveway next to a big white building with a tiny porch. She leaned on the steering wheel. "See that window there, that's our living-room window . . . and that one over there, that's your bedroom . . ."

¶65 We went into the house, down a dim, cool hall. In our new apartment, the wooden floors clicked under our shoes, and my mother showed me everything. Her voice echoed in the empty rooms. I followed her around in a <u>daze</u>. Had I imagined seeing the Other June? Maybe I'd seen another girl who looked like her. A double. That could happen.

"Ho yo, where do you want this chair?" John appeared in the doorway. We brought in boxes and bags and beds and stopped only to eat pizza and drink orange juice from the carton.

Close Reading

Literary Analysis

19. How is June seeing the Other June in **paragraph 63** an example of irony?

Irony

Irony is a conflict between what might be expected and what actually happens.

Writing

20. How does June moving close to the Other June contribute to the rising action of this story's plot?

The event contributes to the rising action because ____, and now ____.

Rising Action

Rising Action is a series of events in a narrative that gradually build up toward the climax.

Words to Know

<u>wheezed</u>: *(v.)* made a whistling sound

<u>daze</u>: *(n.)* state of feeling confused or unable to think clearly

Close Reading

Academic Vocabulary

21. What is Tilly concerned about when she asks in **paragraph 67**, "do you think she'll adjust all right?" How is June's perspective different from Tilly's or her mother's?

Academic Vocabulary

22. How does the Other June mock June in **paragraph 73?**

¶**67** "June's so quiet, do you think she'll **adjust** all right?" I heard Tilly say to my mother.

"Oh, definitely. She'll make a wonderful adjustment. She's just getting used to things."

¶**69** But I thought that if the Other June lived on the same street as I did, I would never get used to things.

That night I slept in my own bed, with my own pillow and blanket, but with floors that creaked in strange voices and walls with cracks I didn't recognize. I didn't feel either happy or unhappy. It was as if I were waiting for something.

¶**71** Monday, when the principal of Blue Hill Street School left me in Mr. Morrisey's classroom, I knew what I'd been waiting for. In that room full of strange kids, there was one person I knew. She smiled her square smile, raised her hand, and said, "She can sit next to me, Mr. Morrisey."

"Very nice of you, June M. OK, June T., take your seat. I'll try not to get you two Junes mixed up."

¶**73** I sat down next to her. She pinched my arm. "Good riddance to bad trash," she **mocked.**

I was back in the Tuesday swimming class, only now it was worse, because every day would be Awfulday. The pinching had already started. Soon, I knew, on the playground and in the halls, kids would pass me, grinning. "Hiya, Fish Eyes."

¶**74** The Other June followed me around during recess that day, droning in my ear, "You are my slave, you must do everything I say, I am your master, say it, say, 'Yes, master, you are my master.'"

I pressed my lips together, clapped my hands over my ears, but without hope. Wasn't it only a matter of time before I said the hateful words?

¶76 "How was school?" my mother said that night.

"OK."

¶78 She put a pile of towels in a bureau drawer. "Try not to be sad about missing your old friends, sweetie; there'll be new ones."

The next morning, the Other June was waiting for me when I left the house. "Did your mother get you that blouse in the garbage dump?" She butted me, shoving me against a tree. "Don't you speak anymore, Fish Eyes?" Grabbing my chin in her hands, she pried open my mouth. "Oh, ha ha, I thought you lost your tongue."

¶80 We went on to school. I sank down into my seat, my head on my arms. "June T., are you all right?" Mr. Morrisey asked. I nodded. My head was almost too heavy to lift.

The Other June went to the pencil sharpener. Round and round she whirled the handle. Walking back, looking at me, she held the three sharp pencils like three little knives.

¶82 Someone knocked on the door. Mr. Morrisey went out into the hall. Paper planes burst into the air, flying from desk to desk. Someone turned on a <u>transistor radio</u>. And the Other June, coming closer, smiled and licked her lips like a cat sleepily preparing to gulp down a mouse.

Close Reading

Writing

23. What information from earlier in the story explains why June doesn't tell her mother about the Other June?

Words and Phrases in Context

24. What is the meaning of the word *pried* in **paragraph 79**? What effect does it have on the paragraph?

Text Structure

25. Find a simile in **paragraph 81 or 82**. What does this simile tell you about how June sees her situation?

Words to Know

<u>transistor radio:</u> *(n.)* small radio that is easy to carry around

Close Reading

Writing

26. Summarize the internal conflict with which June is struggling.

Although June ____, she ____.

June ____, but she ____.

Internal Conflict

The **internal conflict** is an inner struggle or problem that a character faces.

Text Structure

27. What is the climax of this story's narrative? How can you tell?

Climax

The **climax** of a story is the turning point, when the main character's actions change the direction of the story.

I remembered my dream of kicking her, punching, biting her like a dog.

¶84 Then my mother spoke quickly in my ear: Turn the other cheek, my Junie; smile at the world, and the world'll surely smile back.

But I had turned the other cheek and it was slapped. I had smiled and the world hadn't smiled back. I couldn't run home as fast as my feet would take me. I had to stay in school—and in school there was the Other June. Every morning, there would be the Other June, and every afternoon, and every day, all day, there would be the Other June.

¶86 She frisked down the aisle, stabbing the pencils in the air toward me. A boy stood up on his desk and bowed. "My fans," he said, "I greet you." My arm twitched and throbbed, as if the Other June's pencils had already poked through the skin. She came closer, smiling her Tuesday smile.

"No," I whispered, "no." The word took wings and flew me to my feet, in front of the Other June. "Noooooo." It flew out of my mouth into her surprised face.

¶88 The boy on the desk turned toward us. "You said something, my **devoted** fans?"

"No," I said to the Other June. "Oh, no! No. No. No. No more." I pushed away the hand that held the pencils.

¶90 The Other June's eyes opened, popped wide like the eyes of somebody in a cartoon. It made me laugh. The boy on the desk laughed, and then the other kids were laughing, too.

"No," I said again, because it felt so good to say it. "No, no, no, no." I leaned toward the Other June, put my finger against her chest. Her cheeks turned red, she <u>squawked</u> something—it sounded like "Eeeraaghyou!"—and she stepped back. She stepped away from me.

¶92 The door banged, the airplanes disappeared, and Mr. Morrisey walked to his desk. "OK. OK. Let's get back to work. Kevin Clark, how about it?" Kevin jumped off the desk, and Mr. Morrisey picked up a piece of chalk. "All right, class—" He stopped and looked at me and the Other June. "You two Junes, what's going on there?"

I tried it again. My finger against her chest. Then the words. "No—more." And she stepped back another step. I sat down at my desk.

¶94 "June M.," Mr. Morrisey said.

She turned around, staring at him with that big-eyed cartoon look. After a moment she sat down at her desk with a loud slapping sound.

¶96 Even Mr. Morrisey laughed.

And sitting at my desk, twirling my braids, I knew this was the last Tuesday of the Other June.

Words to Know

<u>squawked:</u> *(v.)* made a loud, angry cry

Close Reading

Writing

28. How does June's saying "no" to the Other June in **paragraph 91** change their relationship? What details does Mazer show to illustrate this change?

After June says "no" to the Other June, ____, showing that ____.

LIterary Analysis

29. What does June mean in **paragraph 97** when she says it was "the last Tuesday of the Other June"? What is the resolution of the story's narrative?

Resolution

The **resolution** is outcome or solution to the problem and brings the story to an end.

Identify Evidence | Analyze Characters, Events, and Ideas

Reread **"Tuesday of the Other June,"** highlighting examples and events that Mazer offers to describe June's challenging experiences with the Other June. How does Mazer introduce, describe, and develop characters and events?

- In the Evidence column, record examples from the text that describe June's challenging experiences.
- In the Explanation column, explain how the evidence introduces, illustrates, or develops characters, events, and ideas.

Evidence	Source	Page	Explanation
1. "'What's your name?' She had a deep growly voice."	June	13	This is the first description of the Other June, and it shows that she is not very friendly. Her "growly" voice shows she is animal-like.
2. "'You guys see that bathing suit Fish Eyes was wearing? Her mother found it in a trash can.'"	the Other June	13	
3. "She was training me like a dog. After a few weeks of this, she only had to look at me, only had to growl, 'I'm going to get you, Fish Eyes,' for my heart to slink like a whipped dog down into my stomach."	June	14	
4. "Now at night it wasn't robbers creeping up the stairs, but the Other June, coming to torment me."	June	15	

Evidence	Source	Page	Explanation

Key Ideas and Details

Determining the Central Idea

1. Use the evidence you collected to summarize the key idea of Mazer's short story. What is the central idea of the text? Use evidence.

   _____

2. List three key characters that Mazer introduces in this excerpt. Explain why each character is important to the central idea.

Characters	Significance
June	She is the main character; she has to learn how to balance what her mom taught her about not fighting with her anger at being bullied and her need to protect herself.

3. List three key events that Mazer uses to build the conflict in the story. Explain why each event is important to the central idea.

Events	Significance
June promises her mother she won't get into trouble	June tries to keep her promise, so she does not respond when the Other June targets her.

Craft and Structure

Structure of the Narrative

1. What is the central conflict of this story?

2. Make a list of significant events that build the conflict in order.

3. How does Mazer resolve the central conflict?

Narrator's Perspective

4. How does June see the world at the beginning of the story? How has her perspective changed by the end of the story?

Academic Vocabulary

"Life Doesn't Frighten Me" by Maya Angelou

Rate your understanding of each word. Then read its meaning and write an example sentence.

Word	Meaning	Example
frighten (v.) p. 29 ① ② ③ ④	make someone feel afraid or scared	
counterpane (n.) p. 29 ① ② ③ ④	a quilt or bedspread	
shoo (v.) p. 30 ① ② ③ ④	to make someone or something annoying go away	
charm (n.) p. 31 ① ② ③ ④	an object believed to have special or magical powers	

Word Study

Suffix

A **suffix** is a word part at the end of a word that changes its meaning.

Identify the word that correctly completes the sentence below.

1. The crashing thunder (frightening/ frightened) me.

2. The sight of smoke made the fire seem (frighteningly/frightful) close.

Rating Scale | ① I don't know the word. ② I've seen it or heard it.
③ I know its meaning. ④ I know it and use it.

Life Doesn't Frighten Me

by Maya Angelou

Shadows on the wall
Noises down the hall

Life doesn't frighten me at all
Bad dogs barking loud

5 Big ghosts in a cloud
Life doesn't frighten me at all.

Mean old <u>Mother Goose</u>
Lions on the loose
They don't frighten me at all
10 Dragons breathing flame
On my counterpane
That doesn't frighten me at all.

Words to Know

<u>Mother Goose</u>: *(n.)* an imaginary author of a book of children's poems, rhymes, and fairy tales

Close Reading

Text Structure

1. Why does the speaker of the poem make a list of "bad dogs...big ghosts...Mean old Mother Goose... Lions on the loose"?

Literary Analysis

2. Why does the speaker repeat the refrain "life doesn't frighten me at all"?

Refrain

A repeated phrase or sentence, sometimes called a *chorus*.

Close Reading

Writing

3. How does the poem's speaker react to the things that "don't frighten [her] at all"? What can you infer about her from these actions in **lines 13–21**?

I can infer _____ because the speaker says _____.

Text Structure

4. How are the details in **lines 28–32** different from those in stanzas 1–4?

Text Structure

5. Why is "Kissy little girls / With their hair in curls" in **lines 30–31** in parentheses?

I go boo
Make them shoo
15 I make fun
Way they run
I won't cry
So they fly
I just smile
20 They go wild
Life doesn't frighten me at all.

Tough guys in a fight
All alone at night
Life doesn't frighten me at all.
25 Panthers in the park
Strangers in the dark
No, they don't frighten me at all.

That new classroom where
Boys all pull my hair
30 (Kissy little girls
With their hair in curls)
They don't frighten me at all.

Don't show me frogs and
snakes
And listen for my scream,
35 If I'm afraid at all
It's only in my dreams.

I've got a magic charm
That I keep up my sleeve,
I can walk the ocean floor
40 And never have to breathe.

Life doesn't frighten me at all
Not at all
Not at all.
Life doesn't frighten me at all.

Close Reading

Writing

6. What can you infer about the speaker's reaction to the boys in her class?

Based on ____, the speaker ____.

Words & Phrases in Context

7. Analyze what the speaker means in **lines 37–40**, when she says she has a "magic charm" that she "keep[s] up [her] sleeve."

Text Structure

8. How does the poem's final stanza differ from the ones before it?

Identify Evidence | Analyze Characters, Events, and Ideas

Reread **"Life Doesn't Frighten Me,"** highlighting examples and events that Angelou offers to describe how the speaker deals with challenging experiences. How does she introduce, describe, and develop characters and events?

- In the Evidence column, record examples from the text that describe the speaker's challenging experiences.
- In the Explanation column, explain how the evidence introduces, illustrates, or develops characters, events, and ideas.

Evidence	Source	Lines	Explanation
1. "Bad dogs barking loud / Big ghosts in a cloud / Life doesn't frighten me at all."	speaker	4–6	The speaker isn't afraid of real things that can be terrifying like dogs or imaginary fears, such as ghosts. Nothing scares her in real life or her imagination.
2. "I go boo / Make them shoo / I make fun / Way they run"	speaker	13–16	

Evidence	Source	Lines	Explanation

Key Ideas and Details

Determining the Central Idea

1. Summarize the key idea of Angelou's poem. What is the central idea of the text? Use evidence.

| |
| |
| |

2. List two key images that Angelou introduces in this poem. Explain why each image is important to the central idea.

Image	Significance
"Dragons breathing flame"	The speaker doesn't get scared of the things she imagines or hears in fairy tales.

3. List three key challenging events or experiences that Angelou describes the speaker facing. Explain why each is important to the central idea.

Challenges	Significance
A fight with "tough guys"	

Craft and Structure

Structure of the Poem

1. Make a list of adjectives you would use to describe the speaker in "Life Doesn't Frighten Me."

    -
    -
    -

Narrative Techniques

2. How does Angelou show the reader what her speaker is like?

3. Compare and contrast the way Mazer develops June as a character with the way Angelou develops her speaker.

June	Speaker

Collaborate and Present

Plan and Deliver a Speech

Assignment: Working in small groups, identify and then write a two-minute speech about how June and the Other June interact with each other throughout "Tuesday of the Other June."

Analyze the Content

1. Consider the following questions:
   - What scene or scenes best show how the two characters interact?
   - How do you think the Other June felt during these scenes?

2. Choose at least two examples of how the author shows the two characters interacting. Discuss why you think these examples are particularly effective.

Example	Reason

Write Your Speech

3. Using the chart of examples and reasons as talking points for the body of your speech, draft what you will say.
   - Remember to introduce yourself and your topic to your audience at the beginning of the speech, and to close with a conclusion summarizing your main points.
   - Write your speech on paper or type it using a computer.

Report

Deliver your speech.

Seeking Clarification

- So what you're saying is . . .
- So what you mean is . . .
- In other words, you think . . .
- If I understand you correctly, you are saying . . .

Reporting Ideas

- _____ pointed out . . .
- _____ indicated that . . .
- _____ emphasized . . .

Presentation

- Use good posture.
- Speak loudly and clearly.
- Make eye contact with your audience.

Speech Checklist

Use the checklist below to evaluate your collaboration skills, reasoning, and final presentation.
Think carefully about your work. If you know you completed an item thoroughly, give yourself a check (✓).

COLLABORATE AND PRESENT CHECKLIST

Comprehension & Collaboration	Evidence and Reasoning	Presentation of Knowledge & Ideas
☐ Come to discussions prepared, having read and studied the material.	☐ Explain the purpose of the presentation.	☐ Adapt language to a variety of contexts and tasks to demonstrate knowledge of formal English.
☐ Refer to evidence when contributing to the discussion.	☐ Present information relevant to the task.	☐ Include multimedia components (e.g., graphics, images, music, sound) and visual displays.
☐ Follow rules for discussions and lead by example.	☐ Explain how the two characters interact and describe how these interactions change throughout the story.	☐ Use appropriate volume/tone (clear, not too fast, too slow, or too loud) and avoid using "like" or "ummm."
☐ Ask and answer specific questions.	☐ Explain both characters' perspectives during these interactions.	☐ Have strong posture, a confident stance, and make frequent eye contact.
☐ Make comments that contribute to the topic under discussion.	☐ Use at least two examples from the text about each character.	☐ Occasionally move from one spot to another without fidgeting.
☐ Review the key ideas under discussion and demonstrate understanding of multiple perspectives through reflection and paraphrasing.	☐ Synthesize the key ideas from the speech with a conclusion.	☐ Smile and act relaxed.
Number of ✓s in this category: __	**Number of ✓s in this category:** __	**Number of ✓s in this category:** __

Total # of ✓s: __

Add up the total number of checks (✓) in each category. Then use the scoring guide below to calculate your final score.

Scoring Guide

16 to 18 ✓s	13 to 15 ✓s	11 to 12 ✓s	10 or less ✓s
④ Exemplary	③ Meets Standards	② Needs Work	① Does Not Meet Standards

Read the Model

Writers of fictional narratives use many techniques to craft stories about real or imagined experiences or events. The writer of this short story uses descriptive details, dialogue, and a logical sequence to tell about the challenging experience faced by a character. Read and discuss the model short story below.

The Scar   By Mia Walters

Fictional Narrative

A **fictional narrative** tells about imagined experiences or events.

The **introduction** engages the reader by establishing the setting and introducing the narrator and/or characters.

- Find the clues that describe the point of view of the narrative.

The **body** uses dialogue, description, and transition words and phrases to develop experiences, events, and characters.

- Locate the transition words.

The **conclusion** follows from narrated events and contains the resolution.

- Describe the resolution of this story.

"Quit your crying, boy!" bellowed my father as he stomped into the kitchen. "I myself never cried a tear in my life!" He loomed over me, looking as mad as a hive of hornets that's been knocked out of a tree.

Frightened, I tried to show him the angry, blistering skin on the hand I'd burnt cooking on our grease-splattered pan. He swatted my hand away as if it were an annoying insect.

"You oughta be happy you even got hot food! You hear me? Happy!"

It got so that whenever he looked at me with his eyes spitting venom, I'd back away saying nervously, "I'm happy, daddy!"

Soon enough, Happy became my name.

Years later, while my buddy Weasel and I roamed the streets looking for prey, he said, "What's your real name, Happy?"

I had to think for a long minute. Then I shrugged. "Don't remember."

Later that night, Daddy was waiting for me. As usual.

"Well?" he snarled, looking like that rangy mutt that took a bite out of me once.

I dumped the cash onto the table. "Is that all?" he snapped, grabbing the bills.

"I kept five dollars."

He stopped counting. I saw a flash in his eye. "We got ourselves a little problem then," he said, holding out his hard, beefy hand. "That money's mine."

I held the bill tight in my fist. The scar from my long-ago burn was glossy in the lamplight. Something inside me grew tight and then snapped.

I pushed the bill into my pocket. "Goodbye, Daddy," I said, turning away from his thick, stunned stare. "You always told me I should be happy. Well, I aim to be."

Analyze the Model

A fictional narrative includes characters, setting, plot events, a problem or conflict that a character faces, a climax, and the resolution to the problem.

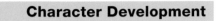

Character Development

Writers develop characters by showing what they think, say, and do over the course of the story.

They also include descriptive details and sensory language to help readers picture characters.

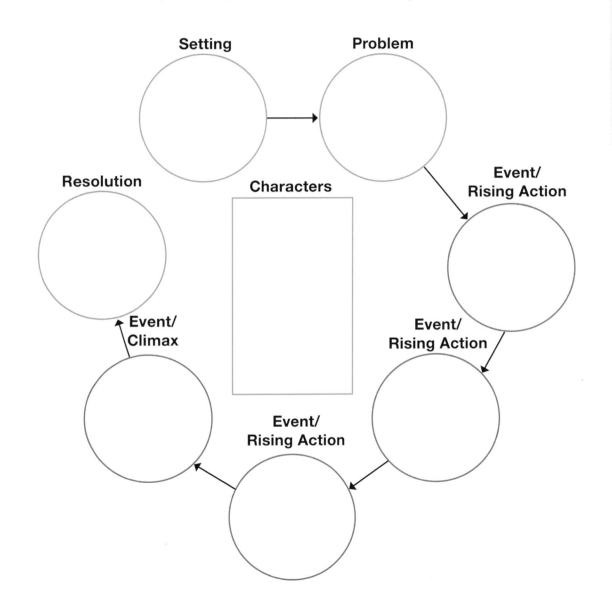

Step 1 | Generate Ideas

[**Write a short story in which a character from one of the Unit texts faces another challenging experience.**]

What You Need to Know | Examine the evidence you have collected about the ways that the characters, events, and ideas are described in "Tuesday of the Other June" and "Life Doesn't Frighten Me." (see pages 24–25 and 32–33).

What You Need to Write | Brainstorm ideas for the characters, problem, and resolution you will write about in your narrative.

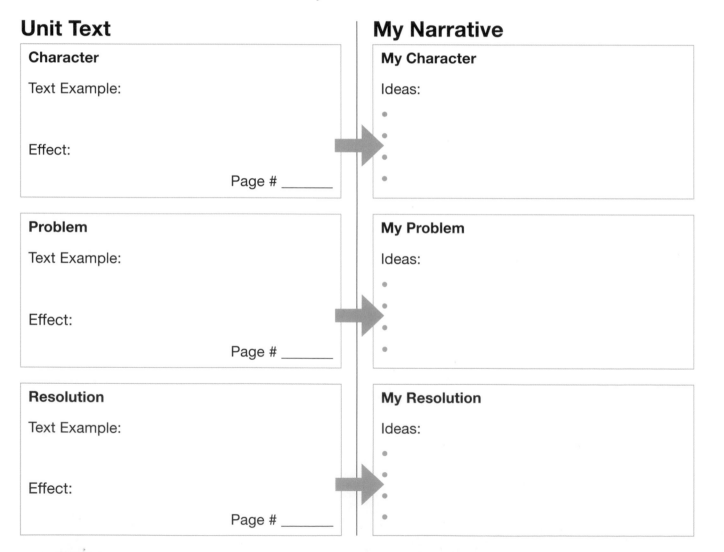

Unit Text

Character

Text Example:

Effect:

Page # _____

Problem

Text Example:

Effect:

Page # _____

Resolution

Text Example:

Effect:

Page # _____

My Narrative

My Character

Ideas:

-
-
-
-

My Problem

Ideas:

-
-
-
-

My Resolution

Ideas:

-
-
-
-

Step 2 | Organize Ideas

What You Need to Know | The big ideas about the challenging experience of the character.

To develop your narrative:

1. Describe the character(s) your narrative will feature and the setting in which it will take place.

2. Select the problem/conflict that your main character will face.

What You Need to Write | Select and describe the important elements of your narrative.

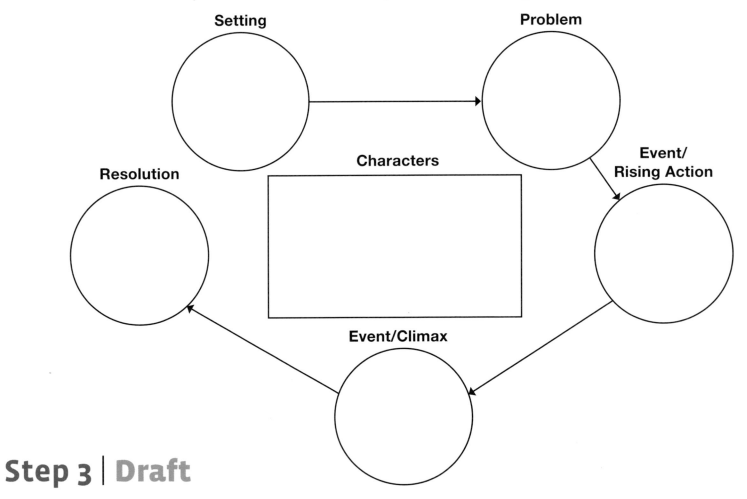

Step 3 | Draft

Write a draft of your essay on the computer or on paper.

Language Study | Character Development

See It | Authors describe their characters' actions, personalities, and dialogue to allow the readers to better understand what these characters are like.

Try It | Each sentence on the left makes a statement about a certain personality trait of a fictional character. The sentences on the right describe actions that illustrate each personality trait. Match each description to the character it describes.

1. Alex is envious.	A. A few miles into their hike, he saw his grandfather struggling to keep up. Without a word, the boy took the older man's backpack and slipped it on his shoulders. It was heavy, but he bore it without complaint.
2. Taylor enjoys solitude.	B. "Are you nervous for the track meet tomorrow?" "No," she shrugged. "I've been training hard. If I focus and run my best, I know I can win."
3. Jordan is selfless.	C. "I wish I could sing as well as Mike," he grumbled. "He gets every solo in chorus. I'd like a chance to be in the spotlight sometimes, too."
4. Cameron is confident.	D. Climbing out of her boat, she surveyed the landscape around her. Miles away from the nearest cabin, she could see nothing but forest. With a contented sigh, she closed her eyes and listened to the peaceful song of the crickets.

Apply It | Describe a character in your narrative using one of the frames below.

1. _____ is _____. _____ enjoys _____. _____ often
       (character)   (adjective)   (character/pronoun)   (action)   (character/pronoun)

   _____.
     (action)

2. _____ is _____. _____ always _____. _____ doesn't
       (character)   (adjective)   (character/pronoun)   (action)   (character/pronoun)

   _____.
     (action)

3. _____ is _____. _____ tries never to _____. When _____
       (character)   (adjective)   (character/pronoun)   (action)   (character/pronoun)

   _____. _____ _____.
     (action)   (character)   (action)

4. When _____ _____, it shows that _____ is _____.
         (character)   (action)   (character/pronoun)   (adjective)

Conventions Study | Using Pronouns

See It | Pronouns help writers avoid repetition by replacing nouns that have already been named. Intensive pronouns emphasize the subject of the sentence.

Try It | Find the pronouns that the writer used in the sentences below, taken from the model. Where did she use a pronoun to avoid repetition? What subject is emphasized by the use of an intensive pronoun?

> "Quit your crying, boy!" bellowed my father. "I myself never cried a tear in my life!" He loomed over me, looking as mad as a hive of hornets that's been knocked out of a tree.

Apply It | Rewrite these sentences using a pronoun for the underlined words.

1. "My dog ran away!" <u>my friend Jessie</u> yelped.

_____

2. We searched all over the neighborhood with <u>her dad and brothers</u>.

_____

3. When we finally found him, <u>the dog's</u> fur was caked in mud.

_____

4. I hope I never lose <u>my dog</u> like that!

_____

Step 4 | Revise and Edit   Revise your draft with a partner.

Organization and Clarity					
Establish the narrator, characters, point of view and setting at the beginning of the story.	Self	1	2	3	4
	Partner	1	2	3	4
Organize the events of the narrative in a clear and logical order.	Self	1	2	3	4
	Partner	1	2	3	4
Develop characters and plot with narrative techniques like dialogue and descriptive details.	Self	1	2	3	4
	Partner	1	2	3	4
Use transition words and phrases to show shifts from one time or setting to another.	Self	1	2	3	4
	Partner	1	2	3	4
Use relevant descriptive details, sensory language, and precise words and phrases.	Self	1	2	3	4
	Partner	1	2	3	4
Provide an ending that comes naturally after the events/experiences in the story.	Self	1	2	3	4
	Partner	1	2	3	4
Evidence and Reasoning					
Introduce a character from either "Tuesday of the Other June" or "Life Doesn't Frighten Me" and develop the character in a way consistent with the Unit text.	Self	1	2	3	4
	Partner	1	2	3	4
Describe a fictional challenge that the character experiences and a resolution that details how the character faces it.	Self	1	2	3	4
	Partner	1	2	3	4
Language and Conventions					
Recognize and correct variations from standard English.	Self	1	2	3	4
	Partner	1	2	3	4
Spell all words correctly and use proper punctuation and pronouns.	Self	1	2	3	4
	Partner	1	2	3	4

Scoring Guide | ① needs improvement   ② average   ③ good   ④ excellent

Step 5 | Publish   Publish your story either in print or digital form.

Publish

Publish your story either in print or digital form. Use the rubric below to assess your final performance task.

PERFORMANCE TASK RUBRIC

Score Point	Organization and Clarity	Evidence and Reasoning	Language and Conventions
Exemplary ④	• beginning of story **effectively** introduces the main character(s) and establishes point of view • middle of the story **describes** the challenging experience facing one character and **expertly develops** the character by showing what he/she thinks, says, and does • uses transition words and phrases to show shifts from one time setting to another • ending of story **wraps up the story by describing** how the challenge/conflict is resolved	• **clearly establishes** a point of view and maintains that point of view throughout the story • develops the conflict and its resolution by precisely **describing** the actions of key characters • **meaningfully** uses narrative strategies such as dialogue, figurative language, and foreshadowing to develop the plot	• **demonstrates a strong command** of the conventions of standard English grammar and usage, as well as of standard English capitalization, punctuation, and spelling • includes **well-chosen** pronouns to avoid repetition • vocabulary is **appropriate** to the plot (a variety of words and phrases to narrate story events; figurative language to describe characters and events; vocabulary that describes the main character and the challenge)
Meets Standards ③	• beginning of story **introduces** the main character(s) and establishes the point of view • middle of story **develops** the challenge/conflict in the story and **describes** what the main character thinks, says, and does • uses transition words and phrases to show shifts from one time setting to another • ending of story **describes** how the challenge/conflict is resolved	• **adequately establishes** and maintains a point of view • develops the conflict and its resolution by **describing** the actions of key characters • **adequately uses narrative strategies** such as dialogue, figurative language, and foreshadowing to develop the plot	• **demonstrates a near command** of the conventions of standard English grammar and usage, as well as of standard English capitalization, punctuation, and spelling **with some errors** • includes pronouns to avoid repetition • vocabulary is **appropriate** to the development of the plot (a variety of words and phrases to narrate story events; figurative language to describe characters and events; vocabulary that describes the main character and challenges)

PERFORMANCE TASK RUBRIC

Score Point	Organization and Clarity	Evidence and Reasoning	Language and Conventions
Needs Work ②	• beginning of story **partially introduces** the main character(s) and point of view • middle of story **somewhat develops** the challenge/conflict in the story; main character is poorly described • uses limited transition words and phrases • ending **attempts to resolve** the conflict and **explain** what the character does	• fails to establish a consistent point of view • partially develops the challenge/conflict by **describing** the actions of key characters • **uses some narrative strategies** such as dialogue, figurative language, and foreshadowing to develop the plot	• demonstrates a **marginal command** of the conventions of English grammar and usage, as well as of standard English capitalization, punctuation, and spelling • there **are many errors, however the text is still understandable** • includes **limited** pronouns to add variety • includes only **one or two examples** of vocabulary that is appropriate to the plot (a variety of words and phrases to narrate story events; figurative language to describe characters and events; vocabulary that describes the main character and the challenge he/she faces)
Does Not Meet Standards ①	• beginning of story **does not establish** the main characters and/or point of view • middle of story is **disorganized and/or lacks description and transitions** • ending is **unclear and/or does not explain** how the character overcomes the challenge/conflict	• **partial story development** without a clear understanding of the challenge facing the main character and how that challenge can be overcome	• demonstrates **almost no command** of the conventions of standard English grammar and usage or standard English capitalization, punctuation, and spelling • there **are many errors that disrupt** the reader's understanding of the text • **does not include** vocabulary that is appropriate to the plot (a variety of words and phrases to narrate story events; figurative language to describe characters and events; vocabulary that describes the main character and the challenge he/she faces)

Questions

Words and Phrases in Context

1. What does the author mean in **paragraph 1** when he writes that he became a "street kid"?

Key Ideas and Details

2. Based on **paragraph 1–5**, describe what Paulsen's life was like during this time.

"Dirk the Protector"

from *My Life in Dog Years* by Gary Paulsen

¶1 For a time in my life I became a street kid. It would be nice to put it another way but what with the drinking at home and the difficulties it caused with my parents I couldn't live in the house.

I made a place for myself in the basement by the furnace and hunted and fished in the woods around the small town. But I had other needs as well—clothes, food, school supplies—and they required money.

¶3 I was not afraid of work and spent most of my summers working on farms for two, three and finally five dollars a day. This gave me enough for school clothes, though never for enough clothes of the right kind; I was never cool or in. But during the school year I couldn't leave town to work the farms. I looked for odd jobs but most of them were taken by the boys who stayed in town through the summer. All the conventional jobs like working in the markets or at the drugstore were gone and all I could find was setting <u>pins</u> in the small bowling alley over the Four Clover Bar.

It had just six alleys and they were busy all the time—there were leagues each night from seven to eleven—but the pay for truly brutal work was only seven cents a line. There weren't many boys willing to do the work but with so few alleys, it was still very hard to earn much money. A dollar a night was not uncommon and three was outstanding.

¶5 To make up the difference I started selling newspapers in the bars at night. This kept me up and out late, and I often came home at midnight. But it added to my income so that I could <u>stay above water</u>.

Words to Know

<u>pins:</u> *(n.)* in bowling, bottle shaped objects that bowlers try to knock down with a heavy ball

<u>stay above water:</u> *(idiom)* earn just enough money to buy what is needed

Unfortunately it also put me in the streets at a time when there was what might be called a rough element. There weren't gangs then, not exactly, but there were groups of boys who more or less hung out together and got into trouble. They were the forerunners of the gangs we have now, but with some singular differences.

¶7 These groups were predatory, and they hunted the streets at night. I became their favorite target in this dark world. Had the town been larger I might have hidden from them, or found different routes. But there was only a small uptown section and it was impossible for me to avoid them. They would catch me walking a dark street and surround me and with threats and blows steal what money I had earned that night.

I tried fighting back but there were usually several of them. I couldn't win. Because I was from "the wrong side of the tracks" I didn't think I could go to the authorities. It all seemed hopeless.

¶9 And then I met Dirk.

The bowling alley was on a second floor and had a window in back of the pit area. When all the lanes were going, the heat from the pin lights made the temperature close to a hundred degrees. Outside the window a ladder led to the roof. One fall evening, instead of leaving work through the front door, I made my way out the window and up the ladder onto the roof. I hoped to find a new way home to escape the boys who waited for me. That night one of the league bowlers had bowled a perfect game—300—and in celebration had bought the pit boys hamburgers and Cokes. I had put the burger and Coke in a bag to take back to my basement. The bag had grease stains and smelled of toasted buns, and my mouth watered as I moved from the roof of the bowling alley to the flat roof over the hardware store, then down a fire escape that led to a dark <u>alcove</u> off an alley.

Questions

Words and Phrases in Context
3. What is the meaning of the word *predatory* in **paragraph 7**? What context clues helped you determine its meaning?

Text Structure
4. Which sentence on **page 49** signals an upcoming shift in Paulsen's situation?

Words to Know

<u>alcove:</u> *(n.)* a part of a room or wall set back further from the wall surrounding it

Questions

Key Ideas and Details

5. What descriptive words and sensory details develop the author's experience in **paragraphs 11–14?**

Key Ideas and Details

6. Explain the example of irony in **paragraph 17**.

¶11 There was a black space beneath the stairs and as I reached the bottom and my foot hit the ground I heard a low growl. It was not loud, more a rumble that seemed to come from the earth and so full of menace that it stopped me cold, my foot frozen in midair.

I raised my foot and the growl stopped.

¶13 I lowered my foot and the growl came again. My foot went up and it stopped.

I stood there, trying to peer through the steps of the fire escape. For a time I couldn't see more than a dark shape crouched back in the gloom. There was a head and a back, and as my eyes became accustomed to the dark I could see that it had scraggly, scruffy hair and two eyes that glowed yellow.

¶15 We were at an <u>impasse</u>. I didn't want to climb up the ladder again but if I stepped to the ground it seemed likely I would be bitten. I hung there for a full minute before I thought of the hamburger. I could use it as a <u>decoy</u> and get away.

The problem was the hamburger smelled so good and I was so hungry.

¶17 I decided to give the beast under the stairs half a burger. I opened the sack, unwrapped the tinfoil and threw half the sandwich under the steps, then jumped down and ran for the end of the alley. I was just getting my stride, legs and arms pumping, pulling air with a heaving chest, when I rounded the corner and ran smack into the latest group of boys who were terrorizing me.

There were four of them, led by a thug—he and two of the others would ultimately land in prison—named, absurdly, "Happy" Santun.

¶19 Happy was built like an upright freezer and had just about half the intelligence but this time it was easy. I'd run right into him.

"Well—lookit here. He came to us this time. . ."

Words to Know

<u>impasse:</u> *(n.)* a situation with no escape or solution

<u>decoy:</u> *(n.)* something used to attract attention away from something else

¶21 Over the months I had developed a policy of flee or die—run as fast as I could to avoid the pain, and to hang on to my hard-earned money. Sometimes it worked, but most often they caught me.

This time, they already had me. I could have handed over the money, taken a few hits and been done with it, but something in me snapped and I hit Happy in the face with every ounce of strength in my puny body.

¶23 He brushed off the blow easily and I went down in a welter of blows and kicks from all four of them. I curled into a ball to protect what I could. I'd done this before, many times, and knew that they would stop sometime—although I suspected that because I'd hit Happy it might take longer than usual for them to get bored hitting me. Instead there was some commotion that I didn't understand and the kicks stopped coming. There was a snarling growl that seemed to come from the bowels of the earth, followed by the sound of ripping cloth, screams, and then the fading slap of footsteps running away.

For another minute I remained curled up, then opened my eyes to find that I was alone.

¶25 But when I rolled over I saw the dog.

It was the one that had been beneath the stairs. Brindled, patches of hair gone, one ear folded over and the other standing straight and notched from fighting. He didn't seem to be any particular breed. Just big and rangy, right on the edge of ugly, though I would come to think of him as beautiful. He was Airedale crossed with hound crossed with alligator.

¶27 Alley dog. Big, tough, mean alley dog. As I watched he spit cloth—it looked like blue jeans—out of his mouth.

Words to Know

brindled: *(adj.)* brown with spots or streaks of another color

Airedale: *(n.)* a large dog with wiry black and brown fur

Questions

Words and Phrases in Context

7. What does the author mean when he writes that "something in me snapped" in **paragraph 22?** What caused him to snap?

Key Ideas and Details

8. What details in **paragraph 23** help you understand why Happy and his gang run away? Why is this event significant?

Questions

Text Structure

9. How is **paragraph 29** different from the previous paragraphs?

Key Ideas and Details

10. What causes the change in the relationship between Paulsen and the dog?

"You bit Happy, and sent them running?" I asked.

¶29 He growled, and I wasn't sure if it was with <u>menace</u>, but he didn't bare his teeth and didn't seem to want to attack me. Indeed, he had saved me.

"Why?" I asked. "What did I do to deserve. . .oh, the hamburger."

¶31 I swear, he pointedly looked at the bag with the second half of hamburger in it.

"You want more?"

¶33 He kept staring at the bag and I thought, Well, he sure as heck deserves it. I opened the sack and gave him the rest of it, which disappeared down his throat as if a hole had opened into the universe.

He looked at the bag.

¶35 "That's it," I said, brushing my hands together. "The whole thing."

A low growl.

¶37 "You can rip my head off—there still isn't any more hamburger." I removed the Coke and handed him the bag, which he took, held on the ground with one foot and deftly ripped open with his teeth.

"See? Nothing." I was up by this time and I started to walk away. "Thanks for the help . . ."

¶39 He followed me. Not close, perhaps eight feet back, but matching my speed. It was now nearly midnight and I was tired and sore from setting pins and from the kicks that had landed on my back and sides.

"I don't have anything to eat at home but crackers and peanut butter and jelly," I told him. I kept some food in the basement of the apartment building, where I slept near the furnace.

Words to Know

<u>menace:</u> (n.) a threatening or dangerous feeling or way of behaving

¶**41** He kept following and, truth be known, I didn't mind. I was still half scared of him but the memory of him spitting out bits of Happy's pants and the sound of the boys running off made me smile. When I arrived at the apartment house I held the main door open and he walked right in. I opened the basement door and he followed me down the steps into the <u>furnace</u> room.

I turned the light on and could see that my earlier judgment had been correct. He was scarred from fighting, skinny and flat sided and with patches of hair gone. His nails were worn down from scratching concrete.

¶**43** "Dirk," I said. "I'll call you Dirk." I had been trying to read a detective novel and there was a tough guy in it named Dirk. "You look like somebody named Dirk."

And so we sat that first night. I had two boxes of Ritz crackers I'd hustled somewhere, a jar of peanut butter and another one of grape jelly, and a knife from the kitchen upstairs. I would smear a cracker, hand it to him—he took each one with great care and gentleness—and then eat one myself.

¶**45** We did this, back and forth, until both boxes were empty and my stomach was bulging; then I fell asleep on the old outdoor lounge I used for furniture.

The next day was a school day. I woke up and found Dirk under the basement stairs, watching me. When I opened the door he trotted up the steps and outside—growling at me as he went past—and I started off to school.

¶**47** He followed me at a distance, then stopped across the street when I went into the front of the school building. I thought I'd probably never see him again.

But he was waiting when I came out that afternoon, sitting across the street by a mailbox. I walked up to him.

¶**49** "Hi, Dirk." I thought of petting him but when I reached a hand out he growled. "All right—no touching."

Questions

Text Structure
11. How does the description of Dirk in **paragraph 42** contrast with the initial description of him in **paragraphs 11–15**?

Key Ideas and Details
12. What details does the author include in **paragraphs 47–48** to help the reader understand why he thinks he will never see Dirk again?

Words to Know

<u>furnace:</u> *(n.)* a large piece of equipment used to heat a building

Questions

Words and Phrases in Context

13. What clue in **paragraph 52** helps you understand the meaning of the word *cohorts* **in paragraph 51**?

Key Ideas and Details

14. Why is Dirk's defense of the author in **paragraph 53** one of the "great moments" in Paulsen's life?

I turned and made my way toward the bowling alley. It was Friday and sometimes on Friday afternoon there were people who wanted to bowl early and I could pick up a dollar or two setting pins.

¶51 Dirk followed about four feet back—closer than before—and as I made my way along Second Street and came around the corner by Ecker's Drugstore I ran into Happy. He had only two of his cohorts with him and I don't think they had intended to do me harm, but I surprised them and Happy took a swing at me.

Dirk took him right in the middle. I mean bit him in the center of his stomach, hard, before Happy's fist could get to me. Happy screamed and doubled over and Dirk went around and ripped into his rear and kept tearing at it even as Happy and his two <u>companions</u> fled down the street.

¶53 It was absolutely great. Maybe one of the great moments in my life. I had a bodyguard.

It was as close to having a live nuclear weapon as you can get. I cannot say we became friends. I touched him only once, when he wasn't looking—I petted him on the head and received a growl and a lifted lip for it. But we became constant companions. Dirk moved into the basement with me, and I gave him a hamburger every day and hustled up dog food for him and many nights we sat down there eating Ritz crackers and he watched me working on stick model airplanes.

¶55 He followed me to school, waited for me, followed me to the bowling alley, waited for me. He was with me everywhere I went, always back three or four feet, always with a soft growl, and to my great satisfaction every time he saw Happy— every time—Dirk would try to remove some part of his body with as much violence as possible.

Words to Know

<u>companions:</u> *(n.)* friends; people you spend time with

He caused Happy and his mob to change their habits. They not only stopped hunting me but went out of their way to avoid me, or more specifically, Dirk. In fact after that winter and spring they never bothered me again, even after Dirk was gone.

¶**57** Dirk came to a wonderful end. I always thought of him as a street dog—surely nobody owned him—and in the summer when I was hired to work on a farm four miles east of town I took him with me. We walked all the way out to the farm, Dirk four feet in back of me, and he would <u>trot</u> along beside the tractor when I plowed, now and then chasing the hundreds of seagulls that came for the worms the plow turned up.

The farmer, whose name was Olaf, was a bachelor and did not have a dog. I looked over once to see Dirk sitting next to Olaf while we ate some sandwiches and when Olaf reached out to pet him Dirk actually—this was the first time I'd seen it—wagged his tail. He'd found a home.

¶**59** I worked the whole summer there and when it came time to leave, Dirk remained sitting in the yard as I walked down the driveway. The next summer I had bought an old Dodge for twenty-five dollars and I drove out to Olaf's to say hello and saw Dirk out in a field with perhaps two hundred sheep. He wasn't herding them, or chasing them, but was just standing there, watching the flock.

"You have him with the sheep?" I asked Olaf.

¶**61** He nodded. "Last year I lost forty-three to <u>coyotes</u>," he said. "This year not a one. He likes to guard things, doesn't he?"

I thought of Dirk chasing Happy down the street, and later spitting bits of his pants, and I smiled. "Yeah, he sure does."

Questions

Key Ideas and Details

15. What does Paulsen mean in **paragraph 57** when he says he "always thought of him as a street dog"?

Words to Know

<u>trot</u>: *(v.)* to run slowly with short, even steps

<u>coyotes</u>: *(n.)* wild animals that are related to dogs and live in North America

Literature Circle Leveled Novels

Bone: Out From Boneville by Jeff Smith
Follow the three Bone cousins—Fone Bone, Phoney Bone, and Smiley Bone—out of Boneville and into a valley peopled with interesting characters and creatures. **Lexile**® measure: GN360L

Shiloh by Phyllis Reynolds Naylor
When Marty Prestor happens upon a mistreated beagle pup, he questions himself and wonders what to do. Should he rescue the pup, help it, or return it to its owner? **Lexile**® measure: 890L

The Graveyard Book by Neil Gaiman
After his parents are murdered, a toddler wanders into a graveyard, where the place's ghastly residents adopt him and dub him "Bod." With help from ghosts, ghouls, and a guardian named Silas, Bod grows up and learns how to fend for himself both inside and outside the graveyard. **Lexile**® measure: 820L

Fiction, Nonfiction, and Novels

Nory Ryan's Song by Patricia Reilly Giff. Read the story of one young girl who refuses to give in to the hunger, exhaustion, and hopelessness of the Irish potato famine. **Lexile**® measure: 600L

Lord of the Flies by William Golding. What happens when a group of boys becomes marooned on an uninhabited island? Attempts at civilization descend into chaos, savagery, and violence. **Lexile**® measure: 770L

Julie of the Wolves by Jean Craighead George. When 13-year-old Julie runs away from her future husband and his parents, she gets stranded on the tundra and has to depend on wolves for help. **Lexile**® measure: 860L

The Worst-Case Scenario: Survival Handbook by Joshua Piven. See how you would fare if you had to land in a Dumpster, wrestle an alligator, escape killer bees, or perform a tracheotomy. **Lexile**® measure: 960L

Island of the Blue Dolphins by Scott O'Dell. Karana is forced to fend for herself when her entire family and village abandon her on an island. **Lexile**® measure: 1000L

Hatchet by Gary Paulsen. A crash landing in the middle of the Canadian wilderness leaves Brian with just the clothes on his back and a small hatchet. Can he learn to survive? **Lexile**® measure: 1020L

Shipwreck at the Bottom of the World by Jennifer Armstrong. After being shipwrecked in Antarctica, Shackleton and his men all survive to tell the tale. **Lexile**® measure: 1090L

SAS Survival Handbook by John Lofty Wiseman. Be prepared for any type of emergency with this book, which includes supply lists and instructions for making camp and finding food.

Films and TV

The American Experience: The Donner Party (PBS, 2004) Experience the gripping story of the Donner Party, which got stranded in the Sierra Nevada mountains in 1846. (90 min.)

Cast Away (20th Century Fox, 2002; rated PG-13) Tom Hanks's character hones his survival skills after a plane crash in the Pacific. (143 min.)

The Crocodile Hunter (Family Home Entertainment, 2001) Dodge the snapping jaws of crocodiles with Steve Irwin as he relives some of his most dangerous adventures. (170 min.)

Gilligan's Island: The Complete Series Collection (Turner Home Entertainment, 2007) Find out what happens when Gilligan, the Skipper, the millionaire and his wife, the movie star, the professor, and Mary Ann are stranded on an island for four TV seasons. (2,507 min.)

Man vs. Wild (Discovery Channel) Tag along after Bear Gryllis as he faces sweltering deserts, raging rivers, poisonous plants, and icy mountain peaks.

Survivorman (Discovery Channel, 2007) Watch survival expert Les Stroud struggle to survive for a week in an extreme environment—with virtually no supplies. (404 min.)

Swiss Family Robinson (Disney, 2002) Watch the Swiss Family Robinson turn their island prison into a paradise, complete with an elaborate tree house and a zoo. But can they defend their home from treacherous pirates? (126 min.)

Treasure Island (Disney, 2003) Strap on your pantaloons and set sail in search of buried treasure with Jim Hawkins and Blind Pew.

Websites

American Hiking Society Learn about hiking throughout the United States, including gear, trails, and preparation.

Backpacker Magazine: How to Do Everything Find out how to cope with bumps along the road, from rattlesnakes and mountain lions to fatigue, blisters, and navigation.

The Iditarod Ride behind the dogsled, track the dog teams, or watch videos of dogs and their mushers attempting to survive in the below-zero temperatures of Alaska.

Man vs. Wild: Bear's Blog Read Bear's thoughts about surviving in extreme environments such as Antarctica, Belize, and Turkey.

Magazines

Outside Find out what it takes to climb mountains, bike through plains, and explore vistas throughout the United States.

National Geographic: Adventure Raft through the Grand Canyon or hike through Bolivia with the writers of this magazine.

National Geographic: Kids Learn about faraway places and how to survive in them.

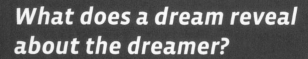

Live YOUR DREAM

What does a dream reveal about the dreamer?

Unit Introduction

In these excerpts from a biography and a memoir, discover the youthful dreams and challenges of two famous individuals.

In an excerpt from his biography *The Life You Imagine*, baseball star Derek Jeter describes setting what may have seemed like an unrealistic goal, and then explains how he achieved that goal.

In his memoir *Dreams From My Father*, President Barack Obama reveals how the challenge to understand his father became his own search for a meaning to life.

WRITING PERFORMANCE TASK

Explain the strategies these writers use to convey their experiences, challenges, and goals.

BIOGRAPHY/MEMOIR _____

from **The Life You Imagine**
by Derek Jeter with Jack Curry

from **Dreams From My Father**
by Barack Obama

Language
- Academic Vocabulary
- Word Study: Context Clues

Language
- Academic Vocabulary
- Word Study: Latin Roots

Reading Informational Text
- Identify Evidence
- Key Ideas and Details
- Craft and Structure

Reading Informational Text
- Identify Evidence
- Key Ideas and Details
- Craft and Structure

SPEAKING AND LISTENING _____

Present a Speech
- Collaborate and Present

Checklist: Speech
- Scoring Guide

WRITING _____

Writing: Informative Essay
- Read the Model
- Analyze the Model
- Gather Evidence
- Organize Ideas

- Language Study: Combining and Rewriting Sentences
- Conventions Study: Using Pronouns Correctly
- Revise, Edit, and Publish
- Performance Task Rubric

EXTENDED READING _____

Magazine Article
"Peak Performance"
by Samantha Larson
from *Teen Vogue*

Academic Vocabulary

from *The Life You Imagine* by Derek Jeter with Jack Curry

Rate your understanding of each word. Then read its meaning and write an example. If the example is given, write the meaning.

Word	Meaning	Example
apply *(v.)* p. 61 ① ② ③ ④	to be relevant or useful toward	
achieve *(v.)* p. 61 ① ② ③ ④	to reach a goal; to successfully complete something good	
envious *(adj.)* p. 62 ① ② ③ ④		I feel envious when my friends are on vacation and I'm stuck at home.
consider *(v.)* p. 62 ① ② ③ ④	to think of someone or something in a particular way; to think deeply	
consume *(v.)* p. 62 ① ② ③ ④	if an idea consumes you, it affects you very strongly, so that you can only focus on that idea	
grand *(adj.)* p. 62 ① ② ③ ④	big or very impressive; intended to achieve something impressive	

Rating Scale
① I don't know the word.
③ I know its meaning.
② I've seen it or heard it.
④ I know it and use it.

Word Study

Context Clues

Context Clues are words in a text that help you figure out the meaning of an unfamiliar word. Sometimes words are defined in the text or meaning is suggested.

The sentences below are from Derek Jeter's biography. Find the context clues to determine the meaning of the bold words.

1. My dream may not **coincide** with your dreams. You may dream about being a detective, a teacher, or the President of the United States.

2. We're talking about life, about **realizing** goals, and about living dreams, no matter what they are.

3. I didn't say anything to my teammates between bench presses. I didn't want them to think I was consumed with myself or that I was being **egotistical**.

From
The Life You Imagine

by Derek Jeter with Jack Curry

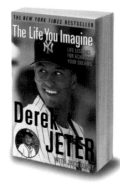

¶1 My dream may not coincide with your dreams. You may dream about being a detective, a teacher, or the President of the United States. But I think what I've learned along the way to becoming <u>shortstop</u> for the Yankees can be **applied** to **achieving** any goal. We're not just talking baseball here— we're talking about life, about realizing goals, and about living dreams, no matter what they are. We all have to start somewhere.

Think About It

¶2 What would you love to do? What are you good at? What would you like to do for the rest of your life?

¶3 These are serious questions that you might not feel like answering before you graduate from high school. But you really should think about them as soon as possible, because when you find that goal that excites you like nothing else, you'll want to open your bedroom window and yell it to anyone with ears!

¶4 If you don't set goals, you're not going to have dreams, either. The goals are the achievements along the way to get to your dreams.

Words to Know

<u>shortstop:</u> *(n.)* a position in baseball between first and second base

---

Close Reading

Key Ideas and Details

1. What is Jeter writing about? Support your answer with details from **paragraph 1**.

Colloquial Language

Colloquial language is a term that describes words and phrases used in everyday conversation.

Text Structure

2. Why does the author include the details in **paragraph 2**? How does this paragraph fit in with the rest of the text in this section?

Questioning

The author asks direct questions of the reader.

Close Reading

Words and Phrases in Context

3. Why does the author use the metaphor *twigs* to describe his arms and legs in **paragraph 5**?

Writing

4. When Jeter tells his mother about his lofty goal, she responds "as matter-of-factly as if I'd asked for another piece of chicken parmesan." Why does the author include this detail?

The author includes this detail because ____.

As a result, the reader ____.

Academic Vocabulary

5. Why did Jeter feel envious in **paragraph 5**? Find evidence that supports your answer.

Key Ideas and Details

6. Find details in **paragraphs 5 and 6** that identify Jeter's goal and the steps he took to achieve it.

¶5 One day, when I was a freshman at Kalamazoo Central High School, I opened up *USA Today* and saw that they had picked Tyler Houston of Las Vegas, Nevada, as the High School Player of the Year. I was **envious**. So I thought ahead three years—how great it would be to be the High School Player of the Year. So I made it a goal. I told my mother. I was 14 years old and looked 12 because of the twigs I had for arms and legs. But, responding as <u>matter-of-factly</u> as if I'd asked for another piece of chicken parmesan, she told me that was an excellent goal.

¶6 Three years later, before my senior year, I was lifting weights at high school with some other baseball players. They were talking about how *USA Today* picks a Player of the Year. I had batted .557 with seven <u>homers</u> in my junior year and was already **considered** one of the finest high school players in the country.

¶7 Now my goal was much more practical than when I had first mentioned it to my mother, but I didn't say anything to my teammates between <u>bench presses</u>. I didn't want them to think I was **consumed** with myself or that I was being egotistical. But I wound up winning it! I still have my photograph of that day.

¶8 When you set a **grand** goal like that and you accomplish it, you become a stronger, more confident person, and it <u>fortifies</u> how smart you were to establish that goal. Don't risk missing a goal because you never thought you could achieve it.

Words to Know

<u>matter-of-factly</u>: *(adv.)* clearly, without emotion

<u>homers</u>: *(n.)* a home run in baseball

<u>bench presses</u>: *(n.)* weight-lifting exercises designed to build upper-body strength

<u>fortifies</u>: *(v.)* makes physically or mentally stronger

Derek Jeter is considered a central figure on the New York Yankees. He debuted in the major leagues in 1995, won the Rookie of the Year award, and since then has left his mark on baseball. He was chosen as the eleventh captain in the history of the Yankees, and has more hits and stolen bases than any Yankee ever. Jeter's teammates and opponents alike recognize him as a highly-skilled professional and one of the best baseball players of his generation.

Close Reading

Text Structure

7. Identify where Jeter uses cause and effect in **paragraphs 5 and 6**. How does this strategy help the reader understand Jeter's goal?

Key Ideas and Details

8. Why does Jeter's goal become "more practical" than it was before?

Writing

9. How does Jeter feel about achieving his goal? Find evidence in **paragraph 7** that illustrates Jeter's feelings.

   Jeter feels ____.

   As an illustration, ____.

   Additionally, ____.

Words and Phrases in Context

10. What details support the meaning of the word *fortifies* in **paragraph 8**? Cite evidence from the text.

Text Structure

11. Why does the author choose to end the passage with the final sentence in **paragraph 8**?

Identify Evidence | Analyze Individuals, Events, and Ideas

Jeter uses a variety of strategies to describe his early experiences, challenges, and goals. How does he illustrate and elaborate on his experiences using these strategies?

- In the Evidence column, record important details from the text that show Jeter's experiences, challenges, and goals.
- In the Explanation column, identify the strategy Jeter is using in his writing. Then, explain how that strategy is being used to illustrate or elaborate on a key individual, event, or idea.

Evidence	Source	Page	Explanation
1. "We're not just talking about baseball here—we're talking about life, about realizing goals, and about living dreams, no matter what they are."	Jeter	61	Jeter uses colloquial language to introduce two central ideas, goals and dreams. Specifically: • the contraction "we're" makes the writing sound informal • the phrase "we're not just talking about baseball here" is another example
2. "What would you love to do? What are you good at? What would you like to do for the rest of your life?"			
3. "I told my mother. I was 14 years old and looked 12 because of the twigs I had for arms and legs."			
4. "But, responding as matter-of-factly as if I'd asked for another piece of chicken parmesan, she told me that was an excellent goal."			

Evidence	Source	Page	Explanation
5.			
6.			
7.			

Key Ideas and Details

Determining the Central Idea

1. Review your notes about Jeter's biography, *The Life You Imagine*. What is the central idea of the excerpt?

2. List three key individuals that Jeter introduces in this excerpt. Explain why each individual is important to the central idea.

Individuals	Significance
Tyler Houston, H.S. Player of the Year	Inspired Jeter to set his own goal to become player of the year

3. List three key events that Jeter introduces. Explain why each event is important to the central idea.

Events	Significance
Reading USA Today	Jeter read the story about the Player of the Year award

Craft and Structure

Structure of the Text

1. How does Jeter begin this excerpt from his biography?

2. What does Jeter share in the second section of the text, after the subheading?

3. What details does Jeter include to illustrate and support the main idea?

4. How does Jeter conclude the text?

Synthesize

5. How does Jeter use language or structure to convey his experiences, challenges, and goals?

Subheadings

A **subheading** is a short phrase used as a title for a small part within a longer piece of writing. For example, Jeter uses the subheading "Think About It."

Cause and Effect

Jeter uses **cause and effect** as a writing strategy to explain why he set this particular goal and what the consequences were.

Academic Vocabulary

from *Dreams from My Father* by Barack Obama

Rate your understanding of each word. Then read its meaning and write an example sentence. If the example is given, write the meaning.

Word	Meaning	Example
accommodate *(v.)* p. 69 ① ② ③ ④	to accept an idea or opinion, especially when it is different from yours	
destiny *(n.)* p. 70 ① ② ③ ④	things that will happen in the future, especially those that cannot be changed or controlled	
inherent *(adj.)* p. 70 ① ② ③ ④	characteristic of; naturally part of someone or something	
contemporaneous *(adj.)* p. 70 ① ② ③ ④		The contemporaneous winds and flooding damaged many of the town's buildings.
composite *(adj.)* p. 70 ① ② ③ ④	made up of several different parts or materials	
opaque *(adj.)* p. 74 ① ② ③ ④	difficult to see through; hard to understand	

Rating Scale | ① I don't know the word. ② I've seen it or heard it.
③ I know its meaning. ④ I know it and use it.

Word Study

The **root word** *mem* comes from the Latin word that means *to remember*.

The **root word** *tempo* or *tempor* comes from the Latin word that means *time*.

Read the definitions below. Then choose the word that goes with each definition.

> contemporary   memoir   tempo
> temporary   memorable   commemorate

1. happening for a limited time

   _____

2. belonging to the present time; modern

   _____

3. to do something to show that you remember and respect someone

   _____

4. a book written about a person's life and experiences

   _____

5. the speed at which something happens

   _____

6. worth remembering

   _____

from
Dreams from My Father

by Barack Obama

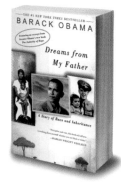

¶1 I don't <u>fault</u> people their suspicions. I learned long ago to distrust my childhood and the stories that shaped it. It was only many years later, after I had sat at my father's grave and spoken to him through Africa's red soil, that I could circle back and evaluate these early stories for myself. Or, more accurately, it was only then that I understood that I had spent much of my life trying to rewrite these stories, plugging up holes in the narrative, **accommodating** unwelcome details, projecting individual choices against the blind sweep of history, all in the hope of extracting some granite slab of truth upon which my unborn children can firmly stand.

¶2 At some point, then, <u>in spite of</u> a stubborn desire to protect myself from scrutiny, in spite of the periodic impulse to abandon the entire project, what has found its way onto these pages is a record of a personal, interior journey—a boy's search for his father, and through that search a workable meaning for his life as a black American. The result is autobiographical, although whenever someone's asked me over the course of these last three years just what the book is about, I've usually avoided such a description. An autobiography promises <u>feats worthy of record</u>, conversations with famous people, a central role in important events. There is none of that here. At the very least, an autobiography implies a summing up, a certain closure, that hardly suits someone of my years, still busy <u>charting</u> his way through the world.

Key Ideas and Details

1. This first section is from the introduction to the book. What is the author writing about in this section? Find details in **paragraphs 1 and 2** that tell about the topic.

Figurative Language

Figurative language is language that departs from the literal meaning of the words in order to achieve an effect or make a point.

Words and Phrases in Context

2. What does the author mean when he writes "a personal interior journey" in **paragraph 2**? Cite evidence from the text.

Academic Language

Academic language describes words and phrases that are formal and scholarly. This kind of language is usually grammatically correct and complex.

Words to Know

<u>fault</u>: *(v.)* to criticize someone for a mistake

<u>in spite of</u>: *(adj.)* without being affected or stopped by something

<u>feats worthy of record</u>: *(n.)* impressive achievements that are worth writing down

<u>charting</u>: *(v.)* making plans for what should be done to achieve a goal

Close Reading

Key Ideas and Details

3. Interpret the meaning of the phrase "affirm a common destiny" in **paragraph 3**. What does this line reveal about the author's perspective?

Academic Vocabulary

4. The author says in **paragraph 4** that he creates characters that are composites, "for the sake of compression." Review the meaning of the word composite. Why would creating composite characters make sense?

Text Structure

5. In **paragraph 5**, how does the author end this introductory section? What is the effect of ending this section of the text in this way?

¶3 I can't even hold up my experience as being somehow representative of the black American experience ("After all, you don't come from an underprivileged background," a Manhattan publisher helpfully points out to me); indeed, learning to accept that particular truth—that I can embrace my black brothers and sisters, whether in this country or in Africa, and affirm a common **destiny** without pretending to speak to, or for, all our various struggles—is part of what this book's about.

¶4 Finally, there are the dangers **inherent** in any autobiographical work: the temptation to <u>color</u> events in ways favorable to the writer, the tendency to overestimate the interest one's experiences hold for others, selective lapses of memory. Such hazards are only magnified when the writer lacks the wisdom of age; the distance that can cure one of certain vanities. I can't say that I've avoided all, or any, of these hazards successfully. Although much of this book is based on **contemporaneous** journals or the oral histories of my family, the dialogue is necessarily an approximation of what was actually said or relayed to me. For the sake of <u>compression</u>, some of the characters that appear are **composites** of people I've known, and some events appear out of precise <u>chronology</u>. With the exception of my family and a handful of public figures, the names of most characters have been changed for the sake of their privacy.

¶5 Whatever the label that attaches to this book—autobiography, memoir, family history, or something else—what I've tried to do is write an honest account of a particular <u>province</u> of my life.

Words to Know

<u>color:</u> *(v.)* to influence something in a particular way

<u>compression:</u> *(n.)* decrease in volume; make smaller, more concise

<u>chronology:</u> *(n.)* the order in which events happened

<u>province:</u> *(n.)* an area; a subject that a person knows a lot about

From Part 1: Origins

¶6 I went to my room and slammed the door, listening as the voices outside grew louder, Gramps insisting that this was his house, Toot saying that my father had no right to come in and bully everyone, including me, after being gone all this time. I heard my father say that they were spoiling me, that I needed a firm hand, and I listened to my mother tell her parents that nothing ever changed with them. We all stood accused, and even after my father left and Toot came in to say that I could watch the last five minutes of my show, I felt as if something had cracked open between all of us, <u>goblins</u> rushing out of some old, sealed-off <u>lair</u>. Watching the green <u>Grinch</u> on the television screen, intent on ruining Christmas, eventually transformed by the faith of the doe-eyed creatures who inhabited Whoville, I saw it for what it was: a lie. I began to count the days until my father would leave and things would return to normal.

¶7 The next day, Toot sent me down to the apartment where my father was staying to see if he had any laundry to wash. I knocked, and my father opened the door, shirtless. Inside, I saw my mother ironing some of his clothes. Her hair was tied back in a ponytail, and her eyes were soft and dark, as if she'd been crying. My father asked me to sit down beside him on the bed, but I told him that Toot needed me to help her, and left after relaying the message. Back upstairs, I had begun cleaning my room when my mother came in.

Words to Know

<u>goblins</u>: *(n.)* mischievous, dwarf-like creatures from folktales

<u>lair</u>: *(n.)* a wild animal's den

<u>Grinch</u>: *(n.)* a fictional character who ruins Christmas and was created by Dr. Seuss

Text Structure

6. What is the significance of the heading at the top of **paragraph 6**? Consider the impact the heading has on the text from this point on.

Key Ideas and Details

7. In **paragraph 6**, why is Gramps insisting that this is his house? Cite evidence from the text.

Writing

8. Explain what the author means by the line: "I felt as if something had cracked open between all of us, goblins rushing out of some old, sealed-off lair" in **paragraph 6**.

The author felt ____ because ____.

The "goblins" represent ____.

He describes the "sealed-off lair" to show ____.

Close Reading

Key Ideas and Details

9. As a child, Obama was called "Barry" by his family. How does Barry feel in this section? Explain your answer using cause and effect.

Words and Phrases in Context

10. Review the meaning of the word *suppress* in **paragraph 13**. How would the meaning of the sentence change if the author replaced the phrase "trying to suppress" with the word *ignoring*?

Words and Phrases in Context

11. What does the author mean by "Each time I remembered, my body squirmed as if it had received a jolt to the nerves" in **paragraph 13**?

Text Structure

12. Why does the author include the line, "I was still trying to figure out how to explain myself when my father walked into class the next day" in **paragraph 14**?

¶8 "You shouldn't be mad at your father, Bar. He loves you very much. He's just a little stubborn sometimes."

¶9 "Okay," I said without looking up. I could feel her eyes follow me around the room until she finally let out a slow breath and went to the door.

¶10 "I know all this stuff is confusing for you," she said. "For me, too. Just try and remember what I said, okay?" She put her hand on the doorknob. "Do you want me to close the door?"

¶11 I nodded, but she had been gone for only a minute when she stuck her head back into the room.

¶12 "By the way, I forgot to tell you that Miss Hefty has invited your father to come to school on Thursday. She wants him to speak to the class."

¶13 I couldn't imagine worse news. I spent that night and all of the next day trying to <u>suppress</u> thoughts of the <u>inevitable</u>: the faces of my classmates when they heard about mud huts, all my lies exposed, the painful jokes afterward. Each time I remembered, my body squirmed as if it had received a jolt to the nerves.

¶14 I was still trying to figure out how I'd explain myself when my father walked into our class the next day. Miss Hefty welcomed him eagerly, and as I took my seat I heard several children ask each other what was going on. I became more <u>desperate</u> when our math teacher, a big, no-nonsense Hawaiian named Mr. Eldredge, came into the room, followed by thirty confused children from his homeroom next door.

Words to Know

<u>suppress:</u> *(v.)* to hold back

<u>inevitable:</u> *(adj.)* impossible to avoid

<u>desperate:</u> *(adj.)* feeling hopeless, in a difficult situation that's impossible to deal with

¶15 "We have a special treat for you today," Miss Hefty began. "Barry Obama's father is here, and he's come all the way from Kenya, in Africa, to tell us about his country."

¶16 The other kids looked at me as my father stood up, and I held my head stiffly, trying to focus on a <u>vacant</u> point on the blackboard behind him. He had been speaking for some time before I could finally bring myself back to the moment. He was leaning against Miss Hefty's thick oak desk and describing the deep gash in the earth where mankind had first appeared. He spoke of the wild animals that still roamed the plains, the tribes that still required a young boy to kill a lion to prove his manhood. He spoke of customs of the Luo, how elders received the utmost respect and made laws for all to follow under great-trunked trees. And he told us of Kenya's struggle to be free, how the British had wanted to stay and unjustly rule the people, just as they had in America; how many had been enslaved only because of the color of their skin, just as they had in America; but that Kenyans, like all of us in the room, longed to be free and develop themselves through hard work and sacrifice.

¶17 When he finished, Miss Hefty was absolutely beaming with pride. All of my classmates applauded <u>heartily</u>, and a few struck up the courage to ask questions, each of which my father appeared to consider carefully before answering. The bell rang for lunch, and Mr. Eldredge came up to me.

¶18 "You've got a pretty impressive father."

¶19 The <u>ruddy-faced</u> boy who asked about cannibalism said, "Your dad is pretty cool."

Words to Know

<u>vacant</u>: *(adj.)* empty

<u>heartily</u>: *(adv.)* in a heartfelt, enthusiastic way

<u>ruddy-faced</u>: *(adj.)* pink and healthy-looking

Close Reading

Text Structure

13. How does the author compare and contrast Kenya and America in **paragraph 16**?

Key Ideas and Details

14. Was the author's father's visit to the school a success? Why or why not?

Writing

15. The author includes descriptive details about his classmates and teacher's reactions to his father. What details are included and why are they important to the story?

The author describes how ____.

Details such as ____ show ____.

Compare/Contrast

A **comparison** tells how two things are similar. A **contrast** tells how they are different.

Close Reading

Key Ideas and Details

16. In **paragraph 21** why does the author include details, "careful to clap whenever he claps"? What does this detail show about the author?

Words and Phrases in Context

17. Interpret the meaning of the phrase "spare equations of sound" in the context of **paragraph 21**. What point is the author making?

Academic Vocabulary

18. Why does the young Obama describe his father as *opaque* in **paragraph 21**? What does this word choice indicate about Obama's relationship with his father?

Text Structure

19. How does this image relate to the information in the text? Explain your answer using specific details.

¶20 And off to one side, I saw Coretta watch my father say good-bye to some of the children. She seemed too intent to smile; her face showed only a look of simple satisfaction.

¶21 Two weeks later he was gone. In that time, we stand together in front of the Christmas tree and pose for pictures, the only ones I have of us together, me holding an orange basketball, his gift to me, him showing off the tie I've bought him ("Ah, people will know that I am very important wearing such a tie"). At a Dave Brubeck concert, I struggle to sit quietly in the dark auditorium beside him, unable to follow the spare equations of sound that the performers make, careful to clap whenever he claps. For brief spells in the day I will lie beside him, the two of us alone in the apartment sublet from a retired old woman whose name I forget, the place full of quilts and doilies and knitted seat covers, and I read my book while he reads his. He remains **opaque** to me, a present mass; when I mimic his gestures or turns of phrase, I know neither their origins nor their consequences, can't see how they play out over time. But I grow accustomed to his company.

Born in 1961, in Honolulu, Hawaii, **Barack Obama** was elected the 44th president of the U.S. in 2008. Barack Obama's father was born in Kenya.

Words to Know

Dave Brubeck: *(n.)* a famous jazz musician and composer

mimic: *(v.)* imitate without necessarily understanding

accustomed: *(adj.)* used to

¶22 The day of his departure, as my mother and I helped him pack his bags, he unearthed two records, <u>forty-fives</u>, in dull brown dust jackets.

¶23 "Barry! Look here—I forgot that I had brought these for you. The sounds of your continent."

¶24 It took him a while to puzzle out my grandparents' old stereo, but finally the disk began to turn, and he gingerly placed the needle on the groove. A tiny <u>guitar lick</u> opened, then the sharp horns, the thump of drums, then the guitar again, and then the voices, clean and joyful as they rode up the back beat, urging us on.

¶25 "Come, Barry," my father said. "You will learn from the master." And suddenly his slender body was swaying back and forth, the lush sound was rising, his arms were swinging as they cast an invisible net, his feet wove over the floor in off-beats, his bad leg stiff but his rump high, his head back, his hips moving in a tight circle. The rhythm quickened, the horns sounded, and his eyes closed to follow his pleasure, and then one eye opened to peek down at me and his solemn face spread into a silly grin, and my mother smiled, and my grandparents walked in to see what all the commotion was about. I took my first tentative steps with my eyes closed, down, up, my arms swinging, the voices lifting. And I hear him still: as I follow my father into the sound, he lets out a quick shout, bright and high, a shout that leaves much behind and reaches out for more, a shout that cries for laughter.

Close Reading

Words and Phrases in Context
20. Why does the author describe the activities in **paragraphs 23–25** as a *commotion*?

Text Structure
21. Consider the line "And I hear him still" in **paragraph 25**. How is the structure of this line different from the rest of this section of the text?

Writing
22. How does the last sentence of **paragraph 25** contribute to the reader's understanding of the author's purpose?

This line primarily ____.

In particular ____.

Therefore ____.

Words to Know

forty-fives: *(n.)* music recorded on vinyl discs, played at 45 rpm on a record player, usually with a single song on each side

guitar lick: *(n.)* a musical passage or phrase performed using a guitar

Identify Evidence | Analyze Individuals, Events, and Ideas

In the excerpt from **Dreams from My Father,** Obama uses a variety of strategies to explain the goal of his book, and to describe his childhood experiences. How does he illustrate and elaborate on ideas using a variety of strategies?

- In the Evidence column, record important details from the text that show Obama's experiences, challenges, and goals.
- In the Explanation column, identify the strategy Obama is using in his writing. Then, explain how that strategy is being used to illustrate or elaborate on a key individual, event, or idea.

Evidence	Source	Page	Explanation
1. "It was only then I understood that I had spent much of my life trying to rewrite these stories, plugging up holes in the narrative, accommodating unwelcome details, projecting individual choices against the blind sweep of history, all in the hope of extracting some granite slab of truth upon which my unborn children can firmly stand."	Obama	69	Obama uses figurative language to describe the difficulties of understanding his background and childhood experiences in order to write a meaningful book. He wanted to try to understand the "holes" in or gaps in his past, some of which he may not even want to hear about (they are "unwelcome"). His goal was to get to some honesty about his family's past and future, and about his journey in particular.
2. "At some point, then, in spite of a stubborn desire to protect myself from scrutiny, in spite of the periodic impulse to abandon the entire project, what has found its way onto these pages is a record of a personal, interior journey— a boy's search for his father, and through that search a workable meaning for his life as a black American."			

Evidence	Source	Page	Explanation
3.			
4.			
5.			

Key Ideas and Details

Determining the Central Idea

1. Use the evidence you have collected to summarize the key idea of Obama's memoir.

2. List three key individuals that Obama introduces in this excerpt. Explain why each individual is important to the central idea.

Individuals	Significance
mother	She also has a difficult relationship with Barry's father.

3. List three key events that Obama introduces. Explain why each event is important to the central idea.

Event	Significance
The family argument about parenting styles (permissive or spoiling the child)	Barry hears his parents and grandparents arguing, upsetting everyone. The fight makes Barry wish his father would leave.

Craft and Structure

Structure of the Memoir

1. What does Obama discuss in the introduction from his memoir? (Paragraphs 1–5)

2. What does Obama describe in the excerpt from Part 1: Origins? (Paragraphs 6–25)

3. How is the voice of the narrator different in Part 1 from the voice in the Introduction?

4. How does the author describe his memories of his father? Why are these memories significant?

Author's Purpose

5. All of these details fit together to communicate a key idea. What is Obama's purpose in sharing these stories about his family history?

Temporal Shift

Temporal shift means time change. In literature, it happens when the story moves suddenly to a different time or time period.

Narrator

The **narrator** is the person telling the story. In a memoir, the narrator is the author. In other genres, this is not always the case.

Collaborate and Present

Plan and Deliver a Speech

As adolescents, both Jeter and Obama wanted to achieve their goals. Young Derek Jeter had a concrete goal to become High School Player of the Year. Young "Barry" Obama wanted to understand who his distant father really was. Did these young men achieve their goals? What challenges did they face along the way?

Assignment: Plan and deliver a short speech about either author's goal and challenges. Explain how he did or did not achieve the end result that he was seeking.

Analyze the Content

1. Consider the following questions:
   - What challenge did the author face? Did he overcome it? If so, how?
   - Was the goal accomplished in the end? Why or why not?

2. Choose one author to write about. Create a chart of the challenges this author faced, the way he approached his challenges, and the outcomes.

Challenge	Approach	Outcome

3. Use the details in the chart you created as talking points for the body of your speech. Draft what you will say in your speech.
   - Remember to introduce yourself and your topic to your audience at the beginning of the speech, and to close with a conclusion summarizing your main points.
   - Write your speech on paper or type it using a computer.

Report

4. Deliver your speech.

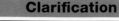

Clarification

- So what you are saying is . . .
- So what you mean is . . .
- In other words, you think . . .
- If I understand you correctly, you are saying . . .

Reporting Ideas

- _____ pointed out
- _____ indicated that
- _____ emphasized

Presentation

- Be still and use good posture.
- Speak loudly and clearly.
- Make eye contact with your audience.

Speech Checklist

Use the checklist below to evaluate your collaboration skills, reasoning, and final presentation.
Think carefully about your work. If you know you completed an item thoroughly, give yourself a check (✓).

COLLABORATE AND PRESENT CHECKLIST

Comprehension and Collaboration	Evidence and Reasoning	Presentation of Knowledge and Ideas
☐ Come to discussions prepared, having read and studied material.	☐ Explain the purpose of the presentation.	☐ Adapt language to a variety of contexts and tasks to demonstrate knowledge of formal English.
☐ Refer to evidence when contributing to the discussion.	☐ Present information relevant to the task.	☐ Include multimedia components (e.g., graphics, images, music, sound) and visual displays.
☐ Follow rules for discussions and lead by example.	☐ State whether the author achieved the end result he was seeking.	☐ Use appropriate volume/tone (clear, not too fast, too slow, or too loud) and avoid using "like" or "ummm."
☐ Ask and answer specific questions.	☐ Explain one author's challenges, approaches, and outcomes.	☐ Have strong posture, a confident stance, and make frequent eye contact.
☐ Make comments that contribute to the topic under discussion.	☐ Use at least three examples from the text.	☐ Occasionally move from one spot to another without fidgeting.
☐ Review the key ideas under discussion and demonstrate understanding of multiple perspectives through reflection and paraphrasing.	☐ Synthesize the key ideas from your speech with a conclusion.	☐ Smile and act relaxed.
Number of ✓s in this category: ___	**Number of ✓s in this category:** ___	**Total # of ✓s in this category:** ___

Total # of ✓s: ___

Add up the total number of checks (✓) in each category. Then use the scoring guide below to calculate your final score.

Scoring Guide

16 to 18 ✓s	13 to 15 ✓s	11 to 12 ✓s	10 or less ✓s
④ Exemplary	③ Meets Standards	② Needs Work	① Does Not Meet Standards

Read the Model

Writers can choose different strategies to share information. The writer of this informative essay explains how an author uses cause and effect and colloquial diction to help readers understand her experiences. Read and discuss the model essay below.

Informative Essay

- An **informative essay** increases a reader's knowledge of a subject.

- The **introduction** states the title and author of the text that the writer will analyze, and includes the thesis statement.

- The two **body paragraphs** express the writer's main points about the text.

- The **conclusion** sums up or restates the thesis. It also explains why the information in the essay matters.

Language and Conventions

- Find two examples of domain-specific or academic vocabulary.

- Find examples of two different citations in the text.

Challenges Reaching the Top   By Marci Kaplan

In "Peak Performance," author Samantha Larson illuminates the challenges she faced as she pursued her goal to climb the world's highest mountains. By using cause and effect and colloquial diction in her writing, Larson helps readers understand her dream and what it took to get there.

First of all, Larson uses cause and effect to tell how she became a mountain climber. She says her father was the reason she climbed her first mountain when she was 12 because "he proposed a family vacation to Africa to climb Mount Kilimanjaro" (92). As a result, she developed a love of climbing. Eventually, she and her father set the goal to climb all Seven Summits, the highest peaks in the world. This explanation helps readers understand how Larson became so interested in mountain climbing and why she set such a lofty goal.

Second of all, Larson uses informal, colloquial language to share her stories and challenges. Contractions, exclamations and slang all contribute to her informal style. For example, she states that climbing Everest would require getting in "serious shape" (93). She adds casually, "I never really went into it thinking I'd be breaking any records!" (93). Then, when sharing details about her excursions, she notes: "Sometimes I'd miss class and be doing my homework on the side of a mountain!" (93). Through Larson's use of colloquial diction, readers understand her voice, glimpse her personality, and comprehend the challenges of her mountain-climbing lifestyle.

Overall, Larson effectively uses cause and effect and informal, colloquial diction to convey her experiences, challenges, and goals to the reader. Her authentic story may even inspire others to pursue their dreams, too.

Analyze the Model

Use the outline below to analyze the model essay. Your notes can be written using shorthand and phrases.

Introduction
¶1 Thesis Statement

Body Paragraphs	
¶2 Topic Sentence/Key Idea	**Relevant Evidence**
¶3 Topic Sentence/Key Idea	**Relevant Evidence**

Conclusion
¶4 Restatement + Why it Matters

Text Structure

- The thesis statement presents a clear plan for the essay.

- The topic sentence of each body paragraph clearly states the main idea of that paragraph. It is the leading or controlling sentence of the paragraph. All the topic sentences support the thesis statement.

- The body paragraphs also contain supporting sentences that build on the idea stated in the topic sentence.

- Supporting sentences include logical reasoning and **relevant evidence**, such as direct quotations from the text, that support the writer's ideas.

- The conclusion should **restate** the thesis and say why **the information matters**.

Step 1 | Gather Evidence

[Explain the strategies these writers use to convey their experiences, challenges, and goals.]

What You Need to Know | Relevant evidence that shows how Jeter and Obama use a variety of writing strategies to explain their experiences and challenges (see pages 64 and 76)

What You Need to Write | Notes that explain your evidence and identify where to find it

Strategies in *The Life You Imagine*

Strategy	Example
Jeter uses colloquial language to introduce two central ideas, goals and dreams	"We're not just talking about baseball here, we're talking about life, about realizing goals, and about living dreams" Page & ¶ _p. 61 ¶1_
Strategy	Example Page & ¶ _____
Strategy	Example Page & ¶ _____

Strategies in *Dreams From My Father*

Strategy	Example
Strategy	Example Page & ¶ _____
Strategy	Example Page & ¶ _____
Strategy	Example Page & ¶ _____

Step 2 | Organize Ideas

Use an outline to record your thesis statement and organize your evidence into paragraphs.

Introduction
¶1 Thesis Statement

Body Paragraphs	
¶2 Topic Sentence/Key Idea	**Relevant Evidence**
¶3 Topic Sentence/Key Idea	**Relevant Evidence**

Conclusion
¶4 Why it Matters

Step 3 | Draft

Write a draft of your essay on the computer or on paper.

Language Study | Combining and Rewriting Sentences

Conjunctions

- Conjunctions are small words that join two or more words, phrases, or clauses.

- Coordinating conjunctions join sentence parts that are the same, such as words, phrases, and clauses. Use the acronym FANBOYS to help you remember them: *for, and, nor, but, or, yet, so.*

Commas

- Use a comma with a coordinating conjunction when each part of the sentence can stand alone.

- Whenever you see one of the FANBOYS, split the sentence around it and see if each sentence makes sense on its own. If so, use a comma.

See It | Sentences can be rewritten and combined using commas and coordinating conjunctions (*for, and, nor, but, or, yet, so*).

Read the examples below:
- **Samantha faced many challenges. She achieved her goal.**
- **Samantha faced many challenges, <u>and</u> she achieved her goal.**
- **Samantha faced many challenges <u>and</u> achieved her goal.**

Try It | Combine the sentences into one sentence. Use an appropriate conjunction.

1. **The author was the youngest non-native person to scale Mount Everest. She was an accomplished mountain climber.**

2. **Samantha received an amazing letter from a girl in Iraq. Samantha wrote her a message back.**

3. **The author cried when she reached the summit. It was strange not to have that goal anymore.**

4. **Samantha could be in school like most students her age. She could be ice-climbing!**

Apply It

Think about the topic you wrote about in your essay. Use the sentence frames below to practice writing about your topic using coordinating conjunctions.

1. The author shares _____, so the reader _____.
   (a key detail)   (what the reader understands)

2. _____ _____, but _____ _____.
   (author's name) (what the author did)   (other author's name) (what the other author did)

3. Since _____ stated _____, the reader can see
   (author's name)   (what the author did)

   that _____.
   (what the reader understands)

Now, **go back to your draft** and select at least two sentences that you could make clearer or less repetitive. Combine and rewrite your sentences using commas and conjunctions.

- _____
  _____

- _____
  _____

- _____
  _____

Conventions Study | Pronoun Antecedents

Pronoun Antecedents

Pronouns:
- Help writers avoid repetition of nouns
- Make writing flow easily

Antecedents:
- The word, phrase, or sentence that is represented by the pronoun

Pronouns must have clear antecedents and agree in number and person with the nouns they replace. Otherwise, writing becomes confusing.

See It | Find the pronouns that the writer used in the sentences below from the model essay on page 82. Then answer the questions.

Larson uses informal, colloquial language to share her stories and challenges. Contractions, exclamations, and slang all contribute to her informal style. For example, she states that climbing Everest would require getting in "serious shape" (93). She adds casually, "I never really went into it thinking I'd be breaking any records!" (93).

1. Whom does the pronoun *she* refer to?

2. What does the pronoun *it* refer to?

Try It | Read the sentences below and identify the antecedents for the underlined pronouns.

3. Samantha grabbed the climbing gear that was in <u>her</u> bag. <u>It</u> was heavy.

4. Mr. Larson reached the bottom of Everest and felt that <u>he</u>, <u>himself</u>, had succeeded.

5. Mrs. Larson met <u>her</u> family members and wondered what <u>they</u> would say.

Apply It | Select and write sentences from the draft of your essay. Note the pronouns you use. Check to see if the antecedents your pronouns are referring to are clear. Write one example below of a pronoun used clearly and correctly.

Step 4 | Revise and Edit   Revise your draft with a partner.

Organization and Clarity					
State the title and author of the texts in the introductory statement and introduce the thesis statement clearly in the introduction.	Self	1	2	3	4
	Partner	1	2	3	4
Include a clear topic sentence with a controlling idea in each body paragraph.	Self	1	2	3	4
	Partner	1	2	3	4
Use appropriate transition words to connect ideas.	Self	1	2	3	4
	Partner	1	2	3	4
Use domain-specific vocabulary to explain the topic.	Self	1	2	3	4
	Partner	1	2	3	4
Conclude by restating the thesis and presenting information about why the information is important to the reader.	Self	1	2	3	4
	Partner	1	2	3	4
Evidence and Reasoning					
Accurately explain and analyze the authors' experiences, challenges, and goals, and the strategies that the authors use in their writing.	Self	1	2	3	4
	Partner	1	2	3	4
Include three or more pieces of evidence to develop the topic in each body paragraph, citing the author and page number accurately.	Self	1	2	3	4
	Partner	1	2	3	4
Language and Conventions					
Establish and maintain a formal style throughout the essay.	Self	1	2	3	4
	Partner	1	2	3	4
Use punctuation/capitalization correctly (e.g., commas, parentheses, and dashes to set off nonrestrictive/parenthetical elements).	Self	1	2	3	4
	Partner	1	2	3	4
Use pronouns correctly and check that antecedents are clear.	Self	1	2	3	4
	Partner	1	2	3	4

Scoring Guide | ① needs improvement   ② average   ③ good   ④ excellent

Step 5 | Publish   Publish your essay either in print or digital form.

Publish

Publish your essay either in print or digital form. Use the rubric below to assess your final performance task.

PERFORMANCE TASK RUBRIC			
Score Point	Organization and Clarity	Evidence and Reasoning	Language and Conventions
Exemplary ④	• introductory paragraph introduces the **thesis clearly** and in an **engaging way** • body paragraphs are **logically organized and strongly develop** how the writers use text structure and language to describe their challenges • concluding statement **wraps up the ideas** in the essay, referring to information from both texts, and summarizes the writers' techniques	• **accurately explains and convincingly analyzes** how the writers use text structure and language to convey information about challenges in their lives • includes **several examples of relevant** factual evidence from each writing that illustrate the techniques the writers use	• demonstrates a **strong command** of the conventions of standard English grammar and usage, as well as of standard English capitalization and punctuation • **consistently** uses a **formal style** throughout the essay • uses **pronouns correctly** and ensures that antecedents are clear • uses **coordinating conjunctions** wherever applicable • vocabulary is **appropriate** to the topic (vocabulary about each challenge; accurate terms for referring to text structure and language)
Meets Standards ③	• introductory paragraph introduces the **thesis clearly** • body paragraphs are **logically organized** and **explain** how the writers use text structure and language to describe their challenges • concluding statement **wraps up the ideas** in the essay, referring to information from both texts	• **accurately explains and generally analyzes** how the writers use text structure and language to convey information about challenges in their lives • includes **relevant** factual evidence from each writing that illustrate the techniques the writers use	• demonstrates **a near command** of the conventions of standard English grammar and usage, as well as of standard English capitalization and punctuation • **often** uses a **formal style** • uses **pronouns correctly** • uses **coordinating conjunctions sometimes** • vocabulary is **appropriate** to the topic (vocabulary about each challenge; terms for referring to text structure and language)

PERFORMANCE TASK RUBRIC

Score Point	Organization and Clarity	Evidence and Reasoning	Language and Conventions
Needs Work ②	• introductory paragraph introduces the **thesis** • body paragraphs are **somewhat logically organized** and **attempt to explain** how the writers use text structure and language to describe their challenges • concluding statement **wraps up the ideas**, but refers to information from only one text	• **accurately explains** how the writers use text structure and language to convey information about challenges in their lives with **limited analysis** • includes **some textual evidence** from each memoir to support analysis	• demonstrates a **marginal command** of the conventions of English grammar and usage, as well as of standard English capitalization and punctuation • **rarely** uses a **formal style** • uses **few pronouns** • uses **coordinating conjunctions rarely** • there **are many errors; however, the text is still understandable** • includes only **one or two examples** of vocabulary that is appropriate to the topic (vocabulary about each challenge)
Does Not Meet Standards ①	• introductory paragraph is **unclear** • body paragraphs are **not organized logically** and/or **do not explain** how the writers use text structure and language to describe their challenges • concluding statement is **unclear or does not wrap up** the ideas in the essay	• response is **partial or inaccurate explanation** of how writers use text structure and language to describe their challenges • includes **no analyses of textual evidence** from each memoir	• demonstrates **almost no command** of the conventions of standard English grammar and usage, as well as of standard English capitalization and punctuation • uses an in**formal style** • **never** uses **pronouns** to refer to antecedents • **does not** use **coordinating conjunctions** • there **are many errors that disrupt** the reader's understanding of the text • **does not include** vocabulary that is appropriate to the topic (vocabulary about each challenge)

Questions

Key Ideas and Details

1. What does **paragraph 1** indicate about the purpose of the text?

Words and Phrases in Context

2. What is the meaning of "up the stakes"? What details in **paragraph 4** help you understand its meaning?

"Peak Performance"

by Samantha Larson from *Teen Vogue*

¶1 Most fathers and daughters have special traditions, something they bond over. My dad and I, we climb mountains.

¶2 It started in 2001 when I was twelve. My dad was an occasional climber. He would climb mainly on short trips near our home in Long Beach, California. But that year, he <u>proposed</u> a family vacation to Africa to climb Mount Kilimanjaro—one of the tallest mountains in the world. I was the only one who thought, "What a great idea!" To be perfectly honest, I didn't even know what it meant to climb 19,300 feet. I figured I'd get to see some zebras and giraffes.

¶3 When my dad and I arrived at the tiny lodge at the base of Kilimanjaro, a group of climbers who'd just finished were talking about how the altitude had gotten to them. The higher you climb, the harder it can be to breathe since there's less pressure in the air. I've been a dancer and a gymnast since I was small. So, until then, I hadn't been concerned about physically doing it. My dad <u>assured</u> me we could go slowly, and that if I changed my mind he'd be happy to turn back. But we didn't need to. And that's how it all began.

Getting Started

¶4 Kilimanjaro is one of seven mountains that together are called the Seven Summits. The Seven Summits are the highest peaks on each of the seven continents. Fewer than 200 people have climbed all seven. At first, my dad and I weren't thinking about completing all of the Summits. Climbing was something we loved. But after each trip, it became natural to want to up the stakes.

Words to Know

<u>proposed:</u> *(v.)* suggested a plan or idea

<u>assured:</u> *(v.)* promised

¶5 In 2002, I became, according to my guide, the youngest person to scale Mount Aconcagua. That's a peak on the border of Argentina and Chile. After that, we tackled Mount Elbrus in Russia. Then Denali in Alaska. Then Kosciuszko in Australia. Most of the trips were taken over school breaks. Sometimes I'd miss class and be doing my homework on the side of a mountain! One time, I even brought along my oboe to practice. More and more, I began to recognize the sense of accomplishment I felt at the end of a successful climb.

¶6 <u>Conditions</u> vary from mountain to mountain. But as a general rule, the higher you go, the colder it gets. The biggest challenge a climber has to face is the change in altitude. If you take a mountain too fast, you can get altitude sickness. This can show up as fatigue and nausea. In extreme cases, fluid starts to collect in your brain. But we always traveled with an experienced guide and took all the precautions we could. I tried not to spend too much time worrying about it. I never felt threatened. While you can't eliminate these risks, if you make good decisions, you can really decrease them.

Training for Everest

¶7 After graduating high school in 2006, I was accepted to Stanford [University]. But I decided to <u>defer</u> for a year to train for Everest. Everest is the highest of the Seven Summits. It was also the last one my dad and I needed to climb to complete the circuit. I never really went into it thinking I'd be breaking any records. Everest is part of the Nepalese Himalayas and is just over 29,000 feet. In 2006, several hikers died trying to reach the top. More than the other mountains, Everest was going to require getting in serious shape. I started running and swimming to build up my stamina and lung <u>capacity</u>. I also spent a lot of time at indoor climbing gyms.

Words to Know

<u>defer</u>: *(v.)* to put something off until later

<u>conditions</u>: (n.) the general state of something

<u>capacity</u>: (n.) the amount something can hold, in this case, air

---

Questions

Text Structure

3. What signal phrase in **paragraph 5** helps you understand how the author has structured the text? How do the headings also help you understand how the author has organized the information in her text?

Words and Phrases in Context

4. What words and phrases on **pages 92–93** help develop the idea that climbing mountains is a challenging activity?

Questions

Key Ideas and Details

5. What is the effect of devoting all of **paragraph 8** to talking about Everest?

Words and Phrases in Context

6. What words and phrases does the author use in **paragraph 9** to create mood? What is the mood?

¶8 In March of this year, we arrived in Kathmandu, Nepal. Each person is usually accompanied by his or her own guide and a Sherpa. A Sherpa is a Tibetan native who carries your equipment, food, and <u>oxygen</u> tanks. The climb takes about eight weeks. Working from a base camp, each day we'd go slightly higher than the day before. We slowly and safely adjusted to each new altitude. There were times when I'd look to the right and the drop would be about 1,000 feet. To the left it'd be about 5,000 feet!

¶9 Early on, I decided to blog about the trip. Base camp had Internet access. Almost every night I'd journal the day and people would post comments. The first entries were from people I knew. Then the Los Angeles Times ran an article about me. Suddenly I was getting 200 messages a day. Some of them were pretty amazing. One came from a girl who said she lived in Iraq in a war zone. She told me she thought my story was inspiring. She hoped that one day an Iraqi girl would be able to climb Everest, too.

Making It To The Top

¶10 At 11:00 P.M. on May 16, we set out for the top of the mountain. By then it was just about 3,000 feet away—less than a mile. At some points, I was going pretty slowly. Every step took so much effort. It's important to keep moving, though. Once you stop, you start to get cold. Everest, at its iciest, was about 30 degrees below zero. I didn't get mountain sickness on Everest, but I did experience a huge loss of appetite. My dad did as well. For the last nine hours of the trip, I ate maybe half of a chocolate bar.

Words to Know

<u>oxygen:</u> *(n.)* a gas that is present in air, and is necessary for most animals and plants to live

¶**11** Eleven hours after starting out from our camp, we made it to the top. I felt a wild mix of emotions, but it wasn't what I had expected to feel. I'd been imagining this moment for a long time. I had this idea I'd be excited and jumping around. I was the youngest non-native person to scale Everest, and the youngest person to climb the Seven Summits. But all I could do was cry. Maybe it was because I'd had this goal for so long. It was strange not to have it anymore. That and the fact that I still had to get back down. It took five days, bringing the entire climb to a total of about seven weeks. Because of the need to slowly <u>acclimatize</u>, going up takes much longer than going down.

¶**12** This fall, I started my <u>freshman</u> year at Stanford. Right before, my dad and I climbed Carstensz Pyramid in Indonesia. It was sort of like a last hurrah. It's been really special to have him as a climbing buddy, and I'm hoping we'll still get to climb together. Then again, it just might be time for a new goal.

Questions

Text Structure

7. How is the **last paragraph** different from all the preceding paragraphs?

Words to Know

<u>acclimatize:</u> *(v.)* to adjust to a new place, situation, or type of weather

<u>freshman:</u> *(adj.)* initial, first

Literature Circle Leveled Novels

Stanford Wong Flunks Big-Time *by Lisa Yee*
Stanford dreams of making the basketball A-Team, but first he has to pass English with the "help" of a pesky girl tutor. **Lexile**® measure: 650L

Diary of a Wimpy Kid *by Jeff Kinney*
Greg, an aspiring cartoonist, is intimidated by junior high and suffers many trials and tribulations—including jealousy over his best friend's popularity and the success of his friend's comics. **Lexile**® measure: 950L

Milagros: Girl From Away *by Meg Medina*
When Milagros's Caribbean island is invaded, Milagros must escape by boat alone, guided by mysterious manta rays that seem to protect her. She lands on an island off the coast of Maine, where she must forge a new life for herself. **Lexile**® measure: 770L

Fiction, Nonfiction, Poetry, and Novels

Kids With Courage: True Stories About Young People Making a Difference *by Barbara A. Lewis.* Read about kids who have committed themselves to making a difference. **Lexile**® measure: 820L

Baseball in April and Other Stories *by Gary Soto.* Choose from 11 short stories about young people overcoming obstacles, solving problems, and trying to achieve their goals. **Lexile**® measure: 830L

Derek Jeter *by Keith Elliot Greenberg.* Learn more about the life and career of baseball great Derek Jeter in this book in the Sports Heroes and Legends series. **Lexile**® measure: 1010L

Life in Ancient China *by Paul Challen.* Part of the Peoples of the Ancient World series, this book relates the history of Chinese society, including the emperor's Forbidden City, dynasties, and Confucius. **Lexile**® measure: GI1030L

The Ballad of Mulan *by Song Nan Zhang.* This Chinese poem has been teaching women for centuries that they can accomplish the same feats as men.

Dare To Dream! 25 Extraordinary Lives *by Sandra McLeod Humphrey.* Read about the lives of famous people in the 20th century who have overcome adversity and become successful.

Poetry for Young People: Langston Hughes *by David Roessel.* Learn about Langston Hughes's life, and read some of his poems.

The Road to TeenVision: How to Find Your Passion and Realize Your Dreams *by Gidget Clayton.* Find your strength and passion and achieve your dreams.

Films and TV

Everest: 50 Years on the Mountain (National Geographic, 2003) Celebrate the 50th anniversary of Edmund Hillary and Tenzing Norgay's historic first journey to the top of Everest. (90 min.)

Everest: Beyond the Limit (Discovery Channel, 2006) Climb with people who have something to prove as they make the harrowing expedition to the world's tallest peak. (287 min.)

Finding Forrester (Sony, 2000) Sixteen-year-old Jamal finds an unlikely mentor in William Forrester, a reclusive Pulitzer-winning novelist who helps Jamal achieve his dreams of being a writer. (136 min.)

Mad Hot Ballroom (Paramount, 2005) In this documentary, preteens are the unlikely but successful participants in a dance competition that tests what they have learned and how far they have come. (105 min.)

Mulan (Disney, 1998) Based on the Chinese tale, this movie tells the story of Mulan, a young girl who takes her father's place in fighting against the Huns. (88 min.)

The No-Guitar Blues (Phoenix Learning Group, 1991) Fausto Sanchez is trying to earn money to buy a guitar, but learns there is no goal worth sacrificing honesty. (27 min.)

October Sky (Universal Studios, 1999) Homer Hickam's early interest in rockets and science is brought to life in this film adaptation of his memoirs. (108 min.)

The Sally Ride Story: A Woman Space Pioneer (Global Science Productions, 2000) Sally Ride follows a difficult training regimen to achieve her goal of flying in space. (50 min.)

Websites

Mount Everest (National Geographic) Navigate this site to find information, games, articles, photos, and more about the National Geographic special on the 50th anniversary of the first ascent of Mount Everest.

The New York Yankees Official site—students can navigate the roster to find player stats and other information on Derek Jeter.

Poets.org Enter Langston Hughes's name in the "Find a Poem or Poet" feature on the left-hand side of the page to find biographical information about Hughes.

Ryan's Well Foundation Learn more about Ryan Hreljac, the boy who has one dream: clean drinking water for everyone around the world.

Magazines

Adventure World Learn about adventure-sport athletes and their dreams of conquering extreme events. Pick up fitness tips that will help you achieve your own goals.

National Geographic Find articles about explorers who are pursuing their dreams of discovering new places, new people, new animals, and new evidence of past civilizations

Sports Illustrated: Kids Read the stories of successful athletes who played their way to the top, never forgetting their dreams to win big.

WORLD WONDERS

Do we have a duty to preserve world wonders for future generations?

Parts of the Great Wall of China, such as this watchtower near Mutianya, China, have been well-preserved. Others, like the portion shown in the background image, have fallen into disrepair.

Unit Introduction

In two magazine articles, discover how two writers present the challenge of protecting the world's greatest monuments for future generations.

In "World's Wonders, Worn Down?" Cody Crane reports on the different factors that threaten to destroy our present-day wonders.

In an excerpt from "How to Save the Taj Mahal?" Jeffrey Bartholet examines the slow decay of one true modern wonder and the challenge of reconciling the duty to preserve history with the economic needs of the present.

WRITING PERFORMANCE TASK

Make an argument for the value of preserving one of the world wonders. Support your claim with clear reasons and relevant evidence.

MAGAZINE ARTICLE

"World's Wonders, Worn Down?" by Cody Crane

Language
- Academic Vocabulary
- Word Study: References

Reading Informational Text
- Identify Evidence
- Key Ideas and Details
- Craft and Structure

from **"How to Save the Taj Mahal?"** by Jeffrey Bartholet

Language
- Academic Vocabulary
- Word Study: Root Words

Reading Informational Text
- Identify Evidence
- Key Ideas and Details
- Craft and Structure

SPEAKING AND LISTENING

Plan and Hold a Class Debate
- Collaborate and Present

Checklist: Debate
- Scoring Guide

WRITING

Writing: Argumentative Essay
- Read the Model
- Analyze the Model
- Gather Evidence
- Organize Ideas

- Language Study: Vary Sentence Patterns
- Conventions Study: Constructing a Thesis Statement
- Revise, Edit, and Publish
- Performance Task Rubric

EXTENDED READING

Interview
"Talking About World Wonders"
by Joy Nolan

Magazine Article
"The Rise and Fall of China's Great Wall: The Race to Save a World Treasure"
from *Current Events*

Academic Vocabulary

"World's Wonders, Worn Down?" by Cody Crane

Rate your understanding of each word. Then read its meaning and write an example sentence. If the example is given, write the meaning.

Word	Meaning	Example
toll *(n.)* p. 101 ① ② ③ ④	the extent of damage or harm to something	
fate *(n.)* p. 101 ① ② ③ ④	final outcome	
canyon *(n.)* p. 103 ① ② ③ ④	a deep, narrow valley with steep sides of rock	
translucent *(adj.)* p. 104 ① ② ③ ④		The water in the lake is translucent enough to see fish swimming along the bottom.
corrosion *(n.)* p. 104 ① ② ③ ④	the weakening or destruction of metal due to water or chemicals	
durable *(adj.)* p. 105 ① ② ③ ④	strong and capable of lasting a long time	

Rating Scale | ① I don't know the word.   ② I've seen it or heard it.
                 ③ I know its meaning.   ④ I know it and use it.

Word Study

References

References are sources that tell the meaning of a word and other information about the word. They include dictionaries, glossaries, and thesauruses in both print and digital form.

Use the dictionary entry for the word *fare* to answer the questions below:

fare 1. (verb) to get by *He will not fare well in the cold weather.* fares, fared, **faring**, 2. (noun) a fee for transportation *The fare for the city bus is going up next month.* fares

1. How many meanings does the word *fare* have?

2. What is the first meaning of the word *fare*?

3. What part of speech is the second meaning of *fare*?

4. What is the past tense form of the first meaning of *fare*?

WORLD'S WONDERS, WORN DOWN?

by Cody Crane

¶1 How do you decide what places to visit when you go on vacation? The ancient Greeks made a list. This ancient travel guide contained the must-see statues, <u>monuments</u>, and places near Greece. These sites came to be known as the Seven Wonders of the World. Since then, wars, accidents, fires, and earthquakes have taken their **toll**, leaving only one ancient wonder—the Pyramids of Giza—still standing.

¶2 A group called the New7Wonders <u>Foundation</u> thinks it's time to update the top-seven list, and they want everyone's opinion to count. They have pared the list to 21 present-day wonders from around the globe. Would-be voters can go online to choose which historical sites should make the final cut.

¶3 How are the top contenders holding up to the test of time? Will they suffer **fates** similar to the original Seven Wonders? *Science World* spoke with experts to find out how some of the sites are faring, and what's being done to protect them.

Text Structure

1. Why does the writer begin the text with the question, "How do you decide what places to visit when you go on vacation?"

Academic Vocabulary

2. What can you infer about the top contenders for the New Seven Wonders based on the author's use of *fate* in **paragraph 3**?

Words to Know

<u>monuments:</u> *(n.)* buildings and statues built to honor an event or a person

<u>foundation:</u> *(n.)* an organization that collects money to use for a special purpose

Close Reading

Text Structure

3. Identify the heading and two subheadings on this page. What does each one tell you?

Text Structure

4. Look at the photo and read the caption. What details about the statues in **paragraph 4** does the image also show?

Caption

Words printed above or below an image to explain what the picture is showing.

Key Ideas and Details

5. Find details in the text that suggest it is possible to preserve the statues.

MYSTERIOUS MOAI

> Easter Island, Chile
> PROBLEM: *WEATHERING*

¶4 This South Pacific island is dotted with hundreds of giant statues, called Moai. Long ago, each statue was carved from blocks of the same igneous, or volcanic, rock that produced the island. Many of the statues are partially buried under shifting soil, so only their heads are visible. "Most people don't realize that the heads have torsos hidden underneath the ground," says Robert J. Koestler, director of the Smithsonian's Museum Conservation Institute. Being covered actually helps protect the statues, he adds. After thousands of years of rain and sea spray pelting the soft igneous stone, weathering has washed away many of the heads' facial features. Plants, bacteria, and fungi growing in cracks in the moist stone also break down the statues. One of the best-preserved Moai is on exhibit in the British Museum in London—far from Easter Island's harsh environment.

Words to Know

weathering: *(n.)* changing color or shape due to exposure to the weather

preserved: *(adj.)* saved; well-taken care of

PHARAOHS' TOMBS

Pyramid of Giza, Egypt
PROBLEM: *WEATHERING*

¶5　These <u>colossal</u> pyramids have stood in the desert outside of Cairo, Egypt, for more than 4,000 years. Ancient Egyptians built the <u>tombs</u> to honor their Pharaohs—the kings whom they believed to be gods. The blocks they used to build the pyramids were cut out of limestone, a sedimentary rock formed when layers of soil are deposited on top of each other. The pyramids once had smooth sides, but wind-blown sand has scoured away most of their outer shell. This weathering has exposed jagged inner layers. Archaeologists have learned much about ancient Egyptian culture by examining the pyramids, though they still debate how builders put the heavy blocks in place. However the pyramids were created, they were built to last.

LOST CITY

Petra, Jordan
PROBLEM: *EARTHQUAKES*

¶6　The city of Petra is hidden deep within a desert **canyon**. To enter, visitors first pass through a narrow crack of rock with walls hundreds of feet high on either side. The Nabataeans, the ancient people who built the city, chiseled many of the buildings right out of the sandstone walls. But Petra's location had a major downfall; it lies in the Great Rift Valley. As the ground moves along this fault, it generates earthquakes. Result: More than 90 percent of the city is now buried in rubble. Archaeologists like Martha Sharp Joukowsky of Brown University in Rhode Island are working to dig out the buildings. "Despite being in an earthquake-prone area, most of the buildings carved out of rock are still standing," she says.

Close Reading

Words and Phrases in Context

6. What context clues help you figure out the meaning of "scoured" in **paragraph 5**?

Writing

7. What evidence supports the idea that the pyramids are an important structure worthy of preservation?

The pyramids are worthy of preservation because _____.

This evidence shows that the pyramids _____.

Key Ideas and Details

8. What details suggest that it is possible to preserve the "Lost City" of Petra, Jordan? What details suggest that it is not possible to preserve it?

Words to Know

<u>colossal</u>: *(adj.)* very big; huge

<u>tombs</u>: *(n.)* graves; places where people are buried

Close Reading

Words and Phrases in Context

9. What is the meaning of the phrase "spared no expense"? Which details help you understand its meaning?

Writing

10. What argument does the author make about what is taking a "toll" on the Taj Mahal? How does the author support this argument?

The author supports his argument that _____ by _____.

Key Ideas and Details

11. Find three details that the author includes to convey the importance of the Eiffel Tower.

MONUMENT TO LOVE

> Taj Mahal, India
> PROBLEM: *POLLUTION*

¶7 When Shah Jehan's wife died, the Muslim emperor spared no expense in building an enormous domed <u>mausoleum</u> fit for his queen. The Taj Mahal's gleaming, white surface is made from marble, a metamorphic rock formed when heat and pressure underground cause minerals to crystallize. Polishing these crystals produces a **translucent**, shining surface. Despite the Taj's romantic history, the modern world may be taking its toll on the monument. Factories, oil refineries, and cars in the nearby city of Agra pump pollution into the air. The pollutants have begun to eat away and discolor the white marble. So far, some of the damaged sections of stone have been replaced and the Indian government is working on ways to improve the city's air quality.

ENGINEERING MARVEL

> Eiffel Tower, France
> PROBLEM: *CORROSION*

¶8 Named after its designer, Alexandre-Gustave Eiffel, this tower is the most visited monument in the world. Eiffel built the tower in 1889 to celebrate the 100th anniversary of the French Revolution. It is the tallest structure in the Paris skyline, standing 324 meters (1,063 feet) tall. The tower is made entirely of metal iron. Since metals are good <u>conductors</u> of heat, when temperatures warm up during the day the tower's metal frame expands, causing it to lean as much as 28 centimeters (7.1 inches). Luckily, the tower was designed to bend easily. A bigger risk: Oxygen from the air and rainwater can cause iron to rust. To prevent this type of **corrosion**, high-climbing workers repaint the tower every seven years.

Words to Know

<u>mausoleum:</u> *(n.)* a large stone building where the dead bodies of important families are kept

<u>conductors:</u> *(n.)* things that allow electrical currents to flow through them easily

SYMBOL OF FREEDOM

Statue of Liberty, United States
PROBLEM: *CORROSION*

¶9 Given as a gift from France to the U.S. in 1886, the Statue of Liberty stands on an island in New York Harbor. "It's the first thing many immigrants saw when they arrived in America and (is) a symbol of freedom," says Pamela Jerome, a professor of historic preservation at Columbia University in New York. The thin copper layer covering the statue was once the color of a penny. This layer is now blue-green—the result of the metal reacting with water and air to create copper carbonate. This naturally occurring coating protects the remaining copper underneath. Water also corroded much of the statue's original iron skeleton. To ensure Lady Liberty's safety, beginning in 1984, iron pieces were replaced with the <u>alloy</u> stainless steel—a **durable** mixture of iron, carbon, and other metals.

CITY IN THE CLOUDS

Machu Picchu, Peru
PROBLEM: *EROSION*

¶10 The ancient city of Machu Picchu sits atop a peak in Peru's Andes Mountains. To create space to grow food, the Incas carved terraces into the steep slopes. These steps prevented erosion by stopping soil from washing down the mountainsides. But a different type of erosion now threatens the city: The pounding feet of tourists are damaging the city's <u>fragile</u> stones. Thousands visit the city every day, says Michelle Berenfeld, a program manager for the World Monuments Fund (WMF). Among other things, the WMF develops plans to help tourists better navigate historical places. "Sites like Machu Picchu are the only things left to tell us about cultures that are now gone. But the more people know and appreciate a site, the more they will want to preserve it," says Berenfeld.

Words to Know

alloy: *(n.)* a mixture of two or more metals

fragile: *(adj.)* easy to break or damage

Close Reading

Text Structure

12. How does the writer support the idea that the Statue of Liberty is a "symbol of freedom"?

Words and Phrases in Context

13. What is the effect of describing the "pounding feet of tourists" on Machu Picchu's "fragile stones" in **paragraph 10**?

Words and Phrases in Context

14. What does the author mean when he writes that the WMF "develops plans to help tourists better navigate historical places"?

Identify Evidence | Analyze Individuals, Events, and Ideas

Reread **"World's Wonders, Worn Down?"** highlighting facts, details, and expert quotations that Crane includes that support the idea that the World Wonders should be preserved.

How does he introduce, illustrate, and elaborate individuals, events, and ideas?

- In the Wonder column, name the wonder.
- In the Problem column, explain one problem detailed in the text that threatens the wonder.
- In the Solution column, explain one way to solve the problem, based on details in the text. Note if no solution is provided in the text.
- In the Argument column, record one detail from the text that could be used to argue for saving the wonder.

Wonder	Problem	Solution	Argument for Saving the Wonder
1. Easter Island (page 102)	"weathering has washed away many of the heads' facial features"	cover the statues; "being covered actually helps," says expert Robert J. Koestler	They have been around for "thousands of years."
2. Pyramid of Giza (page 103)			
3. Lost City of Petra (page 103)			
4. Taj Mahal (page 104)			

Wonder	Problem	Solution	Argument for Saving the Wonder
5. Eiffel Tower (page 104)			
6. Statue of Liberty (page 105)			
7. Machu Picchu (page 105)			

Key Ideas and Details

Determining the Central Idea

1. Use the evidence you collected to summarize the key idea of Crane's article. What is the central idea of the informational article?

2. List the five key problems threatening wonders that Crane explains in this text. Explain how each problem is a threat.

Problem	How It Is a Threat
weathering	wears the surface of a Wonder

Craft and Structure

Structure of the Informational Text

1. What is the purpose of the first three paragraphs of the text?

2. How does the author organize the information that follows those introductory paragraphs?

3. What pattern does the author follow to present information in the body of the article?

Author's Perspective and Purpose

4. Does the author include his opinion about whether the wonders can be saved?

5. Is the author's purpose to inform or to persuade? How do you know?

Author's Purpose

Author's purpose is the reason an author writes a story. Authors write to inform, to entertain, or to persuade.

Perspective

A person's personal opinions or attitudes about something is his or her perspective. Authors communicate their perspectives through the choices they make in their writing.

Academic Vocabulary

"How to Save the Taj Mahal?" by Jeffrey Bartholet

Rate your understanding of each word. Then read its meaning and write an example sentence. If the example is given, write the meaning.

Word	Meaning	Example
skeptical *(adj.)* p. 111 ① ② ③ ④	having feelings of doubt about something	
deteriorate *(v.)* p. 112 ① ② ③ ④	to weaken, fall apart, or grow worse	
degrade *(v.)* p. 114 ① ② ③ ④		Most cars degrade in value over time.
contribute *(v.)* p. 115 ① ② ③ ④	to help or add to something	
priority *(n.)* p. 116 ① ② ③ ④	something that is more important than something else	
endure *(v.)* p. 118 ① ② ③ ④	to last for a long time	

Rating Scale
① I don't know the word.
③ I know its meaning.
② I've seen it or heard it.
④ I know it and use it.

Word Study

Root Word

A **root word** is a word to which prefixes, suffixes, and endings may be added. You can use the root word and its prefixes and suffixes to determine the meaning of a word.

Adding a suffix to a root word changes its meaning.

-ion/-tion is a suffix that means:

- the result, act, or state of something

The word *confuse* means "to cause someone to not think clearly." Adding *-ion* to the end of *confuse* creates the word *confusion*, which means "the state of being confused."

How does the meaning of the following Academic Vocabulary root words change by adding the suffix *-ion/-tion*?

1. *Contribution* means _____.
2. *Degradation* means _____.
3. *Deterioration* means _____.

How to Save the Taj Mahal?
by Jeffrey Bartholet

Close Reading

¶1 To view the Taj Mahal far from the hawkers and crowds, I had hoped to approach it in a small boat on the Yamuna River, which flows in a wide arc along the rear of the majestic 17th-century tomb.

¶2 My guide, a journalist and environmental <u>activist</u> named Brij Khandelwal, was **skeptical**. The river was low, he said; there may not be enough water to float a boat. But he was game. So one morning, we met in downtown Agra, a city of more than 1.4 million people. Eventually we arrived at a spot opposite the Taj. There we hoped to find a fisherman to take us across.

¶3 We stood before a rusty coil of barbed wire, listening to chanting from the nearby shrine, trying to make out the glory of the Taj Mahal through the <u>haze</u>.

Text Structure

1. What is the effect of beginning the text with "To view the Taj Mahal far from hawkers and crowds, I hoped to approach it in a small boat . . ."?

Words to Know

<u>activist:</u> *(n.)* someone who works to make change to improve a situation

<u>haze:</u> *(n.)* smoke or pollution that dirties the air

Close Reading

Text Structure

2. Why does the author shift away from the descriptions of his personal journey in **paragraph 4**?

Academic Vocabulary

3. Describe what is causing the white marble to "deteriorate" in **paragraph 4**. Why is this deterioration described as a "casualty"?

Key Ideas and Details

4. What claim about the Taj Mahal does Bartholet introduce in **paragraph 5**?

Claim

A **claim** is an arguable statement or position.

¶4 The Indian press has been filled with reports that the latest government efforts to control pollution around the Taj are failing and that the gorgeous white marble is **deteriorating**—a possible <u>casualty</u> of India's booming population, rapid economic expansion and lax environmental regulations. Some local preservationists, echoing the concerns of R. Nath, an Indian historian who has written extensively about the Taj, warn that the edifice is in danger of sinking or even collapsing toward the river. They also complain that the Archaeological Survey of India (ASI) has done slipshod repair work and call for fresh assessments of the structure's foundations.

¶5 The criticisms are a measure of how important the complex is to India and the world, as a symbol of historical and cultural glory, and as an architectural marvel. It was constructed of brick covered with marble and sandstone, with elaborate inlays of precious and semiprecious stones. The designers and builders, in their <u>unerring</u> sense of form and symmetry, infused the entire 42-acre complex of buildings, gates, walls and gardens with unearthly grace. "It combines the great rationality of its design with an appeal to the senses," says Ebba Koch, author of *The Complete Taj Mahal*, a careful study of the monument published in 2006. "It was created by fusing so many architectural traditions—Central Asian, Indian, Hindu and Islamic, Persian and European—it has universal appeal and can speak to the whole world."

Words to Know

<u>casualty:</u> *(n.)* a person killed in a war or an accident

<u>unerring:</u> *(adj.)* always right or accurate

¶6 Part of the Taj Mahal's beauty <u>derives</u> from the story the stones **embody**. Though a tomb for the dead, it is also a monument to love, built by the Mughal emperor Shah Jahan, fifth in a line of rulers who had originally come as conquerors from the Central Asian steppes. The Mughals were the dominant power on the Indian subcontinent for much of the 16th to 18th centuries, and the empire reached its cultural zenith under Shah Jahan. He constructed the Taj (which means "crown," and is also a form of the Persian word "chosen") as a final resting place for his favorite wife, Arjumand Banu, better known as Mumtaz Mahal (Chosen One of the Palace). A court poet recorded the emperor's despair at her death in 1631, at the age of 38, after giving birth to the couple's 14th child: "The color of youth flew away from his cheeks; The flower of his countenance ceased blooming." He wept so often "his tearful eyes sought help from spectacles." To honor his wife, Shah Jahan decided to build a tomb so magnificent that it would be remembered throughout the ages.

¶7 For more than 15 years, he directed the construction of a complex of buildings and gardens that was meant to mirror the Islamic vision of Paradise. First he selected the perfect spot: it had to be <u>tranquil</u>, away from the bustle of Agra, even then a thriving commercial center.

¶8 The Taj site was located along a sharp bend in the Yamuna, which slowed the movement of the water and also reduced the possibility of erosion along the riverbank. The water, moreover, provided a glistening mirror to reflect light from the marble, which changes color and tone depending on the hour, day and season.

¶9 Unable to cross the river by boat, I went to the Taj complex in the conventional manner: on foot, and then in a bicycle rickshaw.

Words to Know

<u>derives</u>: *(v.)* comes from

<u>tranquil</u>: *(adj.)* peaceful and calm

Close Reading

Text Structure

5. How does the author tell "the story the stones embody" in **paragraph 6**?

Writing

6. What evidence supports the claims that the Taj Mahal is a "symbol of historical and cultural glory" as well as an "architectural marvel"?

The Taj Mahal is _____ because _____.

Key Ideas and Details

7. What two effects did the construction of the Taj Mahal have on the river, as outlined in **paragraph 8**?

Close Reading

Text Structure

8. What idea in **paragraph 11** is the author commenting on with his statement, "Presumably, the end of time is still a long way off"?

Writing

9. Compare and contrast how Bartholet describes the deterioration of the marble in **paragraph 11** with how Crane describes it in "World's Wonders, Worn Down?"

   Although Bartholet writes ____, Crane ____.

   Both Crane and Bartholet ____.

Key Ideas and Details

10. How does Mehta emphasize his point in **paragraph 13** that more needs to be done to save the Taj Mahal?

¶10 While the Taj is a testament to love, it also embodied the power of Shah Jahan himself. As the emperor's historian wrote: "They laid the plan for a magnificent building and a dome of high foundation which for its <u>loftiness</u> will until the Day of Resurrection remain a memorial to the sky-reaching ambition of His Majesty . . . and its strength will represent the firmness of the <u>intentions</u> of its builder."

¶11 Presumably, the end of time is still a long way off, but the Taj is slowly deteriorating now. Seen up close, the marble has yellow-orange stains in many places; some slabs have small holes where the stone has been eaten away; in a few places, chunks have fallen from the facade; my guide Brij and I even found a bit of recent graffiti on the white marble platform, where two visitors, Ramesh and Bittoo, had signed their names in red ink.

¶12 For decades activists and lawyers have been waging a legal battle to save the Taj Mahal from what they believe is environmental **degradation**. M.C. Mehta, currently one of India's best-known lawyers, has been at the forefront of that fight. I met him twice in New Delhi in a half-finished office with holes in the walls and wires dangling out.

¶13 "The monument gives glory to the city, and the city gives glory to the monument," he tells me, exasperated that more has not been done to clean up Agra and the Yamuna River. "This has taken more than 25 years of my life. I say: 'Don't be so slow! If somebody is dying, you don't wait.'"

Words to Know

<u>loftiness:</u> *(n.)* grandness or arrogance

<u>intentions:</u> *(n.)* plans or what one wants for a situation

¶14 When he began his campaign in the 1980s, one of Mehta's main targets was an oil refinery upwind of the Taj Mahal that spewed sulfur dioxide. Preservationists believed the plant emissions were causing acid rain, which was eating away at the stone of the monument—what Mehta calls "marble cancer." Mehta petitioned the Supreme Court and argued that the Taj was important both to India's <u>heritage</u> and as a tourist attraction that **contributed** more to the economy than an oil refinery. He wanted all polluters, including iron foundries and other small industries in Agra, shut down, moved out or forced to install cleaner technology. In 1996, twelve years after he filed the motion, the court ruled in his favor, and the foundries around Agra were closed, <u>relocated</u> or—as was the case with the refinery—compelled to switch to natural gas.

¶15 But for all his successes, Mehta believes there's much more to be done.

¶16 The river, once such an integral component of the Taj's beauty, is a mess, to put it mildly. I visited one of the city's storm drains where it empties at a spot between the Taj Mahal and the Agra Fort, a vast sandstone-and-marble complex that was once home to Mughal rulers. In addition to the untreated human waste deposited there, the drain belches mounds of litter—heaps of plastic bags, plastic foam, snack wrappers, bottles and empty foil packets that once held herbal mouth freshener. Environmental activists have argued that such garbage dumps produce methane gas that contributes to the yellowing of the Taj's marble.

Close Reading

Words and Phrases in Context

11. What is the meaning of the phrase "ruled in his favor" in **paragraph 14**? Which details help you understand its meaning?

Text Structure

12. What does the transition word *but* in **paragraph 15** indicate that the author will discuss next?

Key Ideas and Details

13. Describe how the author supports his claim in **paragraph 16** that the Yamuna River "is a mess."

Words to Know

<u>heritage</u>: *(n.)* one's history and background

<u>relocated</u>: *(v.)* moved to a new place

Close Reading

Text Structure

14. Why do some in Agra "oppose" the campaign to preserve the Taj Mahal?

Academic Vocabulary

15. In **paragraph 17**, what do some people say are bigger "priorities" than saving the Taj Mahal?

Writing

16. Identify how the author elaborates in **paragraph 18** on the claim he presents in **paragraph 17**?

Elaborating on his claim that ____,
Bartholet writes ____.

¶**17** There are many in Agra who believe that all the worries about the Taj are exaggerated—that far too much attention is paid to the monument at the expense of other **priorities**. They say the restrictions <u>imposed</u> upon the city's several hundred brick kilns, iron foundries and glassworks to reduce air pollution have harmed the local economy. S.M. Khandelwal, a business leader in Agra who opposed Mehta's legal campaign, has long argued that such businesses were responsible for only a tiny fraction of the fumes emitted in the city, and that the more significant polluters were vehicles and power generators. "I was very angry that everyone was so concerned about the Taj Mahal and not about the [livelihoods of the] people of Agra," he says.

¶**18** Even some international experts doubt that air pollution is the <u>prime</u> cause of the discoloring and pitting of the monument's marble. At least some of the yellow marks on the monument, for instance, are rust stains from iron fixtures that hold the marble slabs in place. Marisa Laurenzi Tabasso, an Italian chemist and conservation scientist, has studied the Taj Mahal on behalf of international organizations and Indian authorities. "Most of the problems with the marble are not from pollution, but from climatic conditions," she says. These include heat, sunlight and also moisture, which promotes the growth of algae, leading to biological decay of the stone. Laurenzi Tabasso says the main human impact on the monument probably occurs inside the tomb, where the moist breath of thousands of daily visitors—and their oily hands rubbing the walls—has discolored the marble.

Words to Know

<u>imposed:</u> *(v.)* forced on someone or something

<u>prime:</u> *(adj.)* first, main, or most important

¶19 The main concern, however, is the Yamuna River. Some of the activists I met in Agra cited arguments made by R. Nath, who has written dozens of books on Mughal history and architecture. Nath believes that the river water is essential to maintaining the monument's massive foundation, which is built on a complex system of wells, arches—and, according to Nath—spoked wheels made of sal wood. Nath and some activists worry the groundwater levels beneath the monument are falling—partly the result of a barrier that was constructed upstream to augment public water supplies—and they fear the wood may disintegrate if it isn't kept moist. Nath also believes the Yamuna River itself is part of a complicated engineering feat that provides thrust from different angles as the water wends its way behind the mausoleum. But, due to the lower water level, the Yamuna now dries up for months at a time. Without that <u>stabilizing</u> counterforce of flowing water, the Taj "has a natural <u>tendency</u> to slide or sink into the river," Nath says.

¶20 When I asked ASI officials about the foundation, they said it was fine. ASI officials, however, declined to answer several queries about whether deep boreholes had been drilled.

Close Reading

Words and Phrases in Context

17. Define *foundation* as it is used in **paragraph 19**, and explain how this meaning of the word differs from its meaning in Text 1.

Text Structure

18. In **paragraph 19**, Bartholet varies his sentence pattern using dashes. What effect does this have?

Words to Know

<u>stabilizing:</u> *(adj.)* reinforcing or giving a sense of balance to something

<u>tendency:</u> *(n.)* likely to happen

Close Reading

Text Structure

19. Identify how Bartholet signals to the reader that he is beginning the conclusion to his essay in **paragraph 21**.

Words and Phrases in Context

20. Define *impermanence* as used in **paragraph 21**.

Text Structure

21. How does Bartholet support his claim that Shah Jahan might be "philosophical" about the Taj Mahal's deterioration?

¶21 What would Shah Jahan make of it all? Dixit believes he would be saddened by the state of the river, "but he'd also be happy to see the crowds." Shah Jahan might even be <u>philosophical</u> about the slow deterioration. He had designed the monument to **endure** beyond the end of the world, yet the first report on record of damage and leaks came in 1652. The emperor was certainly familiar with the <u>impermanence</u> of things. When his beloved Mumtaz Mahal died, a court historian wrote:

¶22 *"Alas! This transitory world is unstable, and the rose of its comfort is embedded in a field of thorns. In the dust bin of the world, no breeze blows which does not raise the dust of anguish; and in the assembly of the world, no one happily occupies a seat who does not vacate it full of sorrow."*

Scaffolding surrounds an entryway to the Taj Mahal

Words to Know

<u>philosophical</u>: *(adj.)* believing in intellectual discussion of reality, nature, and humanity

<u>scaffolding</u>: *(n.)* poles and boards built around the outside of a building for workers to stand on

¶**23** If the symbolic power of the Taj can be harnessed to fight for a cleaner river, cleaner air and better living <u>conditions</u>, all the better. But most of the Taj Mahal's flaws don't detract from the overall effect of the monument. In some ways, the yellowing and pocking add to its beauty, just as flaws in a handmade Oriental carpet enhance its aesthetic power, or the patina on an antique piece of furniture is more valued, even with its scratches and scars, than a gleaming restoration job. Standing before the Taj Mahal, it's comforting to know that it is not, in fact, of another world. It is very much part of this ephemeral, <u>unpredictable</u> one we inhabit—a singular masterpiece that will likely be around for many years or even lifetimes to come, but which, despite our best efforts, cannot last forever.

Trash from the Yamuna River washes on shore near the Taj Mahal

Words to Know

<u>conditions:</u> *(n.)* situations or factors of a specific situation

<u>unpredictable:</u> *(adj.)* difficult to know what will happen next

Close Reading

Words and Phrases in Context

22. What is the meaning of *harnessed* in **paragraph 23**? What details help you understand its meaning?

Writing

23. Why does Bartholet claim that the deterioration of the Taj Mahal "add[s] to its beauty"?

Bartholet writes that although _____, the Taj Mahal _____.

Identify Evidence | Analyze Individuals, Events, and Ideas

Reread **"How to Save the Taj Mahal?"** highlighting facts, details, and quotations from experts that Bartholet includes to support the idea that the Taj Mahal can and should be preserved.

How does he introduce, illustrate, and elaborate on individuals, events, and ideas?

- In the Evidence column, record evidence about why or how to preserve the Taj Mahal.
- In the Explanation column, explain how the evidence could be used to support the idea that the Taj Mahal should be preserved.

Evidence	Page	Explanation
1. "a symbol of historical and cultural glory"	112	*shows Taj Mahal is important to India's past and present*
2. "infused the entire 42-acre complex of buildings, gates, walls, and gardens with unearthly grace"		
3. "it is also a monument to love, built by the Mughal emperor Shah Jahan"		
4. "reduced the possibility of erosion along the riverbank"		

Evidence	Page	Explanation
5.		
6.		
7.		

Key Ideas and Details

Determining the Central Idea

1. Use the evidence you collected to summarize the key idea of Bartholet's essay.

2. List four key problematic events that Bartholet introduces in his essay. Explain how each event is important to the central idea.

Events	Significance
pollution	possibly causing marble to deteriorate

3. List three key people that Bartholet introduces in his essay. Explain how each person is important to the central idea.

Individuals	Significance

Craft and Structure

Structure of the Article

1. What topics does Bartholet discuss in his article?

Article

An **article** is a piece of writing about a specific subject, found in a newspaper or magazine.

2. Bartholet weaves back and forth between topics. In what order does he discuss the topics?

Perspective

Someone's personal opinion or attitude about something is his or her **perspective**.

Author's Perspective

3. Make a list of the words and phrases used to describe the Taj Mahal. What do these words and phrases show about Bartholet's views on the Taj Mahal?

4. Whose opinions does Bartholet give about what is damaging the Taj Mahal?

5. What is Bartholet's purpose in writing this article about the Taj Mahal?

6. Based on these details, what is his perspective on the Taj Mahal?

Collaborate and Present

Plan and Hold a Class Debate

Throughout his essay, Bartholet describes M.C. Mehta's frustrations with what he feels is a lack of effort to save the Taj Mahal. Is Mehta right—should the Taj be saved?

Assignment: With a partner, gather evidence supporting your assigned stance on the issue of whether or not to save the Taj Mahal. Then debate a team who has been assigned the opposing stance.

Analyze the Content

1. Consider the following questions:
   - What evidence do Crane and Bartholet include in their texts that suggest the Taj Mahal can be saved? What do they include that suggests the Taj Mahal cannot— or does not need to—be saved?

2. Write down the strongest evidence, the claim you feel this evidence supports, and a potential counterclaim. Discuss why you think your evidence is strong.

Evidence	Claim	Counterclaim

3. Write down your claims, counterclaims and evidence on your debate cards to refer to during the debate.

Prepare Your Points

4. Work with your partner to practice your debate points. Point out when your partner has made an unsupported claim. Take turns arguing the opposing view to prepare for countering your opponents' claim in the official debate.

Debate

5. Participate in the debate.

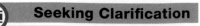

Seeking Clarification

- So, your claim is that . . .
- To clarify, you are saying that . . .
- Can you explain more about why . . .

Reporting Ideas

- _____ argued that . . .
- _____ claimed that . . .
- _____ countered the argument with . . .

Comparing Ideas

- We both believe that . . .
- Although we agree that . . .
- However, one way we disagree is . . .

Debate Checklist

Use the checklist below to evaluate your collaboration skills, reasoning, and debate performance.
Think carefully about your work. If you know you completed an item thoroughly, give yourself a check (✓).

COLLABORATE AND PRESENT CHECKLIST		
Comprehension & Collaboration	**Evidence and Reasoning**	**Presentation of Knowledge & Ideas**
☐ Come to discussions prepared, having read and studied material.	☐ Explain the purpose of the debate.	☐ Adapt language to a variety of contexts and tasks to demonstrate knowledge of formal English.
☐ Refer to evidence when contributing to the debate.	☐ Present information relevant to the task.	☐ Respond to the opposing team in respectful, polite manner.
☐ Follow rules for debate and lead by example.	☐ Explain why the Taj Mahal should or should not be saved.	☐ Use appropriate volume/tone (clear, not too fast, too slow, or too loud) and avoid using *like* or *ummm*.
☐ Ask and answer specific questions.	☐ Support claims with clear reasons and relevant evidence from Unit texts.	☐ Have strong posture, a confident stance, and make frequent eye contact.
☐ Make comments that contribute to the topic under debate.	☐ Respond to opposing claims with clear reasons and relevant evidence.	☐ Occasionally move from one spot to another, without fidgeting.
☐ Review the key ideas under debate and demonstrate understanding of multiple perspectives through reflection and paraphrasing.	☐ Synthesize the key ideas from your debate with a conclusion.	☐ Smile and act relaxed.
Number of ✓s in this category: ___	**Number of ✓s in this category:** ___	**Number of ✓s in this category:** ___
Total # of ✓s: ___		

Add up the total number of checks (✓) in each category. Then use the scoring guide below to calculate your final score.

Scoring Guide			
16 to 18 ✓s	13 to 15 ✓s	11 to 12 ✓s	10 or less ✓s
④ Exemplary	③ Meets Standards	② Needs Work	① Does Not Meet Standards

Read the Model

Writers use many strategies to craft ideas, share information, and persuade readers. The writer of this argumentative essay makes a case for preserving one of the world wonders with specific facts and details about the monument. Read and discuss the model essay below.

Argumentative Essay

An **argument** is a reasoned, logical way of demonstrating the validity of a position, belief, or conclusion.

The introduction introduces the issue and the claim the author is making about that issue.

- Identify the author's claim.

The body paragraphs contain reasons and evidence that supports the author's claim.

- Find two pieces of text evidence the author uses to support his claim.

The conclusion restates the thesis and offers a recommendation.

- Identify the author's recommendation.

Preserve the Great Wall for Future Generations

By Alicia Milos

"Wonder" is defined as "a cause of astonishment or admiration." The Great Wall of China certainly fits this definition. It's considered one of the Seven Wonders of the World. However, years of neglect and misuse have taken their toll. In order to preserve this monument for future generations, we must take action now.

The Great Wall has a rich history that must be shared with future generations. Originally, it was built as a fortress to keep invaders out and protect the Chinese cities and towns. Construction began on the Great Wall as early as 600 BC. The 4,000 mile structure was not completed for almost 22 centuries. The work on this masterpiece was painstakingly done by hand. Construction was overseen by two dynasties.

Today, the great structure is in danger. In the article "The Race to Save a World Treasure," the author writes, ". . . only about 1,500 miles of the wall remain. The rest has fallen apart and disappeared" (140). The progress of the modern world—along with natural elements and neglect—may be slowly wearing away the Wall. In one small village people have taken bricks from the wall to build houses. A highway has "plowed through" another section. Additionally, "…desert sandstorms have worn down much of China's great wonder" (142).

Small steps have been taken to preserve this wonder. The article reports that in an effort to protect what remains of the structure, ". . . the World Monuments Fund placed the Great Wall on its list of 100 Most Endangered Sites" (140). But more work must begin immediately to fix the damage already done and stop further misuse. For centuries the Great Wall has represented the beauty and history of China. How can we preserve it for future generations to enjoy?

Analyze the Model

An argumentative essay states a thesis, or claim, and supports it with logical reasons and evidence from a reliable source in order to persuade readers.

Introduction

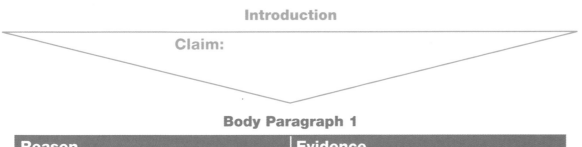

Claim:

Body Paragraph 1

Reason	Evidence
The Great Wall is an important piece of China's history.	•
	•

Body Paragraph 2

Reason	Evidence
	•
	•

Conclusion

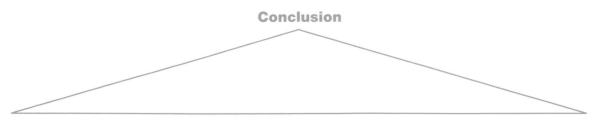

Supporting Evidence

In an **argumentative essay**, the writer presents a claim in the thesis statement.

The writer supports his or her claim with an organizational structure that effectively and logically presents reasons and supporting evidence. The topic sentence of each body paragraph clearly states a reason for the writer's claim. The writer supports these reasons with relevant evidence.

- Evaluate whether each reason supports the thesis.

Relevant evidence includes evidence from relevant sources. This evidence can be a direct quotation or a paraphrase from the text, and should include the text title, author, if given, and page number on which the evidence appears in the source.

- Identify how the writer included evidence from "The Race To Save a World Treasure" in her essay.

Step 1 | Gather Evidence

> Make an argument for the value of preserving one of the world wonders. Support your claim with clear reasons and relevant evidence.

What You Need to Know | Examine the evidence you have collected (see pages 106 and 120).

What You Need to Write | Use a note-taking guide to list facts, data, and details that you will use to support your argument.

TOPIC

Make an argument for the value of preserving one of the world wonders.

Reason #1

Text:

Evidence:

Page # _____

Reason #2

Text:

Evidence:

Page # _____

Reason #3

Text:

Evidence:

Page # _____

Reason #4

Text:

Evidence:

Page # _____

Step 2 | Organize Ideas

What You Need to Know | To write an effective argument, you must support your claim with specific and relevant facts, data, and details.

To develop your topic:

1. List the reasons why you believe this monument should be preserved.

2. Note at least two specific facts, data, or details from the Unit articles that support your reasons.

What You Need to Write | Study the evidence you have gathered and organize the reasons and evidence that best support your claim.

Body Paragraph 1

Reason	Evidence
	• •

Body Paragraph 2

Reason	Evidence
	• •

Step 3 | Draft

Write a draft of your argument on the computer or on paper.

Language Study | Constructing a Thesis Statement

See It | A thesis statement summarizes your entire essay. When writing thesis statements:
- **Present your claim.**
  - **Preview the reasons outlined in your body paragraphs that support this opinion.**

Try It | Read each pair of sentences. Write a thesis statement by combining the sentence that states the writer's claim with the sentence that previews the writer's evidence.

1. **Claim:** Factories near the Eiffel Tower should be closed.

   Evidence: The factories create air pollution that contributes to the corrosion of the Tower.

2. **Claim:** The Statue of Liberty is the most avant-garde structure in the United States.

   Evidence: The skeletal framing under the Statue of Liberty's skirt is the same kind of steel framing now used for many modern skyscrapers.

3. **Claim:** We must work to preserve the pharaohs' tombs in Egypt.

   Evidence: Archaeologists have learned much about ancient Egyptian culture by studying the pyramids and tombs, and there is still much more to discover.

Apply It

Use the frames below to practice writing thesis statements. Then revise your thesis statement or conclusion.

1. _____ must be preserved because _____ and _____.
   (World Wonder)   (reason)   (reason)

2. In order to _____ and _____, we must join forces to preserve _____.
   (reason)   (reason)   (World Wonder)

3. If _____ is not preserved, _____ and _____.
   (World Wonder)   (reason)   (reason)

4. There is great value in preserving _____, because _____ and _____.
   (World Wonder)   (reason)   (reason)

Now, **go back to your draft** and reread your conclusion. Remember that a strong conclusion restates the thesis. Rephrase your thesis statement to use in your revised conclusion.

_____

_____

_____

_____

_____

Conventions Study | Vary Sentence Patterns

See It | Sentence patterns describe how the parts of a sentence are organized. Just like word choice, writers should vary their sentence patterns in order to add variety and avoid repetition in their writing.

Try It | Find the different sentence patterns the writer of the model essay used in the paragraph below.

> Today, the great structure is in danger. In the article "The Race to Save a World Treasure," the author writes on page 140, ". . . only about 1,500 miles of the wall remain. The rest has fallen apart and disappeared." The progress of the modern world—along with natural elements and neglect—may be slowly wearing away the Wall. In one small village, people have taken bricks from the wall to build houses. A highway has "plowed through" another section.

Apply It | Revise these sentences to add variety and avoid repetition.

1. Jake and his family went on vacation. They visited the Eiffel Tower while they were on vacation.

_____

_____

2. They climbed to the top. The climb took a long time. They took pictures at the top.

_____

Step 4 | Revise and Edit   Revise your draft with a partner.

Organization and Clarity					
Introduce a claim and support it with clear, organized reasons and relevant evidence.	Self	1	2	3	4
	Partner	1	2	3	4
Use words, phrases, and clauses to clarify the relationship between the claim and supporting reasons.	Self	1	2	3	4
	Partner	1	2	3	4
Establish and maintain a formal style.	Self	1	2	3	4
	Partner	1	2	3	4
Use words, phrases, and clauses to clarify the relationship between the claim and supporting reasons.	Self	1	2	3	4
	Partner	1	2	3	4
Provide a concluding statement that follows from the evidence presented.	Self	1	2	3	4
	Partner	1	2	3	4

Evidence and Reasoning					
Make a case for preserving one of the potential New World Wonders.	Self	1	2	3	4
	Partner	1	2	3	4
Support claim using evidence from the Unit texts, correctly citing the author and page number for each piece of evidence.	Self	1	2	3	4
	Partner	1	2	3	4

Language and Convention					
Recognize and adjust variations from standard English.	Self	1	2	3	4
	Partner	1	2	3	4
Correctly punctuate, capitalize, and spell all words and phrases.	Self	1	2	3	4
	Partner	1	2	3	4
Vary sentence patterns for meaning, reader interest, and variety.	Self	1	2	3	4
	Partner	1	2	3	4

Scoring Guide | ① needs improvement   ② average   ③ good   ④ excellent

Step 5 | Publish   Publish your essay either in print or digital form.

Publish

Publish your argument either in print or digital form. Use the rubric below to assess your final performance task.

PERFORMANCE TASK RUBRIC			
Score Point	Organization and Clarity	Evidence and Reasoning	Language and Conventions
Exemplary ④	• introductory paragraph includes a **strong thesis statement** that **makes a convincing claim** about why the wonder should be saved • body paragraphs are **effectively organized** and **present logical reasons and evidence** to support the claim • includes **well-chosen** text evidence, precise language, and a variety of sentences • concluding statement **restates the thesis statement** and reasons for the claim	• **accurately explains and convincingly persuades** why the world wonder should be saved • includes **relevant** factual evidence from the magazine article to support each reason for saving the wonder • ends by **effectively restating** the thesis statement and **convincingly persuading** the reader to agree with the author's point of view	• demonstrates a **strong command** of the conventions of standard English grammar and usage, as well as of standard English capitalization, punctuation, and spelling • vocabulary is **appropriate** to the topic (vocabulary about the world wonder; accurate vocabulary for a convincing thesis statement; vocabulary for a variety of sentence patterns)
Meets Standards ③	• introductory paragraph **includes an adequate thesis statement that makes a claim** about why the wonder should be saved • body paragraphs are **logically organized** and **present reasons and evidence** to support the claim • includes **some** text evidence, precise language and sentence variety • concluding statement **restates the thesis statement**	• **adequately explains and generally persuades** why the wonder should be saved • includes **some relevant** factual evidence from the magazine article to support each reason for saving the wonder • ends by **restating** the thesis statement and **persuading** the reader to agree with the author's point of view	• demonstrates **a near command** of the conventions of standard English grammar and usage, as well as of standard English capitalization, punctuation, and spelling **with some errors** • vocabulary is **appropriate** to the topic (vocabulary about the world wonder; accurate vocabulary for a convincing thesis statement; vocabulary for a variety of sentence patterns)

PERFORMANCE TASK RUBRIC

Score Point	Organization and Clarity	Evidence and Reasoning	Language and Conventions
Needs Work ②	• introductory paragraph **includes a weak thesis statement that attempts to make a claim** about why the wonder should be saved • body paragraphs are **somewhat logically organized** and **partially present reasons and evidence** to support the claim • includes **a limited amount** of text evidence, precise language and sentence variety • concluding statement **restates the thesis statement** and some of the reasons for saving the wonder	• **partially explains and minimally persuades** why the wonder should be saved • includes **one or two examples of relevant** factual evidence from the magazine article to support each reason for saving the wonder • ends by **restating** the thesis statement and **partially persuading** the reader to agree with the author's point of view	• demonstrates a **marginal command** of the conventions of English grammar and usage, as well as of standard English capitalization, punctuation, and spelling • there **are many errors, however the text is still understandable** • includes only **one or two examples** of vocabulary that is appropriate to the topic (vocabulary about the world wonder; accurate vocabulary for a convincing thesis statement; vocabulary for a variety of sentence patterns)
Does Not Meet Standards ①	• introductory paragraph is **unclear** and does not include a thesis statement • body paragraphs are **not organized logically** and/or **do not present reasons and evidence** to persuade the reader • essay includes **little text evidence** and minimal sentence variety • concluding statement is **unclear and does not persuade**	• response is **partial or inaccurate explanation** of why the world wonder should be saved • includes **no factual textual evidence** from the magazine article	• demonstrates **almost no command** of the conventions of standard English grammar and usage, as well as of standard English capitalization, punctuation, and spelling • there **are many errors that disrupt** the reader's understanding of the text • **does not include** vocabulary that is appropriate to the topic (vocabulary about the world wonder; accurate vocabulary for a convincing thesis statement; vocabulary for a variety of sentence patterns)

Questions

Questions

Text Structure

1. What is the effect of presenting this article in a Question and Answer format?

Words and Phrases in Context

2. Determine what the phrase "instant gratification" in **answer 2** means using context clues.

"Talking About World Wonders"

by Joy Nolan

Judith DuPré studies buildings, bridges, and other wonders built by humans. In this interview, she discusses amazing buildings and structures of yesterday and today.

Q: What makes people want to build amazing structures?

1 **A:** People have built extraordinary structures throughout history for the same reasons: power, devotion, and pride. Cathedrals were some of the most amazing early wonders. An army of builders joined in with their entire community to create them. <u>Cathedral</u> builders competed to show devotion to their gods with beautiful, tall buildings.

Q: Tell us more about these early wonders of the world. How were they built? By whom?

2 **A:** We don't know the names of the cathedral builders. They worked anonymously on projects they knew would not be completed in their lifetimes. We're more into speed and instant gratification these days.

Q: The American Society of Civil Engineers named the Seven Modern Wonders of the World. The American wonders they chose are the Empire State Building in New York and the Golden Gate Bridge near San Francisco. Do you have a favorite?

Words to Know

<u>cathedral</u>: *(n.)* the main part of a church, usually very large and impressive

3 **A:** I don't agree with either choice. I would nominate the George Washington Bridge (GWB). It was built during the Great Depression and opened in 1931 before most people owned cars. But its engineer, Othmar Ammann, realized the importance of the automobile. He realized that cars were the way of the future. The bridge shows a giant shift in our culture, from trains to cars. I also love that because money was tight, the builders could not afford to cover up the support system of the bridge's pier. It's all still right out there, so we can all see how the bridge is held up.

Q: Do you have any other favorite modern wonders?

4 **A:** Sure I do! The Eiffel Tower in Paris remains an unsurpassed engineering <u>feat</u>. Tall buildings get hit by lots of wind. The shape of the tower was determined by the wind—it has a cage-like design to let the wind through.

Q: Why was the Eiffel Tower built?

5 **A:** Paris wanted an amazing icon—and they got it! Everyone now thinks of the Eiffel Tower when they think of Paris.

Q: How did Eiffel come up with his design for the tower?

6 **A:** Gustave Eiffel was a bridge designer. Also, a few years before he built the tower, he designed the understructure of the Statue of Liberty. It's hidden, but it's incredible! It's a steel cage. Buildings made of stone could go only about ten stories high. Once we had a skeletal cage of iron or steel, a building's weight could be evenly distributed—and it could get immense. It's pretty funny that the most avant-garde structure in the United States—the one that brought about the skeletal steel framing of the modern skyscraper—is hidden under the Statue of Liberty's skirt. It makes me smile.

Words to Know

<u>feat</u>: *(n.)* an impressive achievement

Questions

Key Ideas and Details

3. In **answer 3**, what are the key reasons that DuPré believes the George Washington Bridge is a great wonder?

Words and Phrases in Context

4. In **answer 6**, DuPré calls the Statue of Liberty "the most avant-garde structure [of its time] in the United States." Determine the meaning of this phrase.

Questions

Key Ideas and Details

5. What reasons does DuPré give in **answer 7** to show what makes Crystal Island a wonder?

Words and Phrases in Context

6. Why does DuPré call Norman Foster a "practical visionary" in **answer 7**?

Q: What buildings of today will continue to amaze us?

7 A: The works of Norman Foster are some of the most amazing. His structures are designed to conserve energy and are also pleasing places for people to work and live.

A totally outrageous example is Crystal Island, which is planned for Moscow, Russia. It will be one of the tallest buildings in the world. It will be an indoor city made from glass. The outside of a building is called skin. This building has a "smart" skin to combat the extremely cold, windy climate of Moscow. The building also uses renewable energy resources—sun, wind, geothermal. Energy is harnessed and recycled in a practical way.

I'm also very excited by the way Crystal Island will look. It's sleek and contemporary, very beautiful to look at. Norman Foster is a visionary, but he's a practical visionary. It's not all about the structure. For him, it's about how people interact in these buildings. Some buildings look high-tech and futuristic, but you have to wonder how people are going to like being in them.

Q: What would you say is the most amazing city or place on earth today, architecturally?

8 A: Dubai is a very interesting place to look at. It's part of a desert country in the Middle East. Until recently there was a whole lot of nothing there, and now we see so many amazing new structures going up. It's all because of Sheikh Mohammed, the ruler of Dubai. He is using structures to create an identity for Dubai. He is determined to make Dubai City into a financial capital.

He is also moving the economy away from a petroleum-based one. As of 2008, all buildings built in Dubai had to be sustainable, or "green." We now see more people trying to understand responsible architecture.

Words to Know

geothermal: *(adj.)* having to do with heat from within the earth

Q: Your book tells us that we are living in a time of big innovation in skyscraper design and construction. Can you describe it?

9 **A:** After the attack on the World Trade Center on September 11, 2001, the designing of tall buildings paused momentarily. Then it continued. We are in a race now to build the tallest—the Burj Dubai will be tallest for five years, but architects have already announced buildings that will be taller than that. We're seeing a remarkable meeting of architecture and engineering, helped by computer technology. We're now creating structures that could never have been imagined in the past, even fifty years ago. It's an amazing time to be studying world wonders!

Questions

Text Structure

7. Explain how transition words in **answer 9** help frame DuPre's view of 21st century architecture.

Words to Know

<u>innovation:</u> *(n.)* a new idea, method, or device

Questions

Key Ideas and Details

1. Find the author's main claim in **paragraphs 1–4**, and one reason that supports that claim.

Words and Phrases in Context

2. Determine the meaning of "fortifications" using its context in **paragraph 5**.

"The Rise and Fall of China's Great Wall: The Race to Save a World Treasure"

from *Current Events*

¶1 Made of brick, stone, and dirt, the Great Wall twists and turns across China's landscape like a giant dragon. It seems to rise out of the sea at Bo Hai gulf, a place known to local people as Laolongtou, or "the old dragon's head." The wall then stretches across the plains, crawls along the sides of mountains and scales their peaks as it spans the Asian countryside.

¶2 This ancient wonder, built entirely by hand, often overwhelms visitors. On a trip to the wall in 1909, French scholar Auguste Gilbert de Voisins said, "Nothing stops it, nothing gets in its way; seeing it at this point, one might believe it to be eternal."

¶3 Today however, neglect, misuse, and modernization threaten the giant dragon. Although the wall once stretched nearly 4,000 miles across China's northern border, only about 1,500 miles of China's Great Wall remain. The rest has fallen apart and disappeared.

¶4 This year, the World Monuments Fund placed the Great Wall on its list of 100 Most Endangered Sites. The group hopes to protect what's left of the wall and to encourage the Chinese government and others to save the historic structure. According to a World Monuments Fund report, "[The wall] was built to protect China; now China must protect it."

The Great Wall of Qin

¶5 China's Great Wall didn't start out so great. Begun nearly 2,300 years ago, the structure was a series of small fortifications. As early as 600 BC, people in China built small walls around their homes and cities for protection. Soldiers guarded the gates around the city walls during the day and swung the gates shut at night.

¶6 In the Warring States period (475–221 BC), leaders struggling for control of China built walls around entire kingdoms. Soldiers occupied forts and towers on the wall and fought to protect the borders of the independent states.

¶7 In 221 BC, Qin Shi Huangdi unified the kingdoms and became the first emperor of China. Qin Shi Huangdi gave orders to build the chang cheng, or "long wall," to protect China from northern nomads who were trying to invade China. Laborers built the wall by joining walls constructed earlier and extending the length of the wall to nearly 3,100 miles.

¶8 With the help of General Meng Tian, Qin Shi Huangdi ordered 800,000 men—soldiers, prisoners, and peasants—to build the wall. Where stones were plentiful, workers used stones to build parts of the wall. Where stones were scarce, workers used dirt.

¶9 To build the wall, laborers dug up large amounts of dirt and carried it to the wall. The workers then piled dirt into wooden frames about 6 inches deep. They used wooden instruments to pound the dirt until it became a solid mass. This process was repeated until the wall reached a desired height. Workers then moved the wooden frames to the next section of the wall and began the process again.

¶10 According to legend, Qin Shi Huangdi condemned workers to death for making the slightest construction errors. Today, few traces of the Qin wall remain. After Qin Shi Huangdi's death in 210 BC, workers abandoned the wall and it eventually crumbled into ruins.

The Ming Fortress

¶11 Nearly all of Qin Shi Huangdi's successors built walls along China's northern frontier. The fortifications, however, never fully protected China from invasion. During the early 13th century, Genghis Khan, leader of the Mongols, a nomad group from the north, united several nomad armies and conquered much of Asia.

¶12 In 1279, Genghis Khan's grandson, Kubilai Khan, overthrew the Chinese emperor and established the Yuan dynasty (1279–1368). The Yuan emperors did not maintain the old wall or build a new one, so the wall began to fall into ruins.

Questions

Key Ideas and Details

3. What details explain how the Great Wall was important historically?

Words and Phrases in Context

4. Find the several places on this page where the word *nomads* is used, and determine its meaning using context.

Key Ideas and Details

5. How did the Ming Dynasty make the wall a more permanent and effective structure?

Text Structure

6. What is the effect of using the heading "The Wall At Risk"?

¶**13** After Khan died in 1227, a Chinese farmer named Zu Yuanzhang led a rebel army and helped overthrow the last Yuan emperor. When Zu Yuanzhang seized power, he established the Ming dynasty (1368–1644). Zu and his successors decided to rebuild China's Great Wall, which lay mostly in ruins, to keep the Mongols from returning to re-conquer China. For nearly 200 years, thousands of workers toiled away on the Ming wall—reinforcing the Great Wall with bricks and stone.

¶**14** The Ming wall eventually blocked mountain passes that Mongol soldiers had used to invade China. When Mongol tribes attacked the wall, Chinese soldiers alerted others by lighting signal fires. When guards from a signal tower saw the fire, they built another fire, passing the warning along the wall. The number of smoke plumes and cannon shots fired indicated to Chinese soldiers how many enemy soldiers were approaching.

¶**15** The Ming government taxed the people of China heavily to pay for construction of the Great Wall. In 1644, the Manchus, a nomad tribe from northeast of Peking, helped rebels overthrow the Ming rulers and started the next era in Chinese history—the Qing dynasty. During the Qing dynasty, Manchu forces drove out Mongol invaders and extended China's border farther north beyond the Great Wall. The wall no longer protected China's border, so construction stopped and soldiers abandoned the fortresses.

The Wall At Risk

¶**16** Today, Chinese officials warn that the Great Wall is once again under attack. But this time the wall is not in danger from invaders. Instead local people and tourists alike threaten the wall. Dong Yaohui, head of the Great Wall Society of China, recently persuaded a local government to levy a fine on residents in a small village after they demolished part of the wall to obtain bricks for new houses.

Words to Know

<u>colossal:</u> *(adj.)* very big; huge

And in 1999, officials in the autonomous region of Nei Monggol (once called Inner Mongolia) plowed through the Great Wall to build a highway.

¶**17** Nature has also taken its toll. At the wall's western end, desert sandstorms have worn down much of China's great wonder. Dong Yaohui said, "Saving the Great Wall is now the most urgent task facing our country. Its splendor must be rebuilt."

¶**18** Preservationists also argue that commercial developers are destroying the aesthetic beauty of China's Great Wall. Developers have turned parts of the wall into a tourist destination. Visitors to the wall at the Badaling section near Beijing can take one of five cable cars to the top of the wall, bungee-jump off a section of the wall, paraglide along the wall, or ride a toboggan down the mountain.

¶**19** William Lindesay, an Englishman living in China, organized a group to protect and preserve what is left of the wall. Lindesay's group, the International Friends of the Great Wall, works with local villagers to pick up garbage along the wall and make sure the wall is protected from vandals. "The wall is in grave, grave danger," Lindesay said.

¶**20** The Chinese government also hopes to protect the national treasure. Officials in Beijing are considering legislation that, if passed, would convict anyone caught littering or defacing the Great Wall to a jail term of up to seven years.

¶**21** Arthur Waldron, a historian, wrote, "Whatever the future brings, the image of the wall . . . as a symbol of China . . . seems bound to endure."

Questions

Key Ideas and Details

7. What specific example of "neglect, misuse, and modernization" in **paragraphs 18 and 19** show how the wall is threatened?

Words to Know

aesthetic: *(adj.)* having to do with something's physical appearance

grave: *(adj.)* very serious, with the potential to get worse

Literature Circle Leveled Novels

The 39 Clues: The Maze of Bones *By Rick Riordan*
Siblings compete with less honorable members of the Cahill clan, all distantly related to Benjamin Franklin, to win a fortune by collecting 39 clues. (Only two are found in this first book.) **Lexile**® measure: 610L

All of the Above *By Shelley Pearsall*
Four inner-city teens, inspired by their math teacher, attempt to build the world's largest tetrahedron. **Lexile**® measure: 1000L

The Invention of Hugo Cabret *By Brian Selznick*
An orphaned boy who lives inside the walls of a Paris train station encounters a mystery when he is led to a mechanical man created by his deceased father. **Lexile**® measure: 820L

Nonfiction and Poetry

Built to Last: Building America's Amazing Bridges, Dams, Tunnels, and Skyscrapers *by George Sullivan.* Explore architectural masterpieces from as early as the 18th century, including the Erie Canal and Golden Gate Bridge. **Lexile**® measure: 950L

A Short Walk Through the Pyramids and Through the World of Art *by Phillip Isaacson.* Explore art in all its forms: painting, sculpture, folk art, crafts, and learn why every-day objects can be works of art. **Lexile**® measure: 1110L

Building Big *by David Macaulay.* Celebrate the art of engineering with this book about the constructed wonders of the modern world, including dams, domes, skyscrapers, tunnels, and bridges. **Lexile**® measure: 1260L

Atlas of Lost Cities: Legendary Cities Rediscovered *by Brenda Rosen.* Explore ancient cities with beautiful photography of the archeological sites, detailed reconstructions, and maps. Learn who built these cities and what happened to them.

Engineering in the Ancient World *by J.G. Landels.* Learn more about ancient tools and technology, and how they may have been used in the ancient world.

Machu Picchu *by Barry Brukoff, Pablo Neruda, and Isabel Allende.* Explore the ancient Incan city with the photographs of Barry Brukoff and the poem "Heights of Machu Picchu" by Pablo Neruda.

Pyramid (Fast Forward) *by Henrietta McCall, et al.* Learn about the construction of the Egyptian pyramids and the historical context in which they were built.

The Seventy Great Mysteries of the Ancient World: Unlocking the Secrets of Past Civilizations *by Brian M. Fagan.* The ancient world still contains many mysteries, which are explored through modern scientific techniques.

Films and TV

The 14 Wonders of the World—Ancient and New (Questar Inc., 2008) Visit wonders of the ancient world, including the Chichen Itza pyramid in Mexico and the Taj Mahal. (150 min.)

Ancient Mysteries (A&E Home Video, 1994–1997) Many episodes in this documentary television series explore mysteries, wonders, and monuments of ancient civilizations, such as Atlantis, Pompeii, and Petra.

Empires Collection—The Dynasties (PBS Paramount, 2000) This 5-disc set takes you on an exploration of ancient empires. (990 min.)

In Search of History—Pompeii (A&E Home Video, 2006) Visit this city, preserved by the ash of Mount Vesuvius, and learn about daily life during the Roman Empire. (50 min.)

Modern Marvels—The Great Wall of China (A&E Home Video, 2005) Investigate the planning, construction, and function of the Great Wall and the role it has played in the history of an ancient civilization. (50 min.)

Mystery of the Maya (Razor Digital Entertainment, 1998) Travel to Guatemala and Mexico, including the Yucatán Peninsula, to explore the pyramid temples and palaces of the Maya. (40 min.)

NOVA: Secrets of Lost Empires—Inca (WGBH, 1997) Learn the secrets of the Inca through teams of experts who explore the world they lived in and the structures they left behind. (56 min.)

Seven Wonders of the Industrial World (BBC Warner, 2003) Visit wonders of the ancient world, including the Chichen Itza pyramid in Mexico and the Taj Mahal. (343 min.)

Websites

Building Big Navigate this page on the PBS Web site to learn more about the bridges, domes, skyscrapers, dams, and tunnels featured in the series.

National Geographic Select the "History" link and click on "Mysteries of the Ancient World." Navigate the map to learn about artifacts, legends and myths, temples and tombs, and lost cities of the ancient world.

SIR-C/X-SAR: Space Radar Images of Earth Browse the Web site to view radar images taken from space of archeological sites and cities on Earth.

The History Channel Browse by topic and click on "Mysteries of History" to learn about how scientists and historians are exploring the mysteries of our past.

Magazines

Archaeology This official publication of the Archaeological Institute of America offers the latest information about past civilizations gained by deciphering what they left behind.

National Geographic: Kids Students can explore topics of particular interest to them, written in a way that is easy for them to understand.

Coming to America

What do experiences with others teach people about themselves?

Unit Introduction

In excerpts from two memoirs, discover how two writers experience life in America as immigrants and learn life lessons in their new homes.

In *Funny in Farsi*, Firoozeh Dumas (fi-roo-zay doo-MAH) recounts a series of anecdotes about her experiences as an Iranian immigrant in America and her later years adapting to life in her new country.

Mawi Asgedom tells the story of leaving his native country of Ethiopia and ultimately graduating from Harvard University in *Of Beetles & Angels*.

WRITING PERFORMANCE TASK

Write an essay to compare and contrast the authors' purposes and perspectives. Explain the strategies they use in their writing.

MEMOIRS

from ***Funny in Farsi***
by Firoozeh Dumas

Language
- Academic Vocabulary
- Word Study:
  Context Clues

Reading Informational Text
- Identify Evidence
- Key Ideas and Details
- Craft and Structure

from ***Of Beetles & Angels***
by Mawi Asgedom

Language
- Academic Vocabulary
- Word Study:
  Roots and Suffixes

Reading Informational Text
- Identify Evidence
- Key Ideas and Details
- Craft and Structure

SPEAKING AND LISTENING

Present a Speech
- Collaborate and Present

Checklist: Speech
- Scoring Guide

WRITING

Writing: Informative Essay
- Read the Model
- Analyze the Model
- Gather Evidence
- Organize Ideas

- Language Study: Compare
  and Contrast Statements
- Conventions Study: Transitions
- Revise, Edit, and Publish
- Performance Task Rubric

EXTENDED READINGS

Science Article
from **"1905: Einstein's
Miracle Year"**
by John Schwartz
from *New York Times Upfront*

Nonfiction Excerpt
from ***Shutting Out the Sky:
Life in the Tenements
of New York 1880–1924***
by Deborah Hopkinson

Academic Vocabulary

from *Funny in Farsi* by Firoozeh Dumas

Rate your understanding of each word. Then read its meaning and write an example. If the example is given, write the meaning.

Word	Meaning	Example
upheaval (n.) p. 149 ① ② ③ ④	a very big change that often causes problems	
luxury (n.) p. 149 ① ② ③ ④		Eating dessert twice in one day feels like a luxury.
bucolic (adj.) p. 149 ① ② ③ ④	relating to pleasant countryside	
proximity (n.) p. 149 ① ② ③ ④		We chose our house because of its close proximity to the school.
uncanny (adj.) p. 150 ① ② ③ ④	very strange and difficult to explain	
foreshadowing (v.) p. 151 ① ② ③ ④	indicating or hinting about a future event	

Rating Scale | ① I don't know the word. ② I've seen it or heard it. ③ I know its meaning. ④ I know it and use it.

Word Study

Use context clues to determine the meaning of the bold words below from Dumas's memoir.

1. The Americans we **encountered** were kind and curious, unafraid to ask questions and willing to listen. As soon as I spoke enough English to communicate, I found myself being interviewed nonstop by children and adults alike.

2. Most people in Whittier did not know about the famous **caviar** and once we explained what it was, they'd scrunch up their faces. "Fish eggs?" they would say. "Gross."

3. We tried **mentioning** our proximity to Afghanistan or Iraq, but it was no use. Having **exhausted** our geographical clues, we would say, "You've heard of India, Japan, or China? We're on the same continent."

Funny in Farsi

by Firoozeh Dumas

¶1 I was lucky to have come to America years before the political **upheaval** in Iran. The Americans we encountered were kind and curious, unafraid to ask questions and willing to listen. As soon as I spoke enough English to communicate, I found myself being interviewed nonstop by children and adults alike. My life became one long-running <u>Oprah show</u>, minus the free **luxury** accommodations in Chicago, and Oprah.

¶2 On the topic of Iran, American minds were <u>tabulae rasae</u>. Judging from the questions asked, it was clear that most Americans in 1972 had never heard of Iran. We did our best to educate. "You know Asia? Well, you go south at the <u>Soviet Union</u> and there we are." Or we'd try to be more **bucolic**, mentioning being south of the beautiful Caspian Sea, "where the famous caviar comes from." Most people in Whittier did not know about the famous caviar and once we explained what it was, they'd scrunch up their faces. "Fish eggs?" they would say. "Gross." We tried mentioning our **proximity** to Afghanistan or Iraq, but it was no use. Having exhausted our geographical clues, we would say, "You've heard of India, Japan, or China? We're on the same continent."

Words and Phrases in Context

1. Why does the author describe her life as "one long-running Oprah show"? Support your answer with details from **paragraph 1**.

Hyperbole

Hyperbole is a way of describing something by saying it is much bigger, smaller, worse, etc., than it actually is.

Key Ideas and Details

2. Why is the year 1972 significant to the author? Identify evidence in **paragraph 2**.

Sarcasm

Sarcasm involves saying the opposite of what you really mean in order to make an unkind joke or to show that you are annoyed.

Words to Know

Oprah show *(n.)* an influential daytime television show, featuring many stories and interviews

tabulae rasae: *(n.)* clean slates; an absence of ideas (singular: tabula rasa)

Soviet Union: *(n.)* a former country in Europe and Asia which broke up in the 1990s into smaller countries (like Russia)

Close Reading

Text Structure

3. Why does the author ask three questions in **paragraph 3**? What effect does this have?

Key Ideas and Details

4. Describe two details about Iran that Americans were mistaken about, according to the author.

Writing

5. How do the details in **paragraphs 5 and 6** develop the author's perspective? Analyze Dumas's language and word choice.

The author develops her perspective by _____.

For example _____.

Additionally _____.

Word Choice

Word choice is a phrase used to describe the specific language an author chooses to convey a particular message or idea.

¶3 None of the kids in Whittier, a city an hour outside of Los Angeles, ever asked me about geography. They wanted to know about more important things, such as camels. How many did we own back home? What did we feed them? Was it a bumpy ride? I always disappointed them by admitting that I had never seen a camel in my entire life. And as far as a ride goes, our Chevrolet was rather smooth. They reacted as if I had told them that there really was a person in the Mickey Mouse costume.

¶4 My family and I wondered why Americans had such a mistaken image of Iran. We were offered a clue one day by a neighbor, who told us that he knew about Iran because he had seen *Lawrence of Arabia*. Whoever Lawrence was, we had never heard of him, we said. My father then explained that Iranians are an Indo-European people; we are not Arabs. We do, however, have two things in common with Saudi Arabia, he continued: "Islam and petroleum." "Now, I won't bore you with religion," he said, "but let me tell you about the petroleum industry."

¶5 Another neighbor, a kindly old lady who taught me how to take care of indoor plants, asked whether we had many cats back home. My father, with his **uncanny** ability to forge friendships, said, "We don't keep pets in our homes. They are dirty."

¶6 "But your cats are so beautiful," our neighbor said. We had no idea what she was talking about. Seeing our puzzled expressions, she showed us a picture of a beautiful, long haired cat. "It's a Persian cat," she said. That was news to us; the only cats we had ever seen back home were the mangy strays that ate scraps behind people's houses. From that day, when I told people I was from Iran, I added "where Persian cats come from." That impressed them.

Words to Know

Lawrence of Arabia: *(n.)* an old movie about a British soldier and a writer in the Middle East

petroleum: *(n.)* oil that is obtained from the Earth and is used to make gasoline and other substances

forge: *(v.)* to develop something new, especially a strong relationship with others

¶7 I tried my best to be a worthy representative of my homeland, but, like a Hollywood celebrity relentlessly pursued by <u>paparazzi</u>, I sometimes got tired of the questions. I, however, never punched anybody with my fists; I used words. One boy at school had a habit of asking me particularly stupid questions. One day he inquired about camels, again. This time, perhaps **foreshadowing** a vocation in storytelling, I told him that, yes, we had camels, a one-hump and a two-hump. The one-hump belonged to my parents and the two-hump was our family station wagon.

¶8 His eyes widened.

¶9 "Where do you keep them?" he asked.

¶10 "In the garage, of course," I told him.

Station wagons were originally used as specialized vehicles to carry people and luggage to and from a train *station*. They have been sold worldwide for decades.

Words to Know

<u>paparazzi</u>: *(n.)* photographers who follow famous people in order to take pictures of them

Close Reading

Academic Vocabulary

6. In **paragraph 7**, why does the author say that her experience was "perhaps foreshadowing a vocation in storytelling"?

Key Ideas and Details

7. How does the author's tone change in **paragraph 7**? Use text details to support your analysis.

Writing

8. What does the author mean in **paragraph 7** when she says, "I, however, never punched anybody with my fists"?

   The author means ___. Specifically, ___.

Close Reading

Text Structure
9. Why does the author choose to include the line "I ran away from my geography lesson" in **paragraph 12**? Explain using details from the text.

Words and Phrases in Context
10. Use context clues to determine the meaning of the word *merely* in **paragraph 13**. Why does the author include this word in her anecdote?

Anecdote

An **anecdote** is a short story based on personal experience.

Writing
11. How does Dumas react to her classmates' curiosity? Compose an answer using at least two examples from the text.

Key Ideas and Details
12. Why does the author admit that she "never told them the truth" in **paragraph 13**?

¶11 Having heard what he wanted to hear, he ran off to share his knowledge with the rest of the kids on the playground. He was very angry once he realized that I had fooled him, but at least he never asked me another question.

¶12 Often kids tried to be funny by chanting, "I ran to I-ran, I ran to I-ran." The correct pronunciation, I always informed them, is "Ee-rahn." "I ran" is a sentence, I told them, as in "I ran away from my geography lesson."

¶13 Older boys often asked me to teach them "some bad words in your language." At first, I politely refused. My refusal merely increased their <u>determination</u>, so I solved the problem by teaching them phrases like *man kharam*, which means "I'm an idiot." I told them that what I was teaching them was so nasty that they would have to promise never to repeat it to anyone. They would then spend all of recess running around yelling, "I'm an idiot! I'm an idiot!" I never told them the truth. I figured that someday, somebody would.

Firoozeh Dumas was born in Abadan, Iran, and moved to Whittier, California, at the age of seven. In 2001, Firoozeh decided to write her stories as a gift for her two children. *Funny in Farsi* was a finalist for the PEN/USA award in 2004. Dumas was also a finalist for the prestigious Thurber Prize for American Humor, the first Middle Eastern woman ever to receive this honor.

Words to Know

<u>determination:</u> *(n.)* the quality of trying to do something even when it's difficult

¶**14** But almost every person who asked us a question asked with kindness. Questions were often followed by suggestions of places to visit in California. At school, the same children who inquired about camels also shared their food with me.

¶**15** "I bet you've never tried an Oreo! Have one," or "My mom just baked these peanut butter cookies and she sent you one." Kids invited me to their houses to show me what their rooms looked like. On Halloween, one family brought over a costume, knowing that I would surely be the only kid in the Halloween parade without one. If someone had been able to <u>encapsulate</u> the kindness of these second-graders in pill form, the pills would undoubtedly put many <u>war correspondents</u> out of business.

Close Reading

Text Structure

13. Why does Dumas begin **paragraph 14** with the conjunction *but*? What does the reader understand as a result?

Key Ideas and Details

14. What evidence does Dumas include in **paragraph 15** to support her claim that "almost every person who asked us a question asked with kindness"?

Text Structure

15. Determine the meaning of the last sentence. How does this sentence fit into the larger story that Dumas is telling?

Idiom

An **idiom** is a group of words that has a special meaning that is different from the ordinary meaning of each separate word.

Words to Know

<u>encapsulate:</u> *(v.)* to completely cover or contain something

<u>war correspondents:</u> *(n.)* journalists who report on wars and conflicts, sending news from the front lines

Identify Evidence | Analyze Individuals, Events, and Ideas

Reread the excerpt from *Funny in Farsi*, identifying the strategies Dumas uses to write about her early experiences and her perspective on America. How does she introduce and describe individuals, events, and ideas?

- In the Evidence column, record important details from the text that show Dumas's experiences and reveal her perspective.
- In the Explanation column, identify the strategy Dumas is using in her writing. Then, explain how that strategy is being used to illustrate or elaborate on a key individual, event, or idea.

Evidence	Source	Page	Explanation
1. "Americans we encountered were kind and curious, unafraid to ask questions and willing to listen."	Dumas	149	Dumas introduces the Americans that she meets, using description to highlight their characteristics and telling about the fact they had a lot of questions, but also revealing that they were interested in actually learning about her and her family.
2. "We would say, 'You've heard of India, Japan, or China? We're on the same continent.'"	Dumas	149	
3. "They wanted to know about more important things, such as camels."			
4. "Like a Hollywood celebrity relentlessly pursued by paparazzi, I sometimes got tired of the questions."			

Identify Evidence | Analyze Individuals, Events, and Ideas

Evidence	Source	Page	Explanation
5.			
6.			
7.			

Key Ideas and Details

Determining the Central Idea

1. What is the central idea of the text? Use evidence.

[ ]

2. List three key individuals that Dumas introduces in this excerpt. Explain why each individual is important to the central idea.

Individuals	Significance
the kids in Whittier, California, who wanted to learn about camels	shows American ignorance and childish immaturity

3. List three key events that Dumas introduces in her memoir. Explain why each event is important to the central idea.

Events	Significance
boys run around school yelling, "I'm an idiot"	

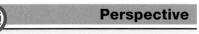

Craft and Structure

Structure of the Memoir

1. Make a list of descriptive words or phrases Dumas used to describe Americans in the paragraphs below. Compare and contrast these words.

Paragraphs 1–2	Paragraphs 7–13

2. Why do you think Dumas's tone changed throughout the excerpt?

Perspective & Point of View

3. Describe the different perspectives in paragraph 6.

The neighbor's perspective is different from the perspective of the narrator and her father in the following ways:

4. What are the advantages and disadvantages of first person point of view?

5. What is Dumas's conclusion about the Americans she met when she immigrated?

Perspective

People's personal opinion or attitude about something is their **perspective**. Authors communicate their perspectives through the choices they make in their writing.

Point of View

Point of view is the lens through which the story is written.

- first person = the narrator is part of the story (I, me, my, mine, we, us, ours)

- second person = the narrator gives information or addresses someone (you, yours)

- third person = the narrator tells another person's story (he, she, her, they, them).

Academic Vocabulary

from *Of Beetles & Angels* by Mawi Asgedom

Rate your understanding of each word. Then read its meaning and write an example sentence. If an example is given, write the meaning.

Word	Meaning	Example
affluent *(adj.)* p. 160 ① ② ③ ④		The affluent family next door had a big house and an expensive car.
commencement *(n.)* p. 160 ① ② ③ ④	a beginning; a graduation ceremony	
fruition *(n.)* p. 161 ① ② ③ ④	the point at which a plan is successfully completed	
obvious *(adj.)* p. 162 ① ② ③ ④	easy to notice or understand	
mutual *(adj.)* p. 163 ① ② ③ ④	shared by two or more people	
reflect *(v.)* p. 163 ① ② ③ ④		On vacation, I always have time to relax and reflect on life.
obligated *(adj.)* p. 164 ① ② ③ ④	feeling that you must do something because it is considered right	

Rating Scale | ① I don't know the word. ③ I know its meaning. ② I've seen it or heard it. ④ I know it and use it.

Word Study

Base Words and Suffixes

A **base word** is the simplest word in a word family. A **suffix** is a word part at the end of a word that changes its meaning. You can use word parts to determine the meaning of a word.

- the base word *commence* means to start or to begin
- the suffix *-ment* is used to make a verb into a noun

Identify the base words and suffixes in the words below. **Question 1** is an example. Then, use the word parts to explain the meaning of the word.

1. commence<u>ment</u>

2. reflection

3. obligation

4. fruition

5. obviously

6. mutually

❖Of Beetles & Angels❖

by Mawi Asgedom

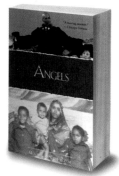

¶1 I may or may not remember seeing my mother look at our house in Adi Wahla, Ethiopia, just before we left. Gazing at it as though it were a person whom she loved and cherished. <u>Trance-walking</u> to the house's white exterior, laying her hands on it for a few moments, feeling its heartbeat—feeling her own heartbeat—then kissing it, knowing that she might never see it again.

¶2 From our very first days in America, my mother and father hammered into our minds the importance of excelling in school.

¶3 RIGHT NOW, WE ARE AMONG THE POOREST IN THE LAND. NEITHER YOUR MOTHER NOR I WILL FIND GOOD WORK BECAUSE WE LACK SCHOOLING. WE WILL HAVE TO WORK BACK-BREAKING JOBS, WE WILL NEVER FULLY UNDERSTAND OUR RIGHTS, AND OTHERS WILL TAKE ADVANTAGE OF US.

¶4 BUT IF YOU, OUR CHILDREN, WORK HARD AT SCHOOL AND FINISH THE UNIVERSITY, MAYBE SOMEDAY YOU CAN HELP YOURSELVES AND HELP YOUR FAMILY, TOO.

Words to Know

<u>trance-walking:</u> *(n.)* walking while you are thinking about something else so deeply that you do not notice what is happening around you

Close Reading

Key Ideas and Details

1. How does Asgedom believe his mother felt about leaving their house in Adi Wahla? What evidence from **paragraph 1** allows you to infer this?

Imagery

Imagery is language used to describe ideas or actions in a way that creates a vivid image in the reader's mind.

Text Structure

2. What is the effect of putting the parents' words in all capital letters in **paragraphs 3 and 4**?

Personal Reflection

Personal reflection is a type of narrative writing that reflects upon personal experiences, memories, values and opinions. Memoirs always involve personal reflection.

Close Reading

Key Ideas and Details

3. Describe what Asgedom has learned from his parents. Use evidence from **paragraphs 5–7** to support your answer.

Academic Vocabulary

4. Explain the significance of Asgedom's commencement speech in **paragraph 8**. Why was it meaningful on multiple levels?

Key Ideas and Details

5. In **paragraph 8**, the author describes how his father would have behaved at his graduation from Harvard, had he been alive. How does Asgedom think his father would have felt that day?

¶5 What's both beautiful and scary about young children is that they will believe most anything that their parents tell them. If our parents had told us that black <u>refugees</u> growing up on <u>welfare</u> in an affluent white community couldn't excel, we probably would have taken them at their word.

¶6 But they told us that we could do anything if we worked hard and treated others with respect. And we believed them.

¶7 It hurt my brother and me to see our parents struggle, and we wanted, more than anything, to be able to help them someday. So we worked hard at school, and after several years, we graduated from the ESL (English as Second Language) program at Longfellow Elementary and entered regular classes full-time.

¶8 Sometimes I wonder what my father would have done at my graduation from Harvard. He probably would have leaped from his seat and interrupted my commencement speech in front of 30,000 spectators. Standing with his back straight, chest out, and right hand pointing forward, he would have shouted, loud enough for everyone to hear:

¶9 THIS IS MY SON, SELAMAWI. A LONG TIME AGO, WHEN HE WAS JUST A LITTLE ONE, I TAUGHT HIM TO WORK HARD AND TO RESPECT OTHERS. NOW LOOK WHERE THAT HAS TAKEN HIM.

Words to Know

welfare: (n.) money that is paid by the government to people who are poor or unemployed

refugee: (n.) someone who has been forced to leave his/her country, especially during a war, or for political or religious reasons

¶10 But like my brother, my father missed my graduation. Ironic, isn't it, that father and son survived disease, war, and famine in Africa, but could not survive something as preventable as drinking and driving in America?

¶11 My father departed before it came to full fruition, but the dream that he and my mother shared has already begun to come true. His children have graduated from college—first me, then Mehret, and one day, Hntsa. Mulu lives in Atlanta and raises two more children with that same dream.

Mawi Asgedom (far right) was born in Ethiopia but fled to Sudan to escape war. After three years living in a Sudanese refugee camp, Mawi and his family moved to the United States in 1983, when Mawi was seven years old. He is the bestselling author of *Of Beetles & Angels: A Boy's Remarkable Journey from a Refugee Camp to Harvard* and *The Code: The 5 Secrets of Teen Success.*

Close Reading

Words and Phrases in Context

6. Who is the "son" in **paragraph 10**? Find the context clues that identify this character.

Text Structure

7. Why does the author include this "ironic" detail in **paragraph 10**? What does the reader understand because of this paragraph?

Writing

8. Explain the "dream" of the author's parents, referred to in **paragraph 11**. How does the author support his claim that this dream "has already begun to come true"?

Close Reading

Key Ideas and Details

9. What was the author's life like in Sudan? Rephrase the text details in your own words.

Text Structure

10. Why does the author ask a question at the end of **paragraph 14**? What is the effect for the reader?

Key Ideas and Details

11. What does the author forget in **paragraph 15**? Why does the author include this detail in the text?

Words and Phrases in Context

12. What is the meaning of *surroundings* in **paragraph 15**?

¶12 I delivered the commencement address at my graduation from Harvard in 1999. This is the text of my speech.

¶13 When I was a child, my mother told me that I should always sleep with the covers over my head. At the time, my family was living in a Sudanese refugee camp, in Africa, and we owned nothing that we did not carry with us. On many a night, we slept out in the open, and my mother warned that if we let the covers down, snakes could slip in and slither into our mouths. We had no trouble following her advice.

¶14 Years later, in the comfort of the United States, my mother gave me another piece of advice, this one less obvious. "Always remember where you came from," she told me just before I left for Harvard. I was puzzled. The first piece of advice had been easy. Who wants a mouth full of snake! But why was it important to remember where I came from?

¶15 When I moved on to Harvard and saw new worlds open before me, I quickly forgot about trying to understand my mother. Before I knew it, I was signed up for the <u>Tae Kwon Do</u> Club, the Harvard African Students' Association, a Phillips Brooks House Program, the Freshman <u>Crew</u> Team (where I totaled a $15,000 boat against the dock), and a Freshman Bible Study (I figured I needed all the prayer that I could get). And, of course, I was taking four classes and trying to meet as many of my 1,600 classmates as wanted to meet me. As I focused my energies on myself and my immediate surroundings, remembering where I had come from seemed far less important than knowing where I was supposed to be every half hour.

Words to Know

<u>Tae Kwon Do:</u> *(n.)* a style of fighting from Korea

<u>Crew:</u> *(n.)* the sport or activity of making a boat move through water with oars

¶16 During my sophomore year, however, something happened to remind me of my mother's advice. I was working as a delivery man for the Harvard Student Agency. One day as I was waiting for my packages in the office, an elderly black woman tottered in and wearily leaned on her cane. She hoped to find someone who would type a short letter for her. Such a simple, easy thing to do. But HSA has no typing service, and the <u>receptionist</u> had to tell her that she had come to the wrong place. As the old woman turned to leave, frustrated and confused, one of my coworkers called her over, gently sat her down, and typed the letter. It was such a simple act. Yet never has a Harvard student seemed so great to me as in that moment of reaching out.

¶17 I began to reflect on what my mother might have meant. In the Sudan, we had carried with us all that we owned, but that included our <u>devotion</u> to one another. In that sense we carried a home, a community, a sense of mutual responsibility wherever we went. On that day in the Harvard Student Agency, my coworker carried a community with her as well: the simple community of human connection and duty.

Close Reading

Words and Phrases in Context

13. Explain the significance of the line in **paragraph 16**: "never has a Harvard student seemed so great to me as in that moment."

Writing

14. What details does the author include in **paragraphs 16 and 17** to support the importance of helping others?

    First, _____. Then _____.

Words and Phrases in Context

15. Interpret the meaning of the line "we carried a home, a community" in **paragraph 17**. What strategy is the author using in this line?

Key Ideas and Details

16. What can you infer from **paragraph 17** about why the author tells the story about his co-worker helping an elderly woman?

Words to Know

<u>receptionist</u>: *(n.)* someone whose job is to welcome and deal with people arriving in an office

<u>devotion</u>: *(n.)* strong love; loyalty

Close Reading

Key Ideas and Details

17. What does Asgedom say is the most important lesson he learned at Harvard? Find the details he uses to express its significance.

Text Structure

18. How does the author explain "remembering where you come from" in **paragraph 19**?

Academic Vocabulary

19. Why does the author choose the word *obligated* in **paragraph 19**? How would the meaning change if another word were used?

Words and Phrases in Context

20. Examine the multiple meanings of the word *covers* in **paragraph 20**. According to the author, what makes "many of us go through life with covers over our heads"?

¶18 So what have I learned from my four years at Harvard? Many facts and formulas, many new ways of thinking, a fresh understanding of the world. But what's most important to me is that after four years at Harvard I'm finally beginning to understand my mother's advice.

¶19 Remembering where you come from means holding on to the vision that you are a part of a human community that you can carry with you every day. That community has given us much. Are we not obligated to give it something back?

¶20 My mother's advice in childhood was to pull the covers over my head—that had been the easy part. But her later advice meant, I now realize, that I should know when to pull the covers down and stick my neck out. That's the hard part. Too many of us go through life with the covers over our heads. We want to reach out, but we fear to make ourselves <u>vulnerable</u>. And we are also busy. We have appointments to keep; we have things to do. We race through a world of demands. And then we ask ourselves almost helplessly, "What can we do as individuals?"

Words to Know

<u>vulnerable:</u> *(adj.)* easily harmed

¶21 Some people say that a butterfly flapping its wings in Japan can cause a hurricane in Louisiana. Anyone of us, however small and helpless we may feel, can spark unimagined changes. Today's small act of kindness can become tomorrow's whirlwind of human progress.

¶22 But as you all know, progress is not easy, and it will not come <u>unsolicited</u>. I hope that many of us will inspire positive change. There is still so much to be done both in distant lands such as the Sudan, and closer to home in our own communities. The big, sweeping, revolutionary actions are always most noticeable. But quite often, it will be the small things that all of us can do that will have the most impact. Yes, we will be busy in our lives. But we can all take a little time to do a little deed of kindness. We can help write a letter; we can inscribe a little goodness on the hard surface of this world.

¶23 In a few minutes we shall be welcomed to the <u>ranks</u> of educated men and women. As we start the journey to wherever our dreams may lead, we must remember where we have come from. We must recall our membership in the human community that has <u>nourished</u> us; we must accept the responsibility to keep that community alive. Improving the quality of life for the entire human community is the single greatest task that faces our generation and generations to come. Of course, no worthy endeavor is without risks and pitfalls—without snakes, if you will—but I know that you, my classmates, are ready to peek out, to see beyond yourselves, and cast off the covers. You are ready to face the snakes and drive them away. You are ready to change the world. Thank you! Good luck! And congratulations!

Close Reading

Writing
21. Explain the meaning of the line "a butterfly flapping its wings in Japan can cause a hurricane in Louisiana" in **paragraph 21**. What examples does the author include to elaborate on this idea?

This line means _____.
The author _____.
Therefore, the reader _____.

Key Ideas and Details
22. What key point does the author make in the text of the commencement speech?

Words and Phrases in Context
23. What does the author mean in **paragraph 23** when he tells his classmates to "face the snakes and drive them away"? Support your answer with text evidence.

Words to Know

<u>unsolicited:</u> *(adj.)* not asked for

<u>ranks:</u> *(n.)* people who belong to a particular group

<u>nourished:</u> *(v.)* given the food and other substances necessary to live

Identify Evidence | Analyze Individuals, Events, and Ideas

Reread the excerpt from *Of Beetles & Angels*, identifying the strategies Asgedom uses to write about his experiences and perspective. How does he introduce and describe individuals, events, and ideas?

- In the Evidence column, record important details from the text that show Asgedom's experiences and reveal his perspective.
- In the Explanation column, identify the strategy Asgedom is using in his writing. Then, explain how that strategy is being used to illustrate or elaborate on a key individual, event, or idea.

Evidence	Source	Page	Explanation
1. "One of my coworkers called her over, gently sat her down, and typed the letter. It was such a simple act. Yet never has a Harvard student seemed so great to me . . ."	Asgedom	163	The author uses imagery to recreate a vivid memory for the reader, one of a Harvard student helping an elderly woman type a letter. The author is reminded of his mother's advice to "remember where you came from."
2. "I TAUGHT HIM TO WORK HARD AND TO RESPECT OTHERS. NOW LOOK WHERE THAT HAS TAKEN HIM."			

Evidence	Source	Page	Explanation
3.			
4.			

Key Ideas and Details

Determining the Central Idea

1. What is the central idea of the text? Use evidence.

2. List three key individuals that Asgedom introduces in this excerpt. Explain why each individual is important to the central idea.

Individuals	Significance
the author's father	the lessons he taught the author lead to success in life

3. List three key events that Asgedom introduces in his memoir. Explain why each event is important to the central idea.

Events	Significance

Craft and Structure

Sequence of a Memoir

1. Make a list of significant events of Asgedom's life in sequential order.

Author's Purpose

2. What are Asgedom's suggestions to the reader about the lessons he learned? Provide evidence from the text.

3. Compare and contrast Asgedom's purpose to Dumas's purpose for writing.

Asgedom   Dumas

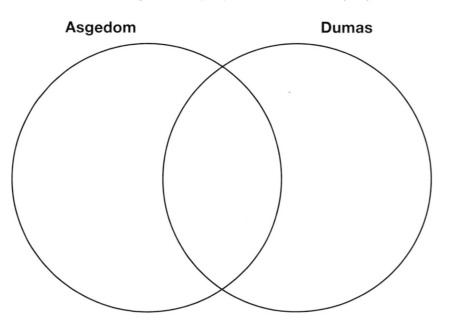

Collaborate and Present

Plan and Deliver a Speech

Assignment: Work with a partner to plan and write a two-minute speech about the effectiveness of humor or reflection in either Dumas's or Asgedom's memoir. Follow the steps below to create a speech and deliver it to the class.

Analyze the Content

1. Consider the following questions:
   - Did any sections make you laugh? What was the author emphasizing in the part that you found humorous?
   - What is the effect of reflection in the memoirs?

2. Go back to the text and choose at least two examples of how either Dumas or Asgedom uses humor/reflection. List the examples and explain the effect.

Example	Effect

Write Your Speech

3. Use your chart of examples and explanations as talking points for the body of your speech.
   - Draft your speech on paper or on the computer.
   - Remember to introduce yourself to your audience and add a conclusion.

Present

4. Deliver your speech.

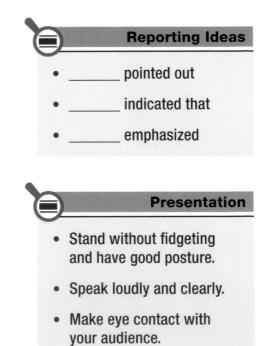

Seeking Clarification

- What you are saying is . . .
- So what you mean is . . .
- In other words . . .
- If I understand you correctly, you are saying . . .

Reporting Ideas

- _____ pointed out
- _____ indicated that
- _____ emphasized

Presentation

- Stand without fidgeting and have good posture.
- Speak loudly and clearly.
- Make eye contact with your audience.

Speech Checklist

Use the checklist below to evaluate your collaboration skills, reasoning, and final presentation.
Think carefully about your work. If you know you completed an item thoroughly, give yourself a check (✓).

COLLABORATE AND PRESENT CHECKLIST

Comprehension & Collaboration	Evidence and Reasoning	Presentation of Knowledge & Ideas
☐ Come to discussions prepared, having read and studied material.	☐ Explain the purpose of the presentation.	☐ Adapt language to a variety of contexts and tasks to demonstrate knowledge of formal English.
☐ Refer to evidence when contributing to the discussion.	☐ Present information relevant to the task.	☐ Include multimedia components (e.g., graphics, images, music, sound), and visual displays.
☐ Follow rules for discussions and lead by example.	☐ Explain how the author uses humor or reflection.	☐ Use appropriate volume/tone (clear, not too fast, too slow, or too loud) and avoid using "like" or "ummm."
☐ Ask and answer specific questions.	☐ Explain why the author's use of humor or reflection is effective/ineffective.	☐ Have strong posture, a confident stance, and make frequent eye contact.
☐ Make comments that contribute to the topic under discussion.	☐ Use at least two examples from the text.	☐ Occasionally move from one spot to another without fidgeting.
☐ Review the key ideas under discussion and demonstrate understanding of multiple perspectives through reflection and paraphrasing.	☐ Synthesize the key ideas from your speech with a conclusion.	☐ Smile and act relaxed.
Number of ✓s in this category: __	Number of ✓s in this category: __	Number of ✓s in this category: __

Total # of ✓s: __

Add up the total number of checks (✓) in each category. Then use the scoring guide below to calculate your final score.

Scoring Guide

16 to 18 ✓s	13 to 15 ✓s	11 to 12 ✓s	10 or less ✓s
④ Exemplary	③ Meets Standards	② Needs Work	① Does Not Meet Standards

Read the Model

The writer of this informative essay uses a compare and contrast structure to show how two authors approach similar topics in different ways. Read and discuss the model essay below.

Informative Essay

An **informative essay** provides an overview of the key topics and ideas of a text.

- The introduction states the title and author of the text that the writer will analyze, and includes the thesis statement.

- The two **body paragraphs** express the writer's main points about the text.

- The conclusion sums up or restates the thesis. It also explains why the information in the essay matters.

- Find two examples of academic and domain-specific vocabulary.

- Find two examples of accurate use of punctuation.

Shared Purpose, Varied Paths   By Declan Wallace

Authors John Schwartz and Deborah Hopkinson both tell the stories of American immigrants. In "1905: Einstein's Miracle Year," Schwartz presents factual information about Albert Einstein's ground-breaking Theory of Relativity and his eventual immigration to the U.S. In *Shutting Out the Sky,* Hopkinson constructs a descriptive narrative to reveal one young Romanian immigrant's experience moving to New York City. While both authors discuss valuable immigrant experiences, they use different strategies to convey their perspectives.

In "1905: Einstein's Miracle Year" Schwartz focuses on the life of one famous American immigrant: Einstein. Specifically, the author explains how Einstein's theory behind $E=MC^2$ changed the foundations of science and enabled America to develop the atom bomb. Schwartz directly states his perspective when he says that Einstein "changed the world forever" (182). To support this key point Schwartz uses historical references, such as newspaper clippings and letters, and expert testimony to show Einstein's impact on science, America, and the world.

In contrast, Deborah Hopkinson focuses on one young immigrant named Marcus. He is not famous, nor has he "changed the world forever." Yet Hopkinson conveys to the reader that Marcus's life and experiences are valuable. For instance, she includes vivid descriptions of the hardships: Marcus arrives unprepared for New York's "bitter cold" and sleeps on a crowded tenement sofa, his feet "propped awkwardly" on a chair. (185). Descriptions like these convey the importance of the immigrant experience.

In closing, each of these authors discusses one immigrant and his place in history, yet they use different approaches to achieve their purposes. Both authors also help readers to remember that America, on many levels, is a nation of immigrants.

Analyze the Model

A **compare/contrast essay** is a type of informative writing that explains similarities and differences between two texts.

Introduction

Which sentence sets up the compare/contrast focus of the essay?

Body Paragraph 1

Purpose: to inform the reader about Einstein's impact on science and the world

Perspective:

Strategies:

Example:

Body Paragraph 2

Purpose:

Perspective:

Strategies:

Example:

Conclusion

How does the writer conclude the essay?

Block Format

In a compare/contrast essay written in block format, a thesis statement in the introduction sets up the compare/contrast focus of the essay.

In **body paragraph 1,** the writer discusses all the key points about one text in the first half of the essay.

Then in **body paragraph 2,** these same key points are analyzed in regard to the second text.

In the conclusion of the essay, the writer ties the ideas together and offers an additional reason why this information may be important to the reader.

Step 1 | Gather Evidence

[**Write an essay to compare and contrast the authors' purposes and perspectives. Explain the strategies they use in their writing.**]

What You Need to Know | The evidence you have collected about the authors' strategies (see pages 154 and 166)

What You Need to Write | The key pieces of evidence that you want to include in your essay

Strategies in *Funny in Farsi*

Strategy	Example
using imagery to recreate a vivid memory for the reader	"One of my coworkers called her over, gently sat her down, and typed the letter. It was such a simple act, yet never has a Harvard student seemed so great to me. . . . p. 163, ¶16
Strategy	Example Page #_____, ¶ # _____
Strategy	Example Page # _____, ¶ #_____

Strategies in *Of Beetles & Angels*

Strategy	Example
Strategy	Example Page #_____, ¶ # _____
Strategy	Example Page #_____, ¶ # _____
Strategy	Example Page #_____, ¶ # _____

Step 2 | Organize Ideas

What You Need to Know | When you compare two things, you describe their similarities. When you contrast them, you focus on their differences.

To develop your topic:
1. Describe Dumas's purpose and strategies.
2. Describe Asgedom's purpose and strategies.

What You Need to Write | Determine which of these authors' purposes and points of view are the same and which are different.

Body Paragraph 1: _____
(author's name)

Purpose: **Perspective:** **Strategies:** **Example:**

Body Paragraph 2: _____
(author's name)

Purpose: **Perspective:** **Strategies:** **Example:**

Step 3 | Draft

Write a draft of your essay on the computer or on paper.

Language Study | Compare and Contrast Statements

See It | **Statements that compare and contrast give details about how two subjects are similar and how they are different.**

When writing statements that compare and contrast:

- Identify the subjects being compared or contrasted.
- Tell how the subjects are similar and different.

Signal Words for Compare and Contrast	
show similarities with signal words such as: _both, also, in addition, likewise, similarly, too, as well as, similar to, much like, each_	**show differences with signal words such as:** _although, but, however, in contrast, otherwise, even though, instead, on the contrary, while_

Now, go back to the model essay and identify the signal words the writer uses to show comparison and contrast.

Try It |
- **Identify which sentences make comparisons and which express contrasts.**
- **Label the signal words that clarify the type of statement being made.**
- **Articulate the meaning of the sentence in your own words.**

1. John Schwartz includes relevant historical details, while Deborah Hopkinson includes rich narrative description.

2. Even though Einstein was an immigrant, he had a different experience from many other immigrants because he moved to the United States later in life.

3. Two new books, _An American Journey_ by Lincoln Petronis and _The Immigrant Life_ by James Hopper, both offer unusual views of the immigrant experience.

4. _Mental Floss_ and _Slate_ are ground-breaking magazines that each challenge the reader to look at American society in a fresh light.

5. Similar to Firoozeh Dumas, the character Marcus moved to America as a child.

Apply It | Compare/contrast Dumas's and Asgedom's purposes and points of view. Try at least three different frames and then choose one that fits with your thinking about these two authors.

1. The differences/similarities between _____ and _____ are _____.
   (author 1)   (author 2)   (state similar or different key ideas)

2. _____ some similarities exist, the differences between _____ and _____
   (Although, While)   (author 1)   (author 2)

   are _____.
   (state similar or different key ideas)

3. Both _____ and _____ tell _____. These two authors present
   (author 1)   (author 2)   (key idea of texts 1 and 2)

   accounts of _____ in _____ ways.
   (detail about their stories)   (similar/different)

4. _____ states _____ in _____, while _____ states _____
   (author 1)   (key idea of text 1)   (title of text 1)   (author 2)   (key idea of text 2)

   in _____.
   (title of text 2)

Now, **go back to your draft** and select at least two statements that you could make clearer or more interesting. Rewrite or combine your sentences using appropriate signal words to show either comparison or contrast.

Conventions Study | Transition Words and Phrases

Illustrate an Idea

Use these transitions to give examples or to explain a statement.

- as an illustration
- expressly
- for example
- for instance
- including
- in particular
- like
- namely
- particularly
- specifically
- such as

Emphasize a Key Point

Use these transitions to highlight a key point or to emphasize an idea.

- above all
- certainly
- especially
- in particular
- keep in mind
- moreover
- most importantly
- notably
- obviously
- particularly
- primarily

See It | Transitions clarify the relationships between ideas and concepts. Go back to the model and identify the transitions that the writer uses to connect ideas and to illustrate and elaborate on key points.

Try It | Complete the paragraph below by selecting appropriate transition words from the boxes to fill in the blanks.

Readers must remember that authors use many strategies to convey their ideas. (1)_____, an author might include expert testimony to support a point they want to make. (2)_____ when an author includes a quotation from a qualified source, that is expert testimony. Readers will (3)_____ understand a text better if they identify the writing strategies the author is using.

Apply It | Go back to your essay and evaluate your use of transition words. Use these questions to guide your evaluation:

- *Do you use meaningful transitions to move your reader from one thought to another?*
- *Do you use transitions to explain examples and emphasize key points?*
- *Does your writing flow smoothly?*

Step 4 | Revise and Edit Revise your draft with a partner.

Organization and Clarity					
State the title and the authors of the texts in the introductory statement.	Self	1	2	3	4
	Partner	1	2	3	4
Introduce ideas about how the authors structured their texts in the introductory statement.	Self	1	2	3	4
	Partner	1	2	3	4
Include controlling ideas in the topic sentences of each body paragraph.	Self	1	2	3	4
	Partner	1	2	3	4
Wrap up ideas in a concluding paragraph.	Self	1	2	3	4
	Partner	1	2	3	4
Include a final thought about why this information is important.	Self	1	2	3	4
	Partner	1	2	3	4
Evidence and Reasoning					
Include three or more pieces of evidence in each body paragraph.	Self	1	2	3	4
	Partner	1	2	3	4
Cite the author and paragraph number for each piece of evidence.	Self	1	2	3	4
	Partner	1	2	3	4
Language and Conventions					
Use appropriate transition words to link sections of the essay and ideas within each paragraph.	Self	1	2	3	4
	Partner	1	2	3	4
Include compare and contrast statements that show similarities and differences.	Self	1	2	3	4
	Partner	1	2	3	4
Use academic and domain-specific vocabulary and establish and maintain a formal, objective tone throughout the essay.	Self	1	2	3	4
	Partner	1	2	3	4

Scoring Guide | ① needs improvement   ② average   ③ good   ④ excellent

Step 5 | Publish Publish your essay either in print or digital form.

Publish

Publish your essay either in print or digital form. Use the rubric below to assess your final performance task.

PERFORMANCE TASK RUBRIC

Score Point	Organization and Clarity	Evidence and Reasoning	Language and Conventions
Exemplary (4)	• introductory paragraph introduces the **topic clearly** and in an **engaging way** and identifies the authors and texts • body paragraphs are **logically organized and effectively explain** each author's purpose and point of view • includes **well-chosen** text evidence and precise language • ends with a **valid conclusion** that **effectively compares and contrasts** the authors' purposes, points of view, and strategies in the two memoirs	• **accurately** introduces Dumas's and Asgedom's points of view on their challenges of living in America as immigrants • includes **three or more examples of relevant** factual evidence from each memoir that illustrate each author's purpose and point of view	• demonstrates a **strong command** of the conventions of standard English grammar and usage, as well as of standard English capitalization, punctuation, and spelling • uses transitions to **effectively link** sections of the essay and ideas within paragraphs • vocabulary is **appropriate** to the topic (vocabulary about the immigrant experience, terms for referring to the structure of a memoir, and language that introduces personal examples)
Meets Standards (3)	• introductory paragraph introduces the **topic clearly** • body paragraphs are **logically organized** and **explain** each author's purpose and point of view • includes **some** text evidence and precise language • ends with a conclusion that **compares and contrasts** the authors' purposes, points of view, and/or strategies in the two memoirs	• **adequately** introduces Dumas's and Asgedom's points of view on the challenges of living in America as immigrants • includes **relevant** factual evidence from each memoir that illustrates each author's purpose, point of view and strategies	• demonstrates **a near command** of the conventions of standard English grammar and usage, as well as of standard English capitalization, punctuation, and spelling **with some errors** • uses **some** transitions to link sections of the essay and ideas within paragraphs • vocabulary is **appropriate** to the topic (vocabulary about the immigrant experience, terms for referring to the structure of a memoir, and language that introduces personal examples)

PERFORMANCE TASK RUBRIC

Score Point	Organization and Clarity	Evidence and Reasoning	Language and Conventions
Needs Work ②	• introductory paragraph introduces the **topic** • body paragraphs are **somewhat logically organized** and **explain** each writer's purpose, points of view, and strategies • includes **a limited amount** of text evidence and precise language • ends with a **partial conclusion** that **refers to some of the ideas** in the essay	• **attempts to introduce** Dumas' and Asgedom's points of view on their challenges of living in America as immigrants • includes **some** factual evidence from each memoir that illustrates each author's purpose, point of view and strategies	• demonstrates a **marginal command** of the conventions of English grammar and usage, as well as of standard English capitalization, punctuation, and spelling • uses **few** transitions to link sections of the essay and ideas within paragraphs • there **are many errors; however, the text is still understandable** • includes only **one or two examples** of vocabulary that is appropriate to the topic (vocabulary about the immigrant experience, terms for referring to the structure of a memoir, and language that introduces personal examples)
Does Not Meet Standards ①	• introductory paragraph is **unclear** • body paragraphs are **not organized logically** and/or **do not explain** each writer's purpose, point of view, and strategies • essay includes **little text evidence** • conclusion is **unclear and/ or does not compare and contrast** the two memoirs	• response is a **partial or inaccurate explanation** of the authors' challenges of living in America as immigrants • includes **no analyses of textual evidence** from each memoir	• demonstrates **almost no command** of the conventions of standard English grammar and usage, as well as of standard English capitalization, punctuation, and spelling. • **does not use** transitions to link sections of the essay and ideas within paragraphs • there **are many errors that disrupt** the reader's understanding of the text • **does not include** vocabulary that is appropriate to the topic (vocabulary about the immigrant experience, terms for referring to the structure of a memoir, and language that introduces personal examples)

Questions

Text Structure

1. What is the effect of using the heading that begins "How an unknown scientist rewrote the rules of physics . . ."?

Key Ideas and Details

2. Why does the author compare Einstein to "rock stars and movie heartthrobs" in **paragraph 5**?

"1905: Einstein's Miracle Year"

by John Schwartz from *The New York Times Upfront*

How an unknown scientist rewrote the rules of physics, and in the process, changed the world forever.

¶1 One hundred years ago, a young patent clerk in Switzerland named Albert Einstein began publishing his revolutionary theories of how the physical universe worked, and the world hasn't been the same since.

¶2 Einstein was 26 and unknown in 1905 when, in the course of a year, he completed three scientific papers that would begin to rewrite the rules of physics and make him a star. While the term *genius* is often overused, Einstein's enormous accomplishments, beginning in what has been called his "miracle year," established him as the most famous genius in the world. And his reputation has only grown in the decades since his death.

¶3 Einstein's "Special Theory of Relativity," one of his accomplishments of 1905, postulated that time and space were not absolute, but instead varied, depending on one's perspective; in other words, they were "relative."

¶4 The same theory yielded modern science's most important equation, $E=MC^2$, which states that energy (E) is equal to mass (M) times the speed of light squared. While deceptively simple, its consequences were monumental because it described the enormous amounts of energy that might be liberated from matter—so much that a penny, if it could be completely converted into energy, would provide all the power used by New York City for two years. The same concept would lead to the idea of harnessing the energy in matter to develop atomic weapons and nuclear power.

¶5 Einstein received the kind of adulation now reserved for rock stars and movie heartthrobs. On his first trip to the United States in 1921, crowds waited for hours at the dock in New York for his ship to come in, and thousands more lined the streets to cheer for him.

¶6 A *Times* reporter described Einstein's arrival: *A man in a faded gray raincoat and a flopping black felt hat that nearly concealed the gray hair that straggled over his ears stood on the boat deck of the steamship Rotterdam yesterday, timidly facing a battery of cameramen. In one hand he clutched a shiny briar pipe and with the other clung to a precious violin. He looked like an artist—a musician. He was. But underneath his shaggy locks was a scientific mind whose deductions have staggered the ablest intellects of Europe.*

¶7 Twelve years later, the world-famous Einstein returned to America for good, fleeing Nazi Germany and its persecution of Jews, and settled in New Jersey to work at Princeton University. His theories, and those of other physicists, led Einstein to believe that science could unlock the promise of $E=MC^2$.

¶8 In August 1939, with World War II looming, he wrote a letter to President Franklin D. Roosevelt that launched the massive effort to build the atomic bomb. Einstein had been a lifelong <u>pacifist</u>.

¶9 The two atom bombs dropped on Japan in August 1945 brought the war to a close, but Einstein was devastated by the resulting destruction and loss of life. "I made one great mistake in my life—when I signed the letter to President Roosevelt recommending that atom bombs be made," he later wrote, adding, "but there was some justification—the danger that the Germans would make them."

¶10 After the war, Einstein and other physicists pushed to control the power they had helped to unleash, calling for arms control. Einstein was offered the presidency of Israel in 1952, but turned it down. He died a U.S. citizen in Princeton, in April 1955, at age 76. In an editorial following his death, the *Times* said that what distinguished Einstein was his passionate devotion to truth, and his great imagination. "Mathematical physicists in Einstein's class are the epic poets of our time," the paper said. "The universe we conceive is their intellectual creation."

Questions

Words and Phrases in Context
3. What words and phrases develop the comparison of Einstein to "an artist—a musician" in both a literal and figurative sense?

Words to Know

pacifist: *(n.)* someone who believes that wars are wrong and refuses to use violence

Questions

Key Ideas and Details

1. What is Marcus's overall impression of his relatives and their life in America? Support your answer with details from the text.

Key Ideas and Details

2. Determine the narrative perspective of the text. What is the effect of including Marcus's inner thoughts in the narration?

from *Shutting Out the Sky: Life in the Tenements of New York 1880–1924*

by Deborah Hopkinson

Settling In: Boarders and Greenhorns

¶1 One early morning in December 1900, a sixteen-year-old boy left Ellis Island and made his way alone into New York City. Struggling with his heavy bundles, Marcus Ravage elbowed his way through the crowded streets of the Lower East Side.

¶2 Marcus shivered in the bitter cold. If only he'd followed his mother's advice and brought his heavy coat to America. He'd been so sure he wouldn't need it. Why should he bother carrying old clothes when he'd soon be rich enough to buy new ones?

¶3 But Marcus had brought something almost as precious as a warm coat. It was just a crumpled bit of paper, but it was a link between his old life in Romania and his new one. On the paper was scribbled the New York address of distant relatives from back home.

¶4 Before long, Marcus found himself in the apartment of the Segal family, who had arrived from Romania just three months before. Mrs. Segal, along with her son and five daughters, lived in a five-room apartment on the third floor of a Rivington Street tenement. Looking around at the sofa, kitchen table, and ever so many chairs, Marcus felt sure that the Segals were already rich. And he wouldn't be far behind.

¶5 Mrs. Segal told Marcus he could stay for free for a few days. After that, he would be expected to find a job and pay fifty cents a week for his bed.

¶6 That evening, people Marcus had never seen before began to stream into the apartment, tired from a long day of work. As the hours ticked by and the strangers didn't leave, Marcus realized they were boarders—they lived there, too! They paid Mrs. Segal for a bed, and perhaps for meals and laundry. Where would everyone sleep? he wondered.

¶7 Marcus soon found out. It wasn't long before everyone began to rush about, lining up chairs in rows to make beds. Marcus and three other young men shared the sofa, sleeping with their heads on the cushions and feet propped awkwardly on chairs. Nine bodies pressed together on the floor, huddling like seals on a rock. In the kitchen, Mrs. Segal and one child cuddled on top of the washtubs while the rest of the children slept on the floor.

¶8 Soon the rooms were filled with deep breathing, dreadful snoring, and smells of all kinds. Yet despite his new, strange <u>circumstances</u>, Marcus fell asleep right away. Next morning he woke to the puffing of steam engines and clatter of wheels outside the windows. Once again the rooms hummed with activity. People raced to put the furniture back into place; the men scrambled to get dressed before the girls awoke.

¶9 After everyone else had hurried off to work or school, Marcus and Mrs. Segal were left alone in the now neat and tidy apartment. He was thoroughly surprised to see Mrs. Segal clean the kitchen floor with precious soap rather than sand, as his mother would have back home.

¶10 When Mrs. Segal came back from the market, Marcus felt more confused than ever. She'd bought the largest eggplant he'd ever seen, as well as an <u>exotic</u> yellow fruit in the shape of a cucumber—a banana. To say nothing of meat—which she cooked for lunch!

¶11 Back home in his village only rich people could indulge in the luxury of meat, eat such extraordinary vegetables, use soap to clean floors, or live on the second floor of such a nice apartment.

¶12 But, Marcus puzzled, if the Segals were rich, why did they share their fine apartment with so many boarders?

¶13 To a newcomer, or "greenhorn," like Marcus, it was all very confusing.

Questions

Words and Phrases in Context

3. Why does the narrator describe the banana Mrs. Segal brings back from the market as "an exotic yellow fruit in the shape of a cucumber"?

Words to Know

<u>circumstances:</u> *(n.)* the conditions or situation

<u>exotic:</u> *(adj.)* something that is exotic seems unusual and interesting because it is related to a foreign country

Literature Circle Leveled Novels

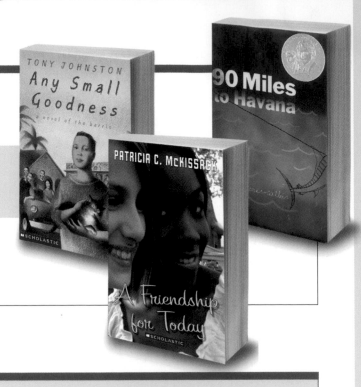

Any Small Goodness: A Novel of the Barrio *by Tony Johnston*
Arturo Rodriguez and his family have just arrived in East L.A. from Mexico. In each chapter, a character performs a random act of kindness. **Lexile**® measure: 600L

A Friendship for Today *by Patricia C. McKissack*
Rosemary is one of the first African Americans to enter the white school in her town. She eventually becomes friends with the white girl who was most cruel to her. **Lexile**® measure: 670L

90 Miles to Havana *by Enrique Flores-Galbis*
When a political revolution takes place in Cuba, Julian's parents send him to Miami, where Julian's older brothers protect him in a refugee camp. The brothers are separated, however, and Julian must make a dangerous journey before being reunited with his mother and his father. **Lexile**® measure: 790L

Fiction, Nonfiction, and Novels

New Kids in Town: Oral Histories of Immigrant Teens *by Janet Bode.* Teenage immigrants from various countries recount the emotional experience of fleeing their homelands and adjusting to a new life in the United States. **Lexile**® measure: 630L

Letters from Rifka *by Karen Hesse.* Rifka journeys from the Ukraine to America, encountering obstacles along the way. **Lexile**® measure: 660L

Esperanza Rising *by Pam Muñoz Ryan.* Esperanza's life is shattered when a tragedy forces her and Mama to flee Mexico to a California farm and work as migrants, facing harsh working conditions and the Great Depression. **Lexile**® measure: 750L

Flight to Freedom *by Ana Veciana-Suarez.* Read about the work camps and prejudice that drive 13-year-old Ana and her family to escape from Communist Cuba in 1967. **Lexile**® measure: 850L

The Star Fisher *by Laurence Yep.* Joan Lee and her family must struggle against old prejudices as they adjust to life as the first Chinese Americans to settle in a West Virginia town. **Lexile**® measure: 850L

The House on Mango Street *by Sandra Cisneros.* A teen girl named Esperanza tells stories about her home in a Hispanic American neighborhood in Chicago. **Lexile**® measure: 870L

Children of the Wild West *by Russell Freedman.* Historical photographs with explanatory text present a picture of life in the American West from 1840 to the early 1900s. **Lexile**® measure: 1010L

Island of Hope: The Story of Ellis Island and the Journey to America *by Martin W. Sandler.* More than 12 million immigrants entered the United States through Ellis Island—the Island of Hope—between 1892 and 1954. Through firsthand accounts and anecdotes, this remarkable book provides perspective and insight into a uniquely American experience.

Films and TV

Dollars and Dreams: West Africans in New York (Blue Saxophone Films, 2007) Follow West African immigrants as they pursue the American Dream in New York City. (56 min.)

Dying to Get In (Mooncusser Films, 2007) Listen to stories from the United States and Mexico border, where undocumented immigrants have to cross miles of the Sonoran Desert to enter the United States. (39 min.)

Immigrants in America, 1970 (National Archives, 2008) Learn about the economic disparities and challenges African, Asian, Italian, and Irish immigrants faced.

Investigative Reports: American Dream, American Nightmare (A&E Home Video, 2006) Learn how mismanagement in the Immigration and Naturalization Service has affected American immigrant families. (50 min.)

Patriot Acts (Thirst Films, 2004). Explore the effects of a program that requires non-immigrant Muslim males over 16 to register with the Department of Homeland Security. (39 min.)

Real Women Have Curves (HBO Independent Productions, 2002) Ana struggles to balance her family's needs, her culture, and her dreams of a college education. (90 min.)

Websites

Crossing the BLVD: Find radio clips, video, stories, images, and songs of recent immigrants living in Queens, a diverse borough of New York City.

Ellis Island Passenger Records: Find out if your ancestors passed through Ellis Island by searching New York passenger records.

New Naturalization Test: Try your hand at this test from the U.S. Citizenship and Immigration Services.

Magazines

Immigration Times: Stay up-to-date on immigration laws and trends.

National Geographic World: Look for articles about the native cultures and societies of people who have immigrated to the United States.

The Immigrant Magazine: Learn more about the lifestyles and cultures of immigrants and their ethnic heritage.

U.S. News and World Report: Search for articles about current issues in immigration and articles about America's diversity.

Cities of GOLD

Why does place matter?

Unit Introduction

In an excerpt from a novel and in three poems, discover how authors use description to convey their perspective about a city.

In the poems "City," "Song of the Builders," and "Our City," poets use descriptive details and sensory language to describe the rhythms of daily life and the challenges found in realistic cities.

L. Frank Baum's fanciful description of the imaginary City of Oz in *The Wonderful Wizard of Oz* allows readers to discover an enchanting city alongside the main character and her friends.

WRITING PERFORMANCE TASK

Choose one writer. Argue which narrative strategies best convey the author's perspective about the city.

🔲 POEMS/NOVEL EXCERPT_____

"City" by Langston Hughes,
"Song of the Builders"
by Jessie Wilmore Murton,
"Our City" by Francisco Alarcón

from ***The Wonderful Wizard of Oz*** by L. Frank Baum

Language
- Academic Vocabulary
- Word Study: Parts of Speech

Language
- Academic Vocabulary
- Word Study: Word Families

Reading Literary Text
- Identify Evidence
- Key Ideas and Details
- Craft and Structure

Reading Literary Text
- Identify Evidence
- Key Ideas and Details
- Craft and Structure

🔲 SPEAKING AND LISTENING_____

Present a Speech
- Collaborate and Present

Checklist: Speech
- Scoring Guide

🔲 WRITING_____

Writing: Argumentative Essay
- Read the Model
- Analyze the Model
- Gather Evidence
- Organize Ideas

- Language Study: Defending a Claim
- Conventions Study: Clarifying
- Revise, Edit, and Publish
- Performance Task Rubric

🔲 EXTENDED READINGS_____

Essay
from ***Here Is New York***
by E. B. White

Memoir
from ***Reading Lolita in Tehran***
by Azar Nafisi

Academic Vocabulary

"City" by **Langston Hughes**

"Song of the Builders" by **Jesse Wilmore Murton**

"Our City" by **Francisco Alarcón**

Rate your understanding of each word. Then read its meaning and write an example. If the example is given, write the meaning.

Word	Meaning	Example
lurk *(v.)* p. 192 ① ② ③ ④		At camp, everyone was afraid that bats lurked in the trees.
stake *(n.)* p. 192 ① ② ③ ④		Before quitting soccer and joining the track team, Jessica considered the stakes.
rivet *(n.)* p. 192 ① ② ③ ④	A metal pin that fastens two pieces of metal together.	
toil *(v.)* p. 192 ① ② ③ ④	to work very hard for a long time	
will *(adj.)* p. 192 ① ② ③ ④	determination to do something, even if it is difficult	

Rating Scale

① I don't know the word.
③ I know its meaning.

② I've seen it or heard it.
④ I know it and use it.

Word Study

Part of Speech

Part of speech is a category a word is assigned to based on how it functions in a sentence. Some common parts of speech are verb, noun, and adjective.

Some words have different meanings depending on how they are used in a sentence. Circle the correct part of speech for *bolts* in the sentences below.

1. Always late for school, Emma **bolts** out the door in the morning.

   verb   noun   adjective

2. He put a **bolt** on the door so he could lock it at night.

   verb   noun   adjective

City

By Langston Hughes

1 *In the morning the city*
Spreads its wings
Making a song
In stone that sings.

5 *In the evening the city*
Goes to bed
Hanging lights
About its head.

Close Reading

Literary Analysis

1. Explain the effect of Hughes's use of personification when he writes that "the city / Goes to bed."

Personification

Personification is the attribution of human qualities to an animal or nonliving object.

Text Structure

2. How do the two stanzas contrast with each other?

Stanza

A **stanza** is a group of lines arranged in a pattern that forms part of a poem.

Close Reading 🔍

Writing

3. What is the effect of the descriptive details Murton uses to describe the "strong men" in the poem?

Academic Vocabulary

4. What is the effect of the word *lurks* in **line 2**?

Text Structure

5. How does the line "And what is life if the goal be won?" reflect the tone of the poem?

SONG OF THE BUILDERS

by Jessie Wilmore Murton

1   O beams of steel are slim and black,

    And danger **lurks** on the skyward track,

    But men are many, men are bold,

    And what is risk when the **stake** is gold?

5   So **riveters** ring,

    And hot bolts fly,

    And strong men **toil**,

    And sweat … and die …

    But the city's towers grow straight and high!

10 O beams of steel are black and slim,

    But the **will** of men are stubborn and grim,

    They reach forever to <u>clutch</u> the sun,

    And what is life if the goal be won?

    So riveters ring,

15 And hot bolts fly,

    And strong men toil,

    And sweat … and die …

    But the city's towers grow straight and high!

Words to Know

<u>beams</u>: *(n.)* a long piece of wood or metal used to build bridges or buildings

<u>clutch</u>: *(v.)* to hold onto something tightly

POEMS

Our City
by Francisco Alarcón

1 Our City
at night
it shines
from afar
5 it looks like
a constellation
of stars
fallen
to the ground
10 Nuestra ciudad
de noche
reluce
de lejos
parece ser
15 constelación
de estrellas
que en la tierra
cayó

Words to Know

constellation: *(n.)* a group of stars

Close Reading

Writing

6. **Lines 10–18** are the Spanish translation of the first **8 lines**. Why does Alarcón include this in his poem?

Alarcón shows that ____ when he ____.

Literary Analysis

7. Describe the effect of the simile "it looks like / a constellation / of stars / fallen / to the ground."

Text Structure

8. What are the similarities between Alarcón's description of a city and the one Hughes writes about in "City"?

Identify Evidence | Analyze Characters, Events, and Ideas

Reread the three poems, highlighting examples that the three poets offer to describe cities. What textual evidence do the poets include to describe these cities?

- In the Evidence column, record examples from the poems that describe cities.
- In the Inference column, explain what you can conclude about the city based on the evidence you selected.

Evidence	Source	Line(s)	Inference
1. "In the morning the city / Spreads its wings"			
2. "Making a song / In stone that sings."	Hughes	3-4	Hughes finds the noises of the city beautiful, like a song.
3. "In the evening the city / Goes to bed / Hanging lights / About its head."			
4. "O beams of steel are slim and black, / And danger lurks on the skyward track"			

Evidence	Source	Line(s)	Inference
5.			
6.			
7.			

Key Ideas and Details

Determining the Central Idea

1. Use the evidence you collected to summarize the central idea of each of the poems.

"City"	"Song of the Builders"	"Our City"

2. List one key image in each poem. Explain why each image is important to the central idea.

Poem	Detail	Significance
"City"		
"Song of the Builders"		
"Our City"		

3. List the perspective that each author has about their respective city.

Poet	Perspective
Langston Hughes	
Jessie Wilmore Murton	Negative—she sees cities as places where some are willing to sacrifice human lives for their own success and wealth.
Francisco Alarcón	

Craft and Structure

Structure of the Poem "Song of the Builders"

Rhyme

A **rhyme** occurs when two words or lines of poetry end with the same sound.

1. What lines are repeated in the poem "Song of the Builders"?

2. What effect does the repetition of these lines have on the central idea?

3. The title of the poem is "Song of the Builders." How does the refrain contribute to the idea that this poem is a song?

4. Murton uses rhyme in "Song of the Builders." What effect does this rhyming have on the poem?

Academic Vocabulary

from *The Wonderful Wizard of Oz* by L. Frank Baum

Rate your understanding of each word. Then read its meaning and write an example. If the example is given, write the meaning.

Word	Meaning	Example
dazzle *(v.)* p. 199 ① ② ③ ④	to be unable to see because of a bright light.	
assorted *(adj.)* p. 199 ① ② ③ ④	many different kinds	
prosperous *(v)* p. 200 ① ② ③ ④		Carla's business was so successful, she had to hire an assistant.
queer *(adj.)* p. 201 ① ② ③ ④	very strange or odd	
manner *(adj.)* p. 203 ① ② ③ ④		The ambulance sped through the city in a rapid manner.
meek *(adv.)* p. 205 ① ② ③ ④	quiet, humble, and obedient	

Rating Scale | ① I don't know the word. ② I've seen it or heard it.
 ③ I know its meaning. ④ I know it and use it.

Word Study

Word Family

A group of words that share the same base word and have related meanings.

Use the words from the word web below to help you complete the sentences.

```
           / wonderful
wonder  <--- wondrous
           \ wondering
```

1. It was _____ to see my family again after two weeks at camp.

2. Don't bother _____ about the answer to the riddle—it's impossible!

3. From the top of the mountain, the view of the city below was _____.

from

The Wonderful Wizard of Oz

by L. Frank Baum

Close Reading

Text Structure

1. How does Baum describe the "wonderful City" Dorothy and her friends visit?

¶1 Even with eyes protected by the green <u>spectacles</u>, Dorothy and her friends were at first **dazzled** by the <u>brilliancy</u> of the wonderful City. The streets were lined with beautiful houses all built of green marble and studded everywhere with sparkling <u>emeralds</u>. They walked over a pavement of the same green marble, and where the blocks were joined together were rows of emeralds, set closely, and glittering in the brightness of the sun. The window panes were of green glass; even the sky above the City had a green tint, and the rays of the sun were green.

There were many people—men, women, and children—walking about, and these were all dressed in green clothes and had greenish skins. They looked at Dorothy and her strangely **assorted** company with wondering eyes, and the children all ran away and hid behind their mothers when they saw the Lion; but no one spoke to them. Many shops stood in the street, and Dorothy saw that everything in them was green. Green candy and green pop corn were offered for sale, as well as green shoes, green hats, and green clothes of all sorts. At one place a man was selling green lemonade, and when the children bought it Dorothy could see that they paid for it with green pennies.

Words to Know

<u>spectacles:</u> *(n.)* glasses

<u>brilliancy:</u> *(adj.)* brightness

<u>emeralds:</u> *(n.)* valuable bright green gemstones

Close Reading

2. How does Baum's description of the workers in **paragraph 3** contrast with the workers in "Song of the Builders"?

While the workers in "Song of the Builders" ____, in Baum's description ____.

Literary Analysis

3. How do the descriptive details and sensory language—like the "dazzling emeralds" and "happy and contented and prosperous people"—contribute to the mood of **paragraphs 1–3**?

Mood

The **mood** is feeling or atmosphere an author creates in the story.

¶3 There seemed to be no horses nor animals of any kind; the men carried things around in little green carts, which they pushed before them. Everyone seemed happy and contented and **prosperous**.

The Guardian of the Gates led them through the streets until they came to a big building, exactly in the middle of the City, which was the Palace of Oz, the Great Wizard. There was a soldier before the door, dressed in a green uniform and wearing a long green beard.

¶5 "Here are strangers," said the Guardian of the Gates to him, "and they demand to see the Great Oz."

"Step inside," answered the soldier, "and I will carry your message to him."

¶7 So they passed through the Palace Gates and were led into a big room with a green carpet and lovely green furniture set with emeralds. The soldier made them all wipe their feet upon a green mat before entering this room, and when they were seated he said politely:

"Please make yourselves comfortable while I go to the door of the Throne Room and tell Oz you are here."

¶9 They had to wait a long time before the soldier returned. When, at last, he came back, Dorothy asked:

"Have you seen Oz?"

¶11 "Oh, no," returned the soldier; "I have never seen him. But I spoke to him as he sat behind his screen and gave him your message. He said he will <u>grant</u> you an audience, if you so desire; but each one of you must enter his presence alone, and he will admit but one each day. Therefore, as you must remain in the Palace for several days, I will have you shown to rooms where you may rest in comfort after your journey."

"Thank you," replied the girl; "that is very kind of Oz."

¶13 The soldier now blew upon a green whistle, and at once a young girl, dressed in a pretty green silk gown, entered the room. She had lovely green hair and green eyes, and she bowed low before Dorothy as she said, "Follow me and I will show you your room."

So Dorothy said good-bye to all her friends except Toto, and taking the dog in her arms followed the green girl through seven passages and up three flights of stairs until they came to a room at the front of the Palace. It was the sweetest little room in the world, with a soft comfortable bed that had sheets of green silk and a green velvet counterpane. There was a tiny fountain in the middle of the room, that shot a spray of green perfume into the air, to fall back into a beautifully carved green marble <u>basin</u>. Beautiful green flowers stood in the windows, and there was a shelf with a row of little green books. When Dorothy had time to open these books she found them full of **queer** green pictures that made her laugh, they were so funny.

Close Reading

Text Structure

4. What can you infer about "the Great Oz" based on the information you know already?

Writing

5. How is Baum's description of the "dazzling" city similar to the description Alarcón gives in his poem?

Text Structure

6. How does Baum indicate in **paragraph 14** that Dorothy has left the "big room" that the soldier brought her and her friends to in **paragraph 7**?

Words to Know

<u>grant</u>: *(v.)* to give or allow

<u>basin</u>: *(n.)* a large bowl used for washing

Close Reading

7. How does Baum's perspective on Oz differ from Murton's perspective on her city?

Text Structure

8. What can you infer about the Scarecrow, the Tin Woodman, and the Lion based on their actions in **paragraph 17**?

¶15 In a wardrobe were many green dresses, made of silk and satin and velvet; and all of them fitted Dorothy exactly.

"Make yourself perfectly at home," said the green girl, "and if you wish for anything ring the bell. Oz will send for you tomorrow morning."

¶17 She left Dorothy alone and went back to the others. These she also led to rooms, and each one of them found himself <u>lodged</u> in a very pleasant part of the Palace. Of course this politeness was wasted on the Scarecrow; for when he found himself alone in his room he stood stupidly in one spot, just within the doorway, to wait till morning. It would not rest him to lie down, and he could not close his eyes; so he remained all night staring at a little spider which was weaving its web in a corner of the room, just as if it were not one of the most wonderful rooms in the world. The Tin Woodman lay down on his bed from force of habit, for he remembered when he was made of flesh; but not being able to sleep, he passed the night moving his joints up and down to make sure they kept in good working order. The Lion would have preferred a bed of dried leaves in the forest, and did not like being shut up in a room; but he had too much sense to let this worry him, so he sprang upon the bed and rolled himself up like a cat and purred himself asleep in a minute.

The next morning, after breakfast, the green maiden came to fetch Dorothy, and she dressed her in one of the prettiest gowns, made of green <u>brocaded</u> satin. Dorothy put on a green silk apron and tied a green ribbon around Toto's neck, and they started for the Throne Room of the Great Oz.

Words to Know

<u>lodged</u>: *(v.)* given a place to stay

<u>brocaded</u>: *(adj.)* woven with a raised overall pattern

¶19 First they came to a great hall in which were many ladies and gentlemen of the court, all dressed in rich costumes. These people had nothing to do but talk to each other, but they always came to wait outside the Throne Room every morning, although they were never permitted to see Oz. As Dorothy entered they looked at her curiously, and one of them whispered:

"Are you really going to look upon the face of Oz the Terrible?"

¶21 "Of course," answered the girl, "if he will see me."

"Oh, he will see you," said the soldier who had taken her message to the Wizard, "although he does not like to have people ask to see him. Indeed, at first he was angry and said I should send you back where you came from. Then he asked me what you looked like, and when I mentioned your silver shoes he was very much interested. At last I told him about the mark upon your forehead, and he decided he would admit you to his presence."

¶23 Just then a bell rang, and the green girl said to Dorothy, "That is the signal. You must go into the Throne Room alone."

She opened a little door and Dorothy walked boldly through and found herself in a wonderful place. It was a big, round room with a high arched roof, and the walls and ceiling and floor were covered with large emeralds set closely together. In the center of the roof was a great light, as bright as the sun, which made the emeralds sparkle in a wonderful **manner**.

Close Reading

Literary Analysis
9. Describe life for people in the City of Oz. Use textual evidence to support your answer.

Words and Phrases in Context
10. What is the meaning of *rich* in **paragraph 19**? How do you know?

Close Reading

Text Structure

11. What is the effect of descriptive details like the "enormous Head, without a body to support it" on the mood of **paragraphs 25–27**?

Words and Phrases in Context

12. What does Oz's title, "the Great and Terrible," reveal about him?

¶25 But what interested Dorothy most was the big throne of green marble that stood in the middle of the room. It was shaped like a chair and sparkled with gems, as did everything else. In the center of the chair was an enormous Head, without a body to support it or any arms or legs whatever. There was no hair upon this head, but it had eyes and a nose and mouth, and was much bigger than the head of the biggest giant.

As Dorothy gazed upon this in wonder and fear, the eyes turned slowly and looked at her sharply and steadily. Then the mouth moved, and Dorothy heard a voice say:

¶27 "I am Oz, the Great and Terrible. Who are you, and why do you seek me?"

It was not such an awful voice as she had expected to come from the big Head; so she took courage and answered:

¶29 "I am Dorothy, the Small and **Meek**. I have come to you for help."

The eyes looked at her thoughtfully for a full minute. Then said the voice:

¶31 "Where did you get the silver shoes?"

"I got them from the Wicked Witch of the East, when my house fell on her and killed her," she replied.

¶33 "Where did you get the mark upon your forehead?" continued the voice.

"That is where the Good Witch of the North kissed me when she bade me good-bye and sent me to you," said the girl.

¶35 Again the eyes looked at her sharply, and they saw she was telling the truth. Then Oz asked, "What do you wish me to do?"

"Send me back to Kansas, where my Aunt Em and Uncle Henry are," she answered <u>earnestly</u>. "I don't like your country, although it is so beautiful. And I am sure Aunt Em will be dreadfully worried over my being away so long."

¶37 The eyes winked three times, and then they turned up to the ceiling and down to the floor and rolled around so queerly that they seemed to see every part of the room. And at last they looked at Dorothy again.

"Why should I do this for you?" asked Oz.

¶39 "Because you are strong and I am weak; because you are a Great Wizard and I am only a little girl."

Close Reading

Academic Vocabulary
13. Explain why Dorothy refers to herself as "the Small and Meek."

Text Structure
14. What is the narrative point of view of this story? List the text clues that help you determine this.

Words to Know

<u>earnestly</u>: *(adv.)* very seriously and sincerely

Identify Evidence | Analyze Characters, Events, and Ideas

Reread the novel excerpt, highlighting examples that Baum offers to describe the City. What textual evidence does Baum include to establish his setting?

- In the Evidence column, record examples from the novel excerpt that describe the City.
- In the Inference column, explain what you can conclude about the City based on the evidence you selected.

Evidence	Page	Inference
1. "Even with eyes protected by the green spectacles, Dorothy and her friends were at first dazzled by the brilliancy of the wonderful City."	199	The City is not the home of Dorothy and her friends; it is very beautiful and sparkling.
2. "The streets were lined with beautiful houses all built of green marble and studded everywhere with sparkling emeralds."	199	
3. "There were many people—men, women, and children—walking about, and these were all dressed in green clothes and had greenish skins."	199	
4. "Many shops stood in the street, and Dorothy saw that everything in them was green."	199	

Evidence	Page	Inference
5.		
6.		
7.		

Key Ideas and Details

Determining the Central Idea

1. Use the evidence you collected to summarize the key idea of the excerpt.

[ ]

2. List three key characters that Baum includes in this novel excerpt. Explain why each character is important to the central idea.

Character	Significance
Palace soldier	leads Dorothy and friends into Palace; says he has never seen Oz

3. Describe Baum's perspective on the City.

[ ]

Craft and Structure

Structure of the Novel Excerpt

1. Make a list of significant events from the story in sequential order.

   1.

   2.

   3.

   4.

2. How do Baum's descriptions of the setting help us visualize and understand the story better?

Author's Purpose

3. What is Baum's purpose in describing the City of Oz?

4. Compare and contrast Baum's purpose for writing about a city to the poets' purpose for writing about a city.

Baum's Purpose	The Poets' Purpose

Collaborate and Present

Plan and Deliver a Speech

Assignment: Prepare a short two-minute speech describing a city or memorable place you have visited or know. Include specific sensory details and personal reflections. Follow the steps below to create a speech and deliver it to the class.

Brainstorm About Your Topic

1. Consider the following questions:
   - What were some things you saw? Tasted? Heard?
   - What did you do while you were there?

2. Choose the most impressive site in the place you chose, and the most exciting thing you did while you were there. Jot down details in the space below.

Most Impressive Site	Most Exciting Experience

Write Your Speech

3. Use your chart of examples and explanations as talking points for the body of your speech.
   - Draft your speech on paper or on the computer.
   - Remember to introduce yourself to your audience and add a conclusion.

Present

4. Deliver your speech.

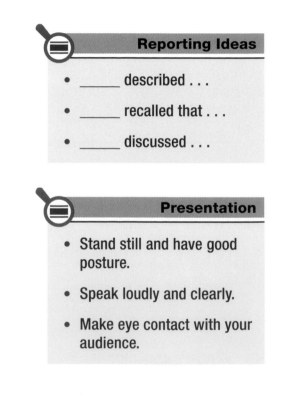

Seeking Clarification

- Could you explain a little more about . . .
- What did you mean when you said . . .
- So, you are saying that . . .

Reporting Ideas

- _____ described . . .
- _____ recalled that . . .
- _____ discussed . . .

Presentation

- Stand still and have good posture.
- Speak loudly and clearly.
- Make eye contact with your audience.

Speech Checklist

Use the checklist below to evaluate your collaboration skills, reasoning, and final presentation.
Think carefully about your work. If you know you completed an item thoroughly, give yourself a check (✓).

COLLABORATE AND PRESENT CHECKLIST		
Comprehension & Collaboration	**Evidence & Reasoning**	**Presentation of Knowledge & Ideas**
☐ Come to discussions prepared, having read and studied material. ☐ Refer to evidence when contributing to the discussion. ☐ Follow rules for discussions and lead by example. ☐ Ask and answer specific questions. ☐ Make comments that contribute to the topic under discussion. ☐ Review the key ideas under discussion and demonstrate understanding of multiple perspectives through reflection and paraphrasing.	☐ Explain the purpose of the presentation. ☐ Present information relevant to the task. ☐ Describe a city or memorable place you have visited. ☐ Use sensory details to describe the sites, sounds, smells, and tastes of that city or place. ☐ Explain the most impressive site you saw and the most exciting experience you had. ☐ Synthesize the key ideas from your speech with a conclusion.	☐ Adapt language to a variety of contexts and tasks to demonstrate knowledge of formal English. ☐ Include multimedia components (e.g., graphics, images, music, sound) and visual displays. ☐ Use appropriate volume/tone (clear, not too fast, too slow, or too loud) and avoid using "like" or "ummm." ☐ Have strong posture, a confident stance, and make frequent eye contact. ☐ Occasionally move from one spot to another without fidgeting. ☐ Smile and appear to be relaxed.
Number of ✓s in this category: ___	**Number of ✓s in this category:** ___	**Number of ✓s in this category:** ___
Total # of ✓s: __		

Add up the total number of checks (✓) in each category. Then use the scoring guide below to calculate your final score.

Scoring Guide			
16 to 18 ✓s	13 to 15 ✓s	11 to 12 ✓s	10 or less ✓s
④ Exemplary	③ Meets Standards	② Needs Work	① Does Not Meet Standards

Read the Model

Writers use many strategies to persuade readers to agree with claims they make in their writing. The writer of this argumentative essay supports her claim with reasons drawn from the texts.

Argumentative Essay

An **argumentative essay** is a reasoned, logical way of demonstrating the validity of a position, belief, or conclusion.

The **introduction** introduces the issue and the claim the author is making about that issue.

- Identify the author's claim.

The **body paragraphs** contain reasons and evidence that supports the author's claim.

- Find two pieces of text evidence the author uses to support her claim.

The **conclusion** restates the thesis and offers a recommendation or final thought.

- Identify the thesis restatement.

The Two Tehrans   By Abbie Francis

What makes a city a home? In the excerpt from *Reading Lolita in Tehran*, Azar Nafisi expresses the sadness and longing she feels living in Tehran. Although she grew up in this city, it has changed so much she no longer feels she is at home. The most effective narrative strategies Nafisi uses to explain this are anecdote and figurative language, because they show how much Tehran has changed and how much she misses the way it was.

Nafisi's anecdote at the beginning of the excerpt is effective because it shows how much Tehran has changed. She describes how she and a friend would go to their "favorite pastry shop, where they had amazing cream puffs" and then walk home together. Nafisi uses descriptive details to describe the setting. She writes about the "protective gleam" of the snow and the "nonsense" they talked about as they walked (226). This contrasts with her description of Tehran now. She writes on that the snow is "polluted" and her friend is "in exile" (227). The reader understands how much Tehran has changed, and how the positive things Nafisi used to enjoy there are gone.

Nafisi's use of figurative language is one of the strategies that conveys her perspective the best because it shows how upset she is about the changes in Tehran. Nafisi writes that she feels like the things she loved about her city are "being crushed like small wildflowers" (227). This simile emphasizes how devastated she is. Later, she writes that she feels she is "squashing the memories . . . underfoot" as she walks home (227). She feels the things she loved about Tehran are suddenly, violently lost to her.

Although Nafisi uses many different narrative strategies in the excerpt, the most effective are her use of anecdote and figurative language. In the end, the reader wonders if Nafisi will ever again feel at home in Tehran.

Analyze the Model

An argumentative essay is a reasoned, logical way of demonstrating the validity of a position, belief, or conclusion.

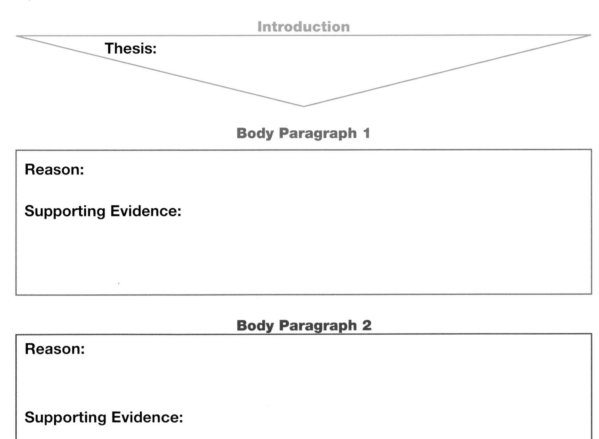

Introduction

Thesis:

Body Paragraph 1

Reason:

Supporting Evidence:

Body Paragraph 2

Reason:

Supporting Evidence:

Conclusion

Structuring an Argument

To structure an argument, put the **reasons** that support your argument in a logical order.

The order in which you discuss these reasons should be the same order you preview them in your **thesis statement**.

- Evaluate whether the reasons in the model are relevant and convincing.

- Explain if the model organizes the reasons in a logical order.

- Determine if the **thesis statement** reflects the order in which the reasons appear in the body of the essay.

Step 1 | Gather Evidence

> Choose one writer. Argue which narrative strategies best convey the author's perspective about the city.

What You Need to Know | Evidence from the texts that gives details about each writer's perspective about cities (see pages 191 and 199).

What You Need to Write | Use a note-taking guide to list authors' perspectives and the key strategies that convey them. Provide an example of the strategy from the text.

"City"

Author's Perspective:

Evidence:

Strategy:

Line # _____

"Our City"

Author's Perspective:

Evidence:

Strategy:

Line # _____

"Song of the Builders"

Author's Perspective:

Evidence:

Strategy:

Line # _____

The Wonderful Wizard of Oz

Author's Perspective:

Evidence:

Strategy:

Page # _____

Step 2 | Organize Ideas

What You Need to Know | Narrative strategies that convey the authors' perspectives

What You Need to Write | Two narrative strategies, with supporting text evidence, that best convey the perspective of one of the authors in the Unit

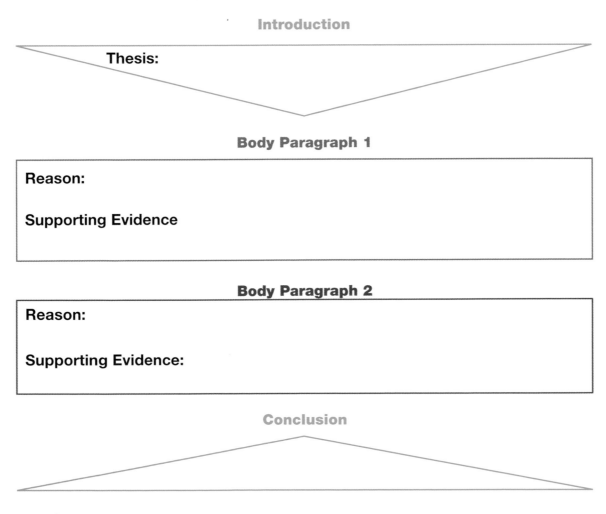

Introduction

Thesis:

Body Paragraph 1

Reason:

Supporting Evidence

Body Paragraph 2

Reason:

Supporting Evidence:

Conclusion

Step 3 | Draft

Write a draft of your essay on the computer or on paper.

Language Study | Defending a Claim

See It

A claim is an arguable statement or position on something. When writers defend their claim, they use clear reasons and relevant evidence to prove their claim is right or to protect it from opposing arguments. The stronger the evidence, the more persuasive the claim.

Try It

Evaluate how well the following claims are defended.

- Put **S** beside claims that are supported with clear reasons and relevant evidence.
- Put **NS** beside claims that are not supported.
- For claims you mark **NS**, rewrite the sentence to include clear reasons and relevant evidence.

1. If I could take my vacation any place, I think Alaska would be the best. _____

_____

_____

2. I like to live in a large city because I enjoy having many people to watch and learn about. _____

_____

_____

3. You don't need a new outfit for the party. You have a brand new pair of jeans that look great. _____

_____

_____

4. It is important to get 7–8 hours of sleep a night. _____

_____

_____

Apply It

Choose one of the frames below to summarize or add additional evidence to a claim you make in your argumentative essay.

1. _____ best shows the author's perspective that _____ because _____.
   (strategy)   (perspective)   (effect of strategy)

2. The author's perspective that _____ is revealed best through the use of _____.
                                  (perspective)   (strategy)

   For example, when the author writes, _____, it _____.
                                        (text evidence)   (effect of strategy)

3. The clearest example that _____ feels _____ is when _____ is used.
                            (author)   (perspective)   (strategy)

   This is because _____.
                   (effect of strategy)

4. The most effective evidence of the author's perspective comes through the use of _____
                                                                                    (strategy)

   because _____.
           (effect of strategy)

Now, **go back to your draft** and examine your reasons and supporting evidence. Choose one place where you could add more supporting evidence and rewrite the sentence.

_____

_____

_____

Conventions Study | Clarifying With Words, Phrases, & Clauses

See It | **Writers use words, phrases, and clauses to connect claims, reasons, and evidence.**

Find the words, phrases, and/or clauses the writer used in the sentences below from the model. How do the words, phrases, and clauses help you understand how the reasons relate to the claim?

> Although she grew up in this city, it has changed so much she no longer feels she is at home. The most effective narrative strategies Nafisi uses to explain this are anecdote and figurative language, because they show how much Tehran has changed and how much she misses the way it was.

Choose a paragraph from your essay. Revise it, being sure to include words, phrases, and clauses that show the relationship between your claim, your reasons, and your evidence. Use the following questions to help you:

- Can I show cause and effect with words and phrases such as *because*, *through*, or *as a result of*?
- Can I add specific evidence using words and phrases such as *specifically*, *in particular*, or *especially*?
- Can I signal an inference or conclusion using words and phrases such as *in conclusion*, *therefore*, or *given these reasons*?

Step 4 | Revise and Edit   Revise your draft with a partner.

Organization and Clarity					
Introduce a claim and support it with clear, organized reasons and relevant evidence.	Self	1	2	3	4
	Partner	1	2	3	4
Establish and maintain a formal style.	Self	1	2	3	4
	Partner	1	2	3	4
Use words, phrases, and clauses to clarify the relationship between the claim and supporting reasons.	Self	1	2	3	4
	Partner	1	2	3	4
Provide a concluding statement that follows from the evidence presented.	Self	1	2	3	4
	Partner	1	2	3	4
Evidence and Reasoning					
Argue which narrative techniques best convey the perspective of one writer featured in the Unit.	Self	1	2	3	4
	Partner	1	2	3	4
Support the claim using evidence from the Unit texts, correctly citing the author and page number for each piece of evidence.	Self	1	2	3	4
	Partner	1	2	3	4
Language and Conventions					
Recognize and adjust variations from standard English.	Self	1	2	3	4
	Partner	1	2	3	4
Correctly punctuate, capitalize, and spell all words and phrases.	Self	1	2	3	4
	Partner	1	2	3	4
Vary sentence patterns for meaning, reader interest, and variety.	Self	1	2	3	4
	Partner	1	2	3	4

Scoring Guide | ① needs improvement   ② average   ③ good   ④ excellent

Step 5 | Publish   Publish your essay either in print or digital form.

Publish

Publish your argumentative essay either in print or digital form. Use the rubric below to consider the success of your final performance task.

PERFORMANCE TASK RUBRIC			
Score Point	Organization and Clarity	Evidence and Reasoning	Language and Conventions
Exemplary ④	• introductory paragraph includes a **strong thesis statement** that **makes a convincing claim** about the strategies that convey an author's perspective • body paragraphs are **effectively organized** and **present logical reasons and evidence** to support the claim • includes **well-chosen** text evidence, precise language, and phrases and clauses that connect claims and reasons • concluding statement **restates the thesis statement**	• **accurately explains and convincingly argues** about one writer's perspective on a city • includes **relevant** factual evidence from the poems or fiction excerpt to explain one writer's perspective about a city and the strategies the writer uses to convey it	• demonstrates a **strong command** of the conventions of standard English grammar and usage, as well as of standard English capitalization, punctuation, and spelling • vocabulary is **appropriate** to the topic (vocabulary about city life; accurate vocabulary for a convincing thesis statement; vocabulary for making a claim and supporting it with logical reasons)
Meets Standards ③	• introductory paragraph **includes an adequate thesis statement that makes a claim** about the strategies that convey an author's perspective • body paragraphs are **logically organized** and **present reasons and evidence** to support the claim • includes **some** text evidence, precise language and phrases and clauses that connect claims and reasons • concluding statement **restates the thesis statement**	• **adequately explains and argues** about one writer's perspective on a city • includes **some relevant** factual evidence from the poems or fiction excerpt to explain one writer's perspective about a city and the strategies the writer uses to convey it	• demonstrates **a near command** of the conventions of standard English grammar and usage, as well as of standard English capitalization, punctuation, and spelling **with some errors** • vocabulary is **appropriate** to the topic (vocabulary about city life; accurate vocabulary for a convincing thesis statement; vocabulary for making a claim and supporting it with logical reasons)

PERFORMANCE TASK RUBRIC

Score Point	Organization and Clarity	Evidence and Reasoning	Language and Conventions
Needs Work ②	• introductory paragraph **includes a weak thesis statement that attempts to make a claim** about the strategies that convey an author's perspective • body paragraphs are **somewhat logically organized** and **partially present reasons and evidence** to support the claim • includes **a limited amount** of text evidence, precise language and phrases and clauses that connect claims and reasons • concluding statement **restates the thesis statement**	• **partially explains and argues** about one writer's perspective on a city • includes **one or two examples of relevant** factual evidence from the poems or fiction excerpt to explain one writer's perspective about a city and the strategies the writer uses to convey it	• demonstrates a **marginal command** of the conventions of English grammar and usage, as well as of standard English capitalization, punctuation, and spelling • there **are many errors; however, the text is still understandable** • includes only one or two examples of vocabulary that is appropriate to the topic (vocabulary about city life; accurate vocabulary for a convincing thesis statement; vocabulary for making a claim and supporting it with logical reasons)
Does Not Meet Standards ①	• introductory paragraph is **unclear** and does not include a thesis statement • body paragraphs are **not organized logically** and/or **do not present reasons and evidence** to persuade the reader • essay includes **little text evidence** and phrases and clauses to connect claims and reasons • concluding statement is **unclear**	• response is **partial or inaccurate explanation** of one writer's perspective about a city and the strategies the writer uses to convey it • includes **no factual textual evidence** from the poems or fiction excerpt	• demonstrates **almost no command** of the conventions of standard English grammar and usage, as well as of standard English capitalization, punctuation, and spelling • there **are many errors that disrupt** the reader's understanding of the text • does not include vocabulary that is appropriate to the topic (vocabulary about city life; accurate vocabulary for a convincing thesis statement; vocabulary for making a claim and supporting it with logical reasons)

Questions

Text Structure

1. White writes in **paragraph 1** that New York can "destroy an individual, or it can fulfill him." What does this show about his opinion of New York City?

Words and Phrases in Context

2. What is the effect of White's use of the word *concentrate* in the first sentence of **paragraph 2**?

from "Here Is New York"

by E. B. White

¶1 On any person who desires such queer prizes, New York will bestow the gift of loneliness and the gift of privacy. It is this <u>largess</u> that accounts for the presence within the city's walls of a considerable section of the population; for the residents of Manhattan are to a large extent strangers who have pulled up stakes somewhere and come to town, seeking sanctuary or fulfillment or some greater or lesser grail. The capacity to make such dubious gifts is a mysterious quality of New York. It can destroy an individual, or it can fulfill him, depending a good deal on luck. No one should come to New York to live unless he is willing to be lucky.

¶2 New York is the concentrate of art and commerce and sport and religion and entertainment and finance, bringing to a single compact arena the gladiator, the evangelist, the promoter, the actor, the trader and the merchant. It carries on its lapel the unexpungeable odor of the long past, so that no matter where you sit in New York you feel the vibrations of great times and tall deeds, of queer people and events and undertakings. I am sitting at the moment in a stifling hotel room in 90-degree heat, halfway down an air shaft, in midtown. No air moves in or out of the room, yet I am curiously affected by <u>emanations</u> from the immediate surroundings. I am twenty-two blocks from where Rudolph Valentino lay in state, eight blocks from where Nathan Hale was executed, five blocks from the publisher's office where Ernest Hemingway hit Max Eastman on the nose, four miles from where Walt Whitman sat sweating out editorials for the Brooklyn Eagle . . . (I could continue this list indefinitely); and for that matter I am probably occupying the very room that any number of exalted and somewise memorable characters sat in, some of them on hot, breathless afternoons, lonely and private and full of their own sense of emanations from without.

Words to Know

<u>largess:</u> *(n.)* money or gifts people give to others who have less than they do

<u>emanations:</u> *(n.)* something that comes from or out of another source

¶3 When I went down to lunch a few minutes ago I noticed that the man sitting next to me (about eighteen inches away along the wall) was <u>Fred Stone</u>. The eighteen inches were both the connection and the separation that New York provides for its inhabitants. My only connection with Fred Stone was that I saw him in *The Wizard of Oz* around the beginning of the century. But our waiter felt the same <u>stimulus</u> from being close to a man from Oz, and after Mr. Stone left the room the waiter told me that when he (the waiter) was a young man just arrived in this country and before he could understand a word of English, he had taken his girl for their first theater date to *The Wizard of Oz*. It was a wonderful show, the waiter recalled—a man of straw, a man of tin. Wonderful! (And still only eighteen inches away.) "Mr. Stone is a very <u>hearty eater</u>," said the waiter thoughtfully, content with this fragile participation in destiny, this link with Oz.

Questions

Key Ideas and Details

3. How are the "eighteen inches" between White and Fred Stone both a "connection" and a "separation"?

Text Structure

4. What is the effect of the waiter's anecdote about when he was "a young man just arrived in this country" in **paragraph 3**?

Words to Know

<u>**Fred Stone:**</u> *(n.)* An American actor who played the Scarecrow in the first stage production of *The Wizard of Oz* in 1902

<u>**stimulus:**</u> *(n.)* something that causes a person to react or change

<u>**hearty eater:**</u> *(n.)* someone who has a large appetite and can eat a lot of food

Questions

Text Structure

5. What does White mean by the "gift of privacy" in **paragraph 4** and why is that an important part of his vision of New York?

Words and Phrases in Context

6. What does White mean when he says that "inches counted heavily" in the last sentence of **paragraph 4**?

¶4 New York blends the gift of privacy with the excitement of participation; and better than most dense communities it succeeds in <u>insulating</u> the individual (if he wants it, and almost everybody wants or needs it) against all enormous and violent and wonderful events that are taking place every minute. Since I have been sitting in this <u>miasmic</u> air shaft, a good many rather splashy events have occurred in town. A man shot and killed his wife in a fit of jealousy. It caused no stir outside his block and got only small mention in the papers. I did not attend. Since my arrival, the greatest air show ever staged in all the world took place in town. I didn't attend and neither did most of the eight million other inhabitants, although they say there was quite a crowd. I didn't even hear any planes except a couple of westbound commercial airliners that habitually use this air shaft to fly over. The biggest oceangoing ships on the North Atlantic arrived and departed. I didn't notice them and neither did most other New Yorkers. I am told this is the greatest seaport in the world, with six hundred and fifty miles of water front, and ships calling here from many exotic lands, but the only boat I've happened to notice since my arrival was a small sloop tacking out of the East River night before last on the ebb tide when I was walking across the Brooklyn Bridge. I heard the Queen Mary blow one midnight, though, and the sound carried the whole history of departure and longing and loss. The <u>Lions</u> have been in convention. I've seen not one Lion. A friend of mine saw one and told me about him. (He was lame, and was wearing a bolero.) At the ballgrounds and horse parks the greatest sporting spectacles have been enacted. I saw no ballplayer, no race horse. The governor came to town. I heard the siren scream, but that was all there was to that—an eighteen inch margin again. A man was killed by a falling cornice. I was not a <u>party</u> to the tragedy, and again the inches counted heavily.

Words to Know

<u>insulating</u>: *(v.)* to protect or keep apart from experiences

<u>miasmic</u>: *(adj.)* containing dirty or unpleasant clouds of air

<u>Lions</u>: *(n.)* Members of the Lions Clubs International, an organization devoted to helping others

<u>party</u>: *(n.)* someone that is involved in an activity, event, or decision

¶**5** I mention these merely to show that New York is peculiarly constructed to absorb almost anything that comes along (whether a thousand-foot <u>liner</u> out of the East or a twenty-thousand-man <u>convention</u> out of the West) without <u>inflicting</u> the event on its inhabitants; so that every event is, in a sense, optional, and the inhabitant is in the happy position of being able to choose his <u>spectacle</u> and so conserve his soul.

Questions

Key Ideas and Details

7. How is the resident of New York City able to "choose his spectacle and so conserve his soul"?

Words to Know

<u>liner</u>: *(n.)* a large passenger ship

<u>convention</u>: *(n.)* a formal gathering for people who all belong to the same organization or share the same interests

<u>inflicting</u>: *(v.)* making someone experience something unpleasant

<u>spectacle</u>: *(n.)* a large, impressive show or scene

Questions

Text Structure

1. Why does Nafisi begin the excerpt with her memory of "a childhood friend" whom she "loved a great deal"? What is the effect of this memory?

Key Ideas and Details

2. What does Nafisi's question, "Was it on this spot that my friend and I had stopped to laugh that day as we licked our cream puffs?" in **paragraph 2** reveal about her feelings?

from *Reading Lolita in Tehran*

by Azar Nafisi

¶1 After the class I felt exhausted. I tried to leave quickly, pretending I had some important business at hand. In fact, I had nothing to do. I put on my coat and hat and gloves and left. I had nowhere to go. It snowed heavily that afternoon, and then the sun came out over piles of clean, fresh white snow. I had a friend, a childhood friend I loved a great deal—she was older than me—when I was very young, before I was sent to England. She and I would sometimes walk in the snow for a long time. We would walk to our favorite pastry shop, where they had amazing <u>cream puffs</u>, made with real cream. We bought the cream puffs and went back out into the snow, in whose protective <u>gleam</u> we ate them as we talked nonsense and walked and walked.

¶2 I left the university and started to walk past the book-lined street. The street vendors selling tapes had turned up the volume, and they hopped from one foot to the other to keep warm, their woolen hats pulled low over their ears, steam escaping from their mouths and appearing to rise with the sound of the music, rising and disappearing into the blue sky. I walked down the street until the bookstores gave way to other shops, and to a movie house where we used to go as children that was now closed. So many movie houses were burned down during those <u>jubilant</u> days of the <u>revolution</u>! I continued down the street until I came to a square called Ferdowsi, named after our greatest epic poet, and paused. Was it on this spot that my friend and I had stopped to laugh that day as we licked our cream puffs?

Words to Know

<u>cream puffs:</u> *(n.)* a light pastry with a cream filling

<u>gleam:</u> *(n.)* the brightness of something shiny

<u>jubilant:</u> *(adj.)* very happy; joyous

<u>revolution:</u> *(n.)* a time when a group of people change the ruler or political system, often with force or violence

¶3 As the years went by, the snow became polluted with the increasing pollution of Tehran; my friend was now in <u>exile</u>, and I had come home. Until then home had been <u>amorphous</u> and elusive: it presented itself in <u>tantalizing</u> glimpses, with the impersonal familiarity of old family photographs. But all of these feelings belonged to the past. Home was constantly changing before my eyes.

¶4 I had a feeling that day that I was losing something, that I was mourning a death that had not yet occurred. I felt as if all things personal were being crushed like small wildflowers to make way for a more <u>ornate</u> garden, where everything would be tame and organized. I had never felt this sense of loss when I was a student in the States. In all those years, my yearning was tied to the certainty that home was mine for the having, that I could go back anytime I wished. It was not until I had reached home that I realized the true meaning of exile. As I walked those dearly beloved, dearly remembered streets, I felt I was squashing the memories that lay underfoot.

Questions

Words and Phrases in Context

3. How does Nafisi's comment in **paragraph 4** that "it was not until I had reached home that I realized the true meaning of exile" show her perspective on Tehran?

Words to Know

exile: *(n.)* a situation in which you are forced to leave your country and live somewhere else, often for political reasons

amorphous: *(n.)* having no clear shape

tantalizing: *(adj.)* to make someone feel the desire to do or have something

ornate: *(adj.)* having a lot of decoration

Literature Circle Leveled Novels

The Thief Lord *by Cornelia Funke*
Two orphaned brothers, Prosper and Bo, have run away to Venice, where crumbling canals and misty alleyways shelter a secret community of street urchins. The leader of this motley crew of lost children is a clever, charming boy with a dark history of his own: He calls himself the Thief Lord. **Lexile**® measure: 640L

The London Eye Mystery *by Siobhan Dowd*
Ted and his older sister Kat become sleuthing partners as they search for their cousin Salim, who disappeared after he boarded the London Eye. The duo must overcome their differences to follow a trail of clues across London in a desperate bid to find their cousin. **Lexile**® measure: 640L

The Wonderful Wizard of Oz *by L. Frank Baum*
Follow the adventures of young Dorothy Gale and her dog, Toto, as their Kansas house is swept up by a cyclone and deposited in a strange land called Oz. **Lexile**® measure: 1030L

Fiction, Nonfiction, and Novels

The Girl Who Owned a City *by O. T. Nelson.* A virus has devastated North America, killing everyone over the age of 12. Ten year-old Lisa must become the ruler of her neighborhood if she and her brother are to survive. **Lexile**® measure: GN420L

The Hunger Games *by Suzanne Collins.* In the ruins of a place once known as North America lies the nation of Panem, a shining Capitol surrounded by twelve districts. Sixteen-year-old Katniss has been dealt a death sentence from the Capitol that she refuses to accept. **Lexile**® measure: 810L

From the Mixed-Up Files of Mrs. Basil E. Frankweiler *by E. L. Konigsburg.* Claudia and her younger brother Jamie have the adventure of a lifetime when they "run away" by spending the night in New York City's Metropolitan Museum of Art. **Lexile**® measure: 700L

A Tree Grows in Brooklyn *by Betty Smith.* An idealistic and sensitive girl, Francie Nolan, comes of age in the slums of Brooklyn at the turn of the 20th century. **Lexile**® measure: 810L

A Wrinkle in Time *by Madeleine L'Engle.* Everything is wrong in Meg Murray's life. One night, the family is visited by a woman named Mrs. Whatsit. She turns out to be the force who spurs on Meg, her brother Charles Wallace, and their friend, Calvin O'Keefe, to embark on a dangerous quest through space to find their father. **Lexile**® measure: 740L

The Great Fire *by Jim Murphy.* Chicago's Great Fire of 1871 was one of the most colossal disasters in American History. **Lexile**® measure: 1130L

Films and TV

Chitty Chitty Bang Bang (Galen Films, 1968) A hapless inventor, his children, and a friend, aided by a flying car, take on a ruthless dictator in a far-off land. (144 min.)

Brooklyn Bridge (Ken Burns America Collection,1981) Learn about the building of this "eighth wonder of the world." (58 min.)

A Wrinkle in Time (Echo Bridge Home Entertainment, 2011) Follow brother and sister Meg and Charles Wallace, and their neighbor Calvin O'Keefe as they embark on a cosmic journey to find the siblings' father. (128 min.)

A Tree Grows in Brooklyn (20th Century Fox, 1945) As she comes of age in Brooklyn in the early 1900s, Francie Nolan and her family experience hard times, good times, change, and renewal. (129 min.)

The Wizard of Oz (Warner Brothers, 1939) Follow young Dorothy, her dog, Toto, and her three companions—the Tin Man, the Cowardly Lion, and the Scarecrow—on the yellow brick road to Emerald City. (102 min.)

Websites

Howstuffworks.com Search for "London Eye" to find out how it works. Check out fascinating information on the building and operation of the London Eye at www.howstuffworks.com/london-eye1.htm

National Geographic: Kids What cities would you like to visit? Find photos, facts, and information on dozens of exciting cities around the world at http://kids.nationalgeographic.com/kids/places

Dubai Architecture Explore the amazing architecture in the city of Dubai, from the Burj Al Arab to the Palm Jumeirah, at http://www.dubai-architecture.info/LIST-MAIN.htm

National Geographic Tour some of the most interesting cities on the planet at http://travel.nationalgeographic.com/travel/city-guides/

Magazines

Architectural Digest Take a peek inside the world's most beautiful homes. This magazine is filled with stunning photographs and exclusive coverage of international interior design, architecture, art, and antiques.

Scholastic News Stay up-to-date with today's news and read about what's happening in cities across the globe.

Dwell The first and only magazine to explore both the interiors and the exteriors of modern home design.

History Lost and Found

How can ancient history teach us about our world today?

Unit Introduction

In a nonfiction article and excerpt, examine how new discoveries about ancient Egypt reveal hidden secrets and affect our view of the past.

In Bryan Brown's article "New Discoveries in Ancient Egypt," evidence confirms suspicions about the burial practices of Egyptian kings.

In an excerpt from his nonfiction book *Curse of the Pharaohs,* archaeologist Zahi Hawass shares his feelings about working amid the tombs of ancient Egyptian rulers and explains one of his discoveries.

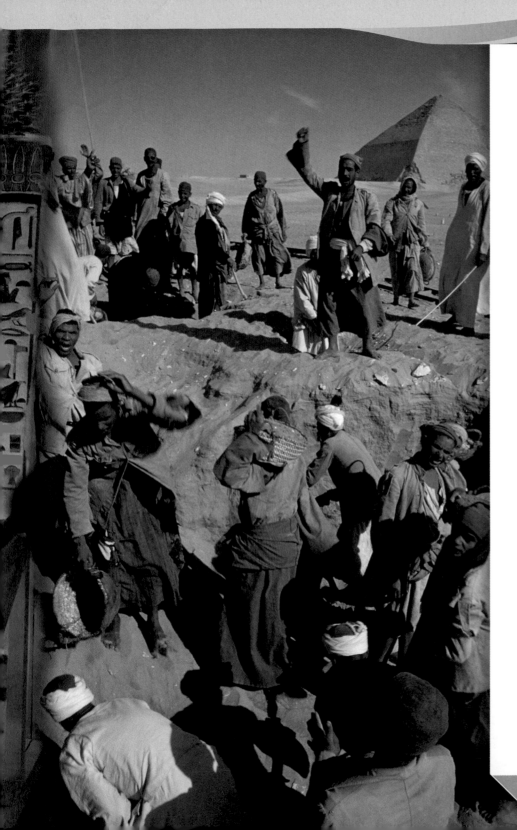

WRITING PERFORMANCE TASK

Compare and contrast how these writers convey the historical importance of recent discoveries. How does each writer support his perspective?

⬛ MAGAZINE ARTICLE/NONFICTION EXCERPT

from **"New Discoveries in Ancient Egypt"** by Bryan Brown from *Junior Scholastic*

from ***Curse of the Pharaohs*** by Zahi Hawass

Language
- Academic Vocabulary
- Word Study: Connotation

Language
- Academic Vocabulary
- Word Study: Roots and Prefixes

Reading Informational Text
- Identify Evidence
- Key Ideas and Details
- Craft and Structure

Reading Informational Text
- Identify Evidence
- Key Ideas and Details
- Craft and Structure

⬛ SPEAKING AND LISTENING _____

Research Project
- Collaborate and Present

Checklist: Research Project
- Scoring Guide

⬛ WRITING _____

Writing: Informative Essay
- Read the Model
- Analyze the Model
- Gather Evidence
- Organize Ideas

- Language Study: Order Supporting Details
- Conventions Study: Pronouns
- Revise, Edit, and Publish
- Performance Task Rubric

⬛ EXTENDED READING _____

Nonfiction Excerpt
from ***Cities of the Dead***
by Denise Rinaldo

Academic Vocabulary

"New Discoveries in Ancient Egypt"
by Bryan Brown

Rate your understanding of each word. Then read its meaning and write an example sentence. If an example is given, write the meaning.

Word	Meaning	Example
reveal *(v.)* p. 233 ① ② ③ ④		The scientist was excited to reveal his discovery to the world.
contain *(v.)* p. 233 ① ② ③ ④		The folder contained all of my homework.
ancient *(adj.)* p. 233 ① ② ③ ④		The ancient gem was recovered from a 500-year-old grave.
unite *(v.)* p. 234 ① ② ③ ④		The two groups united to form one.
eternal *(adj.)* p. 235 ① ② ③ ④		I will be eternally grateful to the woman who saved my life.
conquest *(n.)* p. 237 ① ② ③ ④	a country or land gained by fighting	

Rating Scale | ① I don't know the word. ② I've seen it or heard it.
③ I know its meaning. ④ I know it and use it.

Word Study

Denotation is the literal, or dictionary definition of a word. **Connotation** is what the word suggests, for example:

- positive or negative
- formal or informal

1. Rate the connotation of these synonyms for *long* as negative (-), positive (+), or neutral (n).
   - endless _____
   - enduring _____
   - eternal _____
   - drawn out _____

2. Rate the connotation of these synonyms for *old* as negative (–), positive (+), or neutral (n).
   - decrepit _____
   - ancient _____
   - antique _____
   - mature _____

3. List three or more words that mean *young*. Then rate them using the symbols explained above.

New Discoveries in
Ancient Egypt *by Bryan Brown*

from *Junior Scholastic*

¶1 For years, people have looked with <u>awe</u> upon the burial riches of ancient Egypt's Pharaohs (Kings). The famous tomb of King Tutankhamen *(TOO-tan-KAH-men)*, found in 1922, **contained** so many treasures, it took 10 years for archaeologists to remove them all. More than 5,000 items were found in Tut's four-room burial chamber—everything from jewelry to gold masks to drinking cups!

¶2 But newer discoveries have **revealed** that a few Pharaohs went to the afterlife with more than just objects. Some even brought their servants!

¶3 Recently, archaeologists from New York University, Yale University, and the University of Pennsylvania Museum have made some <u>startling</u> discoveries at the **ancient** graveyard of Abydos *(eh-BYE-des)*. Near the 5,000-year-old tomb of the Pharaoh Aha, they found six connected graves.

¶4 Archaeologists think the bones in the graves are those of officials, craftsmen, and servants in Aha's royal court. The discoveries <u>confirm</u> a long-held suspicion among historians—that individuals were sacrificed in order to serve their ruler's needs in the afterlife.

Close Reading

Key Ideas and Details
1. Identify where the author's main claim is introduced. What is the author's purpose in writing this article?

Academic Vocabulary
2. Why does the author choose to use the word *ancient* in **paragraph 3**?

Parentheses

Parentheses (like this) indicate that the reader should place less emphasis on the enclosed material.

Key Ideas and Details
3. Explain what was startling about the discovery in the ancient graveyard. Use details from **paragraph 4** to support your answer.

Dashes

Dashes—like this—usually show emphasis. They are often used in the middle of a sentence.

Words to Know

<u>awe</u>: *(n.)* a feeling of great respect or admiration

<u>startling</u>: *(adj.)* very unusual or surprising

<u>confirm</u>: *(v.)* to show that something is definitely true, especially by providing more proof

Expert Testimony

Text Structure

4. Why does the author use the subheading "A Gigantic Leap" above **paragraph 5**? Use evidence from the text to support your answer.

Key Ideas and Details

5. Identify details that the author uses to elaborate on his claim about servants being sacrificed. What new information is offered in **paragraphs 5–7**?

Writing

6. Review the details in **paragraphs 5–7**. What type of information does the author include to convey the importance of Aha?

Text Structure

7. How does the time period that is discussed in this section relate to the time line on the opposite page?

A Gigantic Leap

¶5 The kingdom of ancient Egypt lasted for 3,000 years, beginning around 3100 B.C. Historians often call Aha, also known as Menes *(MEE-nez)*, the first Pharaoh. Many <u>credit</u> him with **uniting** Lower Egypt and Upper Egypt into one kingdom.

¶6 Egyptian civilization "took a gigantic leap under the ruler Aha," says David O'Connor, who is leading the excavations at Abydos.

¶7 The human sacrifices offered for Aha also "indicate a great change of royal power," says Laurel Bestock, a member of the Abydos team. During Aha's time, Egyptians began to view their king as a god, or a <u>divine</u> representative.

Workmen excavate the Valley of the Kings.

Words to Know

<u>credit:</u> *(v.)* to give someone credit for; to acknowledge that someone did or said something

<u>divine:</u> *(adj.)* god-like

¶8   Experts think individuals in Aha's court were poisoned during the royal ritual. Still, tests on the skeletons do not reveal any signs of physical trauma. Court members may have thought they were gaining **eternal** life by following their King into death.

¶9   There are also bodies in graves linked to the tomb of King Djer, Aha's successor. But O'Connor believes that the Pharaohs stopped making human sacrifices by the end of Egypt's First Dynasty, in about 2986 B.C.

Time line

3100 B.C.	**Early Period** Aha unites Upper and Lower Egypt.
2686–2181 B.C.	**Old Kingdom** The first great pyramids are built.
1991–1786 B.C.	**Middle Kingdom** The arts flourish during this time of prosperity.
1554–1070 B.C.	**New Kingdom** Egypt is at the height of its power. Tutankhamen rules from 1347 to 1339 B.C.
1070–332 B.C.	**Late Period** Ruled by a series of foreign powers, Egypt is in decline.
332–30 B.C.	**Alexander and the Ptolemies** Egypt is ruled by Alexander the Great, King of the Macedonians, and the dynasty (powerful group or family) of his successor, Ptolemy (TAH-leh-me).
30 B.C.–395 A.D.	**Roman Period** Egypt is part of the Roman Empire.

Words to Know

ritual: *(n.)* a ceremony that is always performed in the same way, in order to mark an important occasion

trauma: *(n.)* serious injury

dynasty: *(n.)* rulers from the same family

Close Reading

Academic Vocabulary

8. What does the evidence in **paragraph 8** reveal about how and why humans were sacrificed?

Key Ideas and Details

9. How does the author further develop the idea that servants were sacrificed for their kings?

Words and Phrases in Context

10. Explain the significance of the phrase "following their King into death" in **paragraph 8**. What does the author mean by *following*?

Text Structure

11. What information is provided by the time line that is not given elsewhere in the article?

Close Reading

Key Ideas and Details

12. What is the historical importance of this new discovery in the Abydos cemetery? How is it different compared to previous discoveries?

Words and Phrases in Context

13. Describe the "boat graves" that the author mentions in **paragraph 11**. Why were they created?

Writing

14. Why does the author include quotations in **paragraphs 11 and 12**? Explain why the strategy is useful in this context.

Key Ideas and Details

15. How does the information about the disturbed graves emphasize the importance of the discovery?

A Jumble of Bones

¶10 Abydos was one of the most important burial grounds in ancient Egypt. The city was also a major center for worship of Osiris *(oh-SY-rihs)*, the god of the dead.

¶11 O'Connor has been digging at Abydos since 1967. His teams have <u>excavated</u> fleets of full-size wooden boats in "boat graves," and even the bones of donkeys. "The king would need transportation in the afterlife," archaeologist Matthew Adams explains.

¶12 The graves of Aha's servants were discovered about a mile from the Pharaoh's tomb. Among the bones, archaeologists found jars with Aha's royal <u>seals</u>. Bestock told JS that the graves have been "heavily disturbed" by ancient tomb robbers. "In three cases we found parts of a single body," she says. "In two cases there were only jumbled [mixed-up] bones."

Words to Know

<u>excavated</u>: *(v.)* carefully dug up in order to find ancient objects, bones, etc.

<u>seal</u>: *(n.)* a stamp made of metal or wax with a distinctive design used to authenticate a document or container

¶**13** <u>Scholars</u> divide the time line of ancient Egypt into as many as 10 historical <u>periods</u>. The kingdom was ruled by 31 dynasties until Alexander the Great conquered it in 332 B.C. One of the greatest generals in history, Alexander spread Greek culture across much of the known world with his **conquests**.

¶**14** In 30 B.C., the Romans defeated Queen Cleopatra, the last of the rulers who followed Alexander. Roman rule began to weaken when the empire split apart in 395 A.D. After that, the glory of ancient Egypt began to disappear under <u>waves</u> of new conquests and foreign control.

¶**15** Today, clues to the great mysteries of one of the world's great civilizations are being dug out of the desert bit by bit. In Abydos, archaeologists have uncovered the tombs of all eight kings of the First Dynasty. But O'Connor's team believes that there are many more bones of the First Dynasty officials and servants to be found.

¶**16** "There is still a lot of exciting work to do!" says Bestock.

Close Reading

Text Structure

16. What important information about the grave site at Abydos does the author save for the last section? What might his purpose have been in doing so?

Academic Vocabulary

17. Explain why "waves of new conquests" ended Egyptian rule.

Words and Phrases in Context

18. Why does the author use the word *glory* in association with ancient Egypt in **paragraph 14**? What does the word's connotation reveal about the author's perspective?

Writing

19. How does the work of archaeologists like Bestock change the way people look at history? Explain your answer using details from the text.

Words to Know

<u>scholars:</u> *(n.)* intellectual, well educated people; people who know a lot about a specific topic

<u>periods:</u> *(n.)* particular lengths of time, with beginning and end points

<u>waves:</u> *(n.)* sudden increases in a particular behavior, activity, or feeling

Identify Evidence | Analyze Individuals, Events, and Ideas

Reread **"New Discoveries in Ancient Egypt,"** identifying details that show how the author conveys the historical importance of the discoveries in Abydos. How does the author introduce, illustrate, and elaborate upon how important these discoveries are?

- As you read, use the Evidence Column to record examples from the text that show the significance of the discoveries.
- In the Explanation column, explain how the author uses the evidence to convey the historical importance.

Evidence	Source	Page	Explanation
1. "For years, people have looked with awe upon the burial riches of ancient Egypt's pharaohs."	Brown	233	Brown is establishing the great interest and respect people have for the archaeological findings he is going to discuss.
2. "The discoveries confirm a long-held suspicion among historians—that individuals were sacrificed in order to serve their ruler's needs in the afterlife."			
3. "The human sacrifices offered for Aha also 'indicate a great change of royal power,' says Laurel Bestock, a member of the Abydos team."			
4. "Still, tests on the skeletons do not reveal any signs of physical trauma."			

Evidence	Source	Page	Explanation

Key Ideas and Details

Determining the Central Idea

1. Use the evidence you collected to summarize the key idea of the text.

Analyzing Details

2. List three details that tell about the historical context for what was found at the graveyard of Abydos. Explain why each detail is important to the central idea.

Detail about Historical Context	Significance

3. Brown gives quotes from experts—archaeologists and members of the team that found the grave site. List two people quoted and explain the significance of including their perspective.

Expert Quoted	Significance

Craft and Structure

Structure of the Magazine Article

1. How do the three subheadings in the article help explain the article's structure? List each heading, and tell what it helps convey about the section it labels.

Section Header	What Header Conveys

Primary Source

A **primary source** is a document that contains information that has been obtained by people's experiences and not taken from other documents.

2. The article includes facts and explanations, as well as quotes from experts. Explain how including these quotations from experts adds validity to the article.

Secondary Source

A **secondary source** interprets or reviews previously discovered or previously discussed information.

Author's Purpose and Perspective

3. Describe the author's purpose in writing this article.

4. Is Bryan Brown an expert or a reporter? Is this article a primary source or a secondary source?

Academic Vocabulary
from *Curse of the Pharaohs* by Zahi Hawass

Rate your understanding of each word. Then write its meaning and an example sentence. If the example is given, write the meaning.

Word	Meaning	Example
sacred (adj.) p. 243 ① ② ③ ④	very important; of special religious value	
central (adj.) p. 243 ① ② ③ ④	in the middle of an area; more important than anything else	
symmetrical (adj.) p. 244 ① ② ③ ④		The auditorium was completely symmetrical: both sides looked the same.
disintegrate (v.) p. 244 ① ② ③ ④		After being left out in the rain, my homework folder disintegrated into pieces.
represent (v.) p. 244 ① ② ③ ④	to be a symbol of something; to be a sign or mark that means something	
delicate (adj.) p. 246 ① ② ③ ④		When I bumped into the delicate glass statue, it fell to the ground and broke.

Rating Scale | ① I don't know the word. ② I've seen it or heard it. ③ I know its meaning. ④ I know it and use it.

Word Study

The **root word** *integer* comes from the Latin word that means "whole" or "entire."

The **prefix** *dis-* means "not" or "the opposite of."

Use roots and prefixes as clues to determine the meaning of the words.

1. *integrate* means _____

2. *disintegrate* means _____

3. *disintegrated* means _____

4. Why would paper disintegrate in the rain?

5. List at least five more words that use the root *integer* or the prefix *dis-*.

from

Curse of the Pharaohs

by Zahi Hawass

Hidden Statues

¶1 One of the many wonderful discoveries we made in this cemetery was a group of four beautiful statues belonging to a man named Inty-Shedu. He lived during the Old Kingdom, the age when the pyramids at Giza were built, about 4,500 years ago. Inty-Shedu was the <u>overseer</u> of the **sacred** boat at the temple of a goddess named Neath. This would have been an important job, since the boat had to be kept ready for the goddess to use whenever she left her temple. While we were excavating Inty-Shedu's tomb, we found what we call a *serdab*. This is an Arabic word that means "cellar." Archaeologists use the term to refer to a small, <u>enclosed</u> chamber without a door.

¶2 The discovery of four statues, *in situ* (a fancy way of saying "in their original place"), is very unusual. The statue we had seen first, showing a man with shoulder-length hair and a moustache seated on a chair, was in the center. It was large, about 30 inches tall. To its left were a standing statue and a sitting statue, and to its right was a second standing statue. The statues on the sides were all smaller than the **central** figure. These four statues were carved out of limestone and painted with bright colors.

Words to Know

<u>overseer:</u> *(n.)* person in charge

<u>enclosed:</u> *(adj.)* closed in

Close Reading

Words and Phrases in Context

1. Use context clues to determine the meaning of the italicized words *serdab* and *in situ* in **paragraphs 1 and 2**.

Appositives

An **appositive** is a noun or phrase that renames another noun right beside it. Appositives can be short or long.

Key Ideas and Details

2. In **paragraph 2**, the author notes that the discovery of the statues is unusual. What makes it unusual?

Chronology

Chronology is the order in which events happened in the past.

Close Reading

Academic Vocabulary

3. Explain why one statue mentioned in **paragraph 3** *disintegrated* while the others remained intact.

Key Ideas and Details

4. How does the beginning of **paragraph 5** confirm the importance of the discovery?

Writing

5. What is the author's purpose in **paragraphs 5**? What key idea is he illustrating for the reader?

Text Structure

6. What is significant about the author's use of the word *Strange* in the heading "Strange Coincidences"?

¶3   The ancient Egyptians were always careful to do things **symmetrically**, and I found it strange that there would be two statues on one side of the main figure and only one on the other. So I looked carefully, and I saw that there had once been a second statue on the right, but it had been made of wood and had **disintegrated** into powder.

¶4   I felt sad at the loss of the fifth statue, but I began to examine the four extraordinary statues left in front of me. Each was inscribed with the name Inty-Shedu. I knew that they were meant to **represent** one person at various stages of his life.

Strange Coincidences

¶5   This is when strange things began to happen. On the day that the announcement was to be made, October 12, 1992, a big earthquake struck Cairo. I was sitting in my office at Giza when I felt the ground shake so hard that some of my books fell off their shelves. I immediately thought about the Sphinx, which is already in great danger of crumbling to pieces, and all our new discoveries, so I ran outside to see if everything was OK. I was very happy to find everything still standing, but we had to postpone the announcement—after the earthquake, the people of Egypt were very upset, and the mood of the country was very gloomy. Everyone had the earthquake on their minds, so this would not have been a good time to announce our discovery.

Words to Know

inscribed: *(v.)* carved; carefully written

postpone: *(v.)* to put off

gloomy: *(adj.)* dark and sad

¶6   We set a new date, on a Friday, which is the weekend in Egypt. I usually sleep a little bit late on Fridays then go to a cafe to write. But that day, because of the announcement about the statues, I got up early. My driver picked me up, and we drove off to the pyramids. As a government <u>official</u>, I have my own car and someone to drive me wherever I need to go. I sat in the front seat, reading the paper as I like to do in the morning. Suddenly the sky began to spin, and I fainted—I was having a heart attack!

¶7   I was very lucky because my driver was smart enough to take me right to the hospital, only a few minutes away. I was rushed to the emergency room, where I was given a shot of heart medicine that saved my life. But of course we had to cancel the announcement again. I stayed in the hospital for about two weeks, thinking of Inty-Shedu.

¶8   So we never made an official announcement of the statues. Maybe Inty-Shedu was shy and didn't want everyone paying so much attention to him. Some people might say that the earthquake and my heart attack were the result of an ancient curse, to which they like to <u>ascribe</u> all unusual events connected with <u>Egyptology</u>. But if there is a "Curse of Inty-Shedu," it holds no terror for me. It probably saved my life. If I had been home in bed when I had my heart attack, there would have been no one to notice that I needed medical help, and I might well have died!

Words to Know

<u>official:</u> *(n.)* someone who is in a position of authority

<u>ascribe:</u> *(v.)* give credit to, say that something caused something else

<u>Egyptology:</u> *(n.)* the study of ancient Egypt

Close Reading

Words and Phrases in Context

7. What is the author describing when he says "the sky began to spin" in **paragraph 6**?

Writing

8. How does Hawass develop and then conclude his discussion of the announcement?

Text Structure

9. The author claims in **paragraph 8** that "maybe Inty-Shedu was shy and didn't want everyone paying so much attention to him." What is the purpose of including this line in the text?

Key Ideas and Details

10. Why does the author say that a curse might have saved his life? Paraphrase his reasoning.

Close Reading

Key Ideas and Details

11. What is the author's purpose in the section "Treasuring the Past"?

Words and Phrases in Context

12. In **paragraph 10,** why does the author say that he is "always mindful" of the person buried inside?

Writing

13. Determine Hawass's perspective on archaeologists. Why might he be biased in his assessment?

Academic Vocabulary

14. Why is it important to protect the *delicate* bones of mummies?

Treasuring the Past

¶**9** What we do as archaeologists is to study the past, with care and love. We search for remains of the ancients that have been left in place. We treat each grave that we find with respect. We pay attention to the context of each object—exactly where and how it was left. The information that we gather in this way tells us stories about the people who left the objects behind.

¶**10** When I discover a new tomb, I am always mindful of the person buried inside. I move and touch the mummies I find as little as possible. And I use all of the latest technologies, such as x-rays and CAT scans, so that I can study them without disturbing their **delicate** bones. Using these tools can give us detailed pictures of the mummies and provide us with lots of information.

Dr. Zahi Hawass is an Egyptian archaeologist who has written many books relating to Egyptology.

Words to Know

context: *(n.)* the situation, events, or information that are related to something and that help you to understand it

CAT scan: *(n.)* a special type of X-ray machine

¶11 By studying ancient bones and <u>artifacts</u> in this way, I can learn so much—the age people were when they died, whether they were sick or healthy, and even what killed them. For example, several of the skeletons from the pyramid builders' cemetery have wounds that suggest that they were hurt or killed during their work on the pyramid site, perhaps by falling blocks. We even know something about the medical care available: One man had his arm amputated and lived for many years afterward.

¶12 By studying groups of mummies or tombs or houses, I can find out about families and groups of people, and even the society as a whole. By reading the texts that ancient people have left behind, I can learn about things such as their religious beliefs and how their <u>economy</u> worked.

¶13 As an archaeologist, I cause the names of the dead to be remembered, not forgotten. So if there is a curse, it should follow the thieves and robbers who destroy the past, not the scholars who try to preserve it.

Close Reading

Words and Phrases in Context

15. Explain the context clues that help define the word *suggest* in **paragraph 11**.

Text Structure

16. Why does Hawass end the passage with a reference to "the thieves and robbers who destroy the past"?

Key Ideas and Details

17. Use Hawass's perspective to analyze why learning about history matters. Why would Hawass think it's important to study ancient culture? Use evidence from the text to support your answer.

Words to Know

<u>artifacts</u>: *(n.)* objects from the past

<u>economy</u>: *(n.)* a system of how money and goods are traded in a society

Identify Evidence | Analyze Individuals, Events, and Ideas

Reread the excerpt from **Curse of the Pharaohs,** identifying details that show how the author conveys the historical importance of the discovery he describes. How does the author introduce, illustrate, and elaborate upon individuals, events, and ideas that show how important these discoveries are?

- As you read, use the Evidence column to record evidence from the text that shows the importance of the discoveries.
- In the Explanation column, explain how the evidence reveals or contributes to the author's perspective.

Evidence	Source	Page	Explanation
1. "He lived during the Old Kingdom, the age when the pyramids at Giza were built, about 4,500 years ago."	Hawass	243	Hawass is showing that this grave is very ancient, and therefore probably a rare discovery.
2. "Inty-Shedu was the overseer of the sacred boat at the temple of a goddess named Neath. This would have been an important job, since the boat had to be kept ready for the goddess to use whenever she left her temple."			
3. "The discovery of four statues, *in situ* (a fancy way of saying "in their original place"), is very unusual."			

Evidence	Source	Page	Explanation
4. "Each [statue] was inscribed with the name Inty-Shedu. I knew that they were meant to represent one person at various stages of his life."			
6.			
7.			

Key Ideas and Details

Determining the Central Idea

1. Use the evidence you collected to summarize the key idea of this excerpt.

Analyzing Significant Details

2. Record two specific details that show what archaeologists do to help increase our knowledge of the past. Explain how each detail supports the central idea of the text.

What Archaeologists Do	Significance

3. In the section "Strange Coincidences," Hawass writes about how he kept trying to announce his discovery but was delayed several times because of things outside of his control. How is this section tied to the central idea of the text?

Craft and Structure

Structure of the Text

1. How do the three subheadings help to create a clear text structure? List each one and explain what it helps convey about the section it heads.

Section Header	What Header Means

2. The article is a combination of two writing forms: narrative and expository. Explain how these two forms are different in this article.

Form	What Material Is Presented in This Form

Author's Perspective and Purpose

3. Describe the author's purpose in writing this article.

Collaborate and Present

Research and Present a Project

Assignment: In groups, create a website, PowerPoint, or poster giving more information about the tomb of Inty-Shedu. Be sure to include an annotated map, relevant images, and informational captions.

Research

1. Using a web browser or library database, find additional information about the tomb of Inty-Shedu. Look for sources that contain images and maps. Copy images and maps into your own presentation document, attributing them to their sources.

URL address	Author of Content	Information	Trustworthy?

Decide and Create

2. As a group, decide what should be included in your presentation and who is going to create each part. Then, each teammate should put together their element of the presentation.

Element of the Presentation	Point Person

Present

3. Present your research project. Each team member should explain the part they worked on. Listen for questions and respond clearly with additional information.

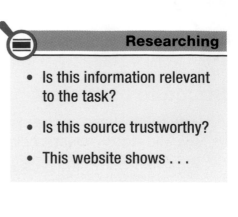

Researching

- Is this information relevant to the task?
- Is this source trustworthy?
- This website shows . . .

Making Decisions

- Is the work divided evenly?
- I volunteer to . . .
- From my perspective . . .

Presentation

- Face your audience.
- Take turns speaking.
- Speak loudly and clearly.
- Avoid using "like" or "ummm."

Research Project Checklist

Use the checklist below to evaluate your collaboration skills, reasoning, and final presentation.
Think carefully about your work. If you know you completed an item thoroughly, give yourself a check (✓).

COLLABORATE AND PRESENT CHECKLIST		
Comprehension & Collaboration	**Evidence & Reasoning**	**Presentation of Knowledge & Ideas**
☐ Come to discussions prepared, having read and researched material.	☐ Explain the purpose of the research project.	☐ Adapt language to a variety of contexts and tasks to demonstrate knowledge of formal English.
☐ Refer to evidence when contributing to the discussion.	☐ Present information relevant to the task.	☐ Include multimedia components (e.g., graphics, images, music, sound) and visual displays.
☐ Follow rules for discussions and lead by example.	☐ Explain how the project conveys new information about the tomb of Inty-Shedu.	☐ Use appropriate volume/tone (clear, not too fast, too slow, or too loud) and avoid using "like" or "ummm."
☐ Ask and answer specific questions.	☐ Include at least three relevant images with informative, accurate captions.	☐ Have strong posture, a confident stance, and make frequent eye contact.
☐ Make comments that contribute to the topic under discussion.	☐ Include one example of a map with a key.	☐ Occasionally move from one spot to another without fidgeting.
☐ Review the key ideas under discussion and demonstrate understanding of multiple perspectives through reflection and paraphrasing.	☐ Synthesize new information that helps the viewer understand more about the topic.	☐ Smile and act relaxed.
Number of ✓s in this category: ___	**Number of ✓s in this category:** ___	**Number of ✓s in this category:** ___
Total # of ✓s: ___		

Add up the total number of checks (✓) in each category. Then use the scoring guide below to calculate your final score.

Scoring Guide			
16 to 18 ✓s	**13 to 15 ✓s**	**11 to 12 ✓s**	**10 or less ✓s**
④ Exemplary	③ Meets Standards	② Needs Work	① Does Not Meet Standards

Read the Model

The writer of this informative essay uses a compare and contrast structure to show how two writers convey the historical importance of different archaeological discoveries. Read and discuss the model essay below.

Informative Essay

- An **informative essay** increases a reader's knowledge of a subject.

- The introduction states the title and author of the text that the writer will analyze, and includes the thesis statement.

- The two body paragraphs express the writer's main points about the text.

- The conclusion sums up or restates the thesis. It also explains why the information in the essay matters.

- Find three examples of words and phrases that signal either comparison or contrast.

Two Authors, Three Discoveries by Cameron Hoffman

In "New Discoveries in Ancient Egypt" and *Cities of the Dead*, authors Bryan Brown and Denise Rinaldo describe several recent archaeological discoveries. The authors themselves feel that these discoveries are important and give evidence to support that perspective.

In both texts, the authors cite teams of experts who came together to make the discoveries. Brown mentions archaeologists, while Rinaldo mentions scientists, explorers, and historians. The reader can assume that the discoveries are important partly because of the professional expertise behind them.

However, since the discoveries vary greatly, so does supporting evidence for their importance. In "New Discoveries in Ancient Egypt," Brown suggests that graves near a 5,000-year-old tomb are important because they confirm the long-held suspicion that Egyptians made human sacrifices. In addition, artifacts found nearby, such as boats for the king's "transportation in the afterlife," enforce the site's significance (236). In *Cities of the Dead*, Rinaldo describes the search for the legendary city of Ubar and a mission to determine the fate of Easter Island. As in Brown's article, Rinaldo helps support the importance of the Ubar site with descriptions of buried artifacts that indicate a once-thriving trading center. In contrast, however, she goes further and supports the significance of the discoveries by explaining how scientists, using "NASA's technology," aided in these searches (267).

Although Brown and Rinaldo describe different discoveries, they both cite experts and elaborate on the historical significance of each. Inspired by these texts, readers themselves may want to learn even more about these fascinating ancient cultures.

Analyze the Model

Informative essays often use a compare-and-contrast structure to tell how two texts are alike and different.

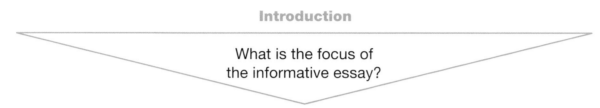

Introduction

What is the focus of the informative essay?

Topic: _____

"New Discoveries in Ancient Egypt"	Cities of the Dead
• Point	• Point
• Evidence	• Evidence

Topic: _____

"New Discoveries in Ancient Egypt"	Cities of the Dead
• Point	• Point
• Evidence	• Evidence

Conclusion

What does the writer include in the conclusion?

Point-by-Point Format

In a compare/contrast essay written in a **point-by-point format**, the writer discusses points from both texts in each paragraph.

Body paragraph 1 focuses on one topic and discusses how that topic applies to both texts.

Body paragraph 2 focuses on a second topic and discusses how it applies to both texts.

In the conclusion of the essay, the writer ties the ideas together and offers an additional reason why this information may be important to the reader.

Step 1 | Gather Evidence

[
Compare and contrast how these writers convey the historical importance of recent discoveries. How does each writer support his perspective?
]

What You Need to Know | The author's perspectives on why the discoveries are important, how each author conveys the historical importance of the discoveries

What You Need to Write | The main discovery discussed by each author and evidence from the text that shows why the discovery matters and reveals the author's perspective

"New Discoveries in Ancient Egypt"	*Curse of the Pharaohs* excerpt
Main Discovery _____	Main Discovery _____

Importance: Text Evidence: Page # _____	Importance: Text Evidence: Page # _____
Importance: Text Evidence: Page # _____	Importance: Text Evidence: Page # _____
Importance: Text Evidence: Page # _____	Importance: Text Evidence: Page # _____

Step 2 | Organize Ideas

What You Need to Know | Each authors' perspective on why the discoveries were important and the strategies they use to support that perspective

What You Need to Write | The key similarities and differences between the texts on these topics

Thesis Statement_____

Topic:_____

"New Discoveries in Ancient Egypt"	*Curse of the Pharaohs* excerpt
• Point • Evidence	• Point • Evidence

Topic:_____

"New Discoveries in Ancient Egypt"	*Curse of the Pharaohs* excerpt
• Point • Evidence	• Point • Evidence

Conclusion_____

Step 3 | Draft

Write a draft of your essay on the computer or on paper.

Language Study | Order Supporting Details

See It

A writer may want to include many interesting facts about the history of Egypt in his or her essay. However, depending on the topic, some details may be more relevant than others. Writers usually want to include the *most* important details that support their point.

Read each topic sentence and supporting details. Then, rate the supporting details from most important (1), to less important (2), to least important (3).

1. **Topic Sentence:** The discovery of the tomb of King Tutankhamen has great historical significance.

   Supporting Details:

   - There were newer discoveries made after Tut's tomb was found.
   - The tomb of King Tutankhamen contained so many treasures that it took ten years to remove them all.
   - Items in the tomb included jewelry, gold masks, and drinking cups.

Try It

Read each topic sentence and supporting details. Then, rate the supporting details from most important (1), to less important (2), to least important (3).

2. **Topic Sentence:** The ancient graveyard of Abydos is an important archaeological site.

   Supporting Details:

   - Archaeologists made startling discoveries near the tomb of Pharaoh Aha at Abydos.
   - There is still a lot of work to do at Abydos.
   - Abydos was also a major center for worship of Osiris, the god of the dead.

3. **Topic Sentence:** Alexander the Great was one of the greatest generals in history

   Supporting Details:

   - Queen Cleopatra was the last of the rulers who followed Alexander.
   - Alexander conquered the kingdom of Egypt in 332 BC.
   - Alexander the Great spread Greek culture across much of the known world.

Apply It | Follow the steps and use the questions below to help you improve your supporting details.

1. Reread the topic sentence of your first body paragraph.

   • *What is the point you are trying to make?*

2. Go back to your notes and review the evidence from both texts that relates to this topic. Order the supporting details from most important to least important.

   • *How clearly does each detail relate to the topic? Would another detail be more appropriate?*

3. Go back to your essay and make sure that you have included the most important details in your first paragraph.

   • *Do you have relevant details about each text, on the same topic?*

4. Repeat the process for each of your body paragraphs.

Conventions Study | Using Pronouns with Collective Nouns

See It

A Collective Noun is the name for a collection (or group) of people or things taken together and spoken of as one whole. For example, in the phrase "a class of students," *class* is a collective noun.

To use pronouns with collective nouns, remember these rules:

- When the group is acting as one (doing the same thing at the same time) the noun is singular. So the pronoun and verb used with it are also singular.
  Example: <u>The army was</u> on the move. <u>It was</u> heading to Cairo.

- If the group is doing different things, then the collective is broken into parts. So the pronoun and verb used with it are made plural.
  Example: <u>Some troops in the army</u> were heading North. <u>Others were</u> heading South.

- For multiple collective nouns, use plural pronouns and verbs.
  Example: <u>The armies were</u> invading the capital. <u>They were</u> moving in from all sides.

Try It

Read the examples. Identify the singular nouns, plural nouns, and collective nouns. Then, identify the pronouns and verbs and correct them if necessary.

1. Some students in the class read its history books quietly.

2. A fleet of ships was buried for the King to use in the afterlife.

3. A group of mummies were dug out of the ruins.

4. The team was carefully recording each and every discovery.

5. The set of statues were incomplete without the fourth one.

Apply It

Go back to your draft and make sure that your nouns and pronouns agree in number (singular/plural) if you use any collective nouns.

Step 4 | Revise and Edit Revise your draft with a partner.

Organization and Clarity						
State the authors and titles of the texts in the introductory statement.	Self	1	2	3	4
	Partner	1	2	3	4
Introduce ideas about how the authors structured their texts in the introductory statement.	Self	1	2	3	4
	Partner	1	2	3	4
Include a controlling idea in the topic sentences of each body paragraph.	Self	1	2	3	4
	Partner	1	2	3	4
Wrap up ideas in a concluding paragraph and include a final thought about why this information is important.	Self	1	2	3	4
	Partner	1	2	3	4
Evidence and Reasoning						
Include three or more pieces of evidence in each body paragraph.	Self	1	2	3	4
	Partner	1	2	3	4
Cite the author and page number for each piece of evidence.	Self	1	2	3	4
	Partner	1	2	3	4
Language and Conventions						
Use appropriate transition words to link sections of the essay and ideas within each paragraph.	Self	1	2	3	4
	Partner	1	2	3	4
Include compare and contrast statements that show similarities and differences.	Self	1	2	3	4
	Partner	1	2	3	4
Use academic and domain-specific vocabulary and establish and maintain a formal, objective tone throughout the essay.	Self	1	2	3	4
	Partner	1	2	3	4

Scoring Guide | ① needs improvement   ② average   ③ good   ④ excellent

Step 5 | Publish Publish your essay either in print or digital form.

Publish

Publish your compare/contrast essay either in print or digital form. Use the rubric below to consider the success of your final performance task.

PERFORMANCE TASK RUBRIC			
Score Point	Organization and Clarity	Evidence and Reasoning	Language and Conventions
Exemplary ④	• introductory paragraph introduces the **topic clearly** and in an **engaging way** • body paragraphs are **logically organized and compare and contrast** the writers' perspectives by ordering points from least important to most important • includes **well-chosen** text evidence, precise language, and pronouns • concluding statement **restates the focus** and leaves the reader with something to think about	• **accurately explains** each writer's perspective about the historical significance of recent discoveries by explaining **several similarities and differences** • includes **several examples of relevant** factual evidence from each nonfiction text that illustrate each writer's perspective	• demonstrates a **strong command** of the conventions of standard English grammar and usage, as well as of standard English capitalization, punctuation, and spelling • vocabulary is **appropriate** to the topic (vocabulary about recent historical discoveries; vocabulary to compare and contrast; accurately using pronouns to add variety)
Meets Standards ③	• introductory paragraph introduces the **topic clearly** • body paragraphs are **logically organized** but points of **comparison and contrast** are ordered without consideration of the most important point • includes **some** text evidence, precise language and pronouns • concluding statement **wraps up the ideas** in the essay	• **explains** each writer's perspective about the historical significance of recent discoveries by explaining **at least one similarity and difference** • includes **some relevant** factual evidence from each nonfiction text that illustrate each writer's perspective	• demonstrates **a near command** of the conventions of standard English grammar and usage, as well as of standard English capitalization, punctuation, and spelling **with some errors** • vocabulary is **appropriate** to the topic (vocabulary about recent historical discoveries; vocabulary to compare and contrast; accurately using pronouns to add variety)

PERFORMANCE TASK RUBRIC

Score Point	Organization and Clarity	Evidence and Reasoning	Language and Conventions
Needs Work ②	• introductory paragraph introduces the **topic** • body paragraphs are **somewhat logically organized,** but points of comparison and contrast are ordered without consideration of the most important point and unnecessary details are included • includes **a limited amount** of text evidence, precise language and pronouns • concluding statement **attempts to restate** the focus statement	• **with limited analysis, attempts to explain** the similarities and differences in the writers' perspectives about the historical significance of recent discoveries • includes **some textual evidence** from each nonfiction text to support each perspective	• demonstrates a **marginal command** of the conventions of English grammar and usage, as well as of standard English capitalization, punctuation, and spelling • there **are many errors; however, the text is still understandable** • includes only **one or two examples** of vocabulary that is appropriate to the topic (vocabulary about recent historical discoveries; vocabulary to compare and contrast; accurately using pronouns to add variety)
Does Not Meet Standards ①	• introductory paragraph is **unclear** • body paragraphs are **not organized logically** and/or **do not compare and contrast** the writer's points of view • essay includes **little text evidence** and few pronouns • concluding statement is **unclear or does not wrap up** the ideas in the essay	• response is a **partial or inaccurate explanation** of the writers' perspectives about the historical significance of recent discoveries • includes **no analyses of textual evidence** from each nonfiction text	• demonstrates **almost no command** of the conventions of standard English grammar and usage, as well as of standard English capitalization, punctuation, and spelling • there **are many errors that disrupt** the reader's understanding of the text • **does not include** vocabulary that is appropriate to the topic (vocabulary about recent historical discoveries; vocabulary to compare and contrast; accurately using pronouns to add variety)

Questions

Key Idea and Details

1. Describe the lost city of Ubar. Why does the author introduce this topic through an anecdote about Bertram Thomas?

Text Structure

2. What is the purpose of the subheadings in this text? Why is the first heading different than the others on **pages 264 and 265**?

from *Cities of the Dead*

by Denise Rinaldo

Ancient Ubar: Lost City of Arabia

¶1 The year is 1930. Bertram Thomas, a British explorer, has been trekking for days through the vast Rub' al-Khali desert, in southern Arabia. "Look!" says Thomas's guide. He is pointing to a wide path in the sand. "There's the road to Ubar!"

¶2 Thomas knew the legend: the rich, beautiful trading city had been built by a powerful king. He wanted it to be a paradise on Earth. It became the world's largest supplier of frankincense, a kind of incense used in perfume and medicine.

¶3 According to the legend, the people of Ubar became wealthy from their trade in frankincense. They also became greedy and filled with pride. God became so angry with them that he made the city vanish beneath the sands.

¶4 Thomas didn't turn down the path that day. He was running low on water. And his goal was to become the first European to cross the Rub' al-Khali desert. Still, he made careful notes about the location of the road.

A Modern Searcher

¶5 Flash forward to California in the 1980s. Nicholas Clapp, a filmmaker and amateur archeologist, is obsessed with Ubar. Clapp read everything he could about the legendary city. He first learned about it in an old book of stories called *The Book of the One Thousand and One Nights,* as well as in ancient Roman texts and in the Koran, the Muslim holy book.

¶6 Clapp became convinced that Ubar was real. He decided to plan an expedition to find the lost city. But the Rub' al-Khali desert is huge—the size of Texas. How could Clapp narrow his search?

¶7 He decided to call the National Aeronautics and Space Administration (NASA) the U.S. space agency.

¶8 NASA's mission is to explore space. But it also studies Earth from space. Scientists use spacecraft equipped with high-tech cameras to take photos of the planet. And some of NASA's imaging technology can actually see through sand. When Clapp told NASA scientists about Ubar, they were fascinated—and they wanted to help. As one researcher said to Clapp, "What's science for, if not to find out what exists or doesn't?" So NASA took photos from space of the Rub' al-Khali desert and searched the images for evidence of Ubar.

¶9 These images didn't show signs of a lost city in the desert. But they did show a wide, ancient road under the sand. Maybe it was the road to Ubar, covered by drifting sands!

¶10 Caravans of traders would have ridden into the city on camels to buy the precious frankincense and then fanned out through the ancient world to sell it.

¶11 This constant trekking would have created roads across the desert. Even though they hadn't been used for a long time, these ancient roads might have left permanent marks on the earth. If scientists could find where all these roads met, perhaps they could locate Ubar.

Off to Oman

¶12 Now Clapp had enough evidence to convince experienced explorers and archeologists to join an expedition. He put together a team that included Juris Zarins, an archeology professor with years of experience in the Arabian desert, and Sir Ranulph Fiennes, a man described by the *Guinness Book of World Records* as the world's greatest living explorer.

¶13 Using ancient documents, plus the NASA information, the team chose five places to search. All were in Oman—a desert nation on the Arabian peninsula. In the summer of 1990, Clapp's team spent two weeks in the scorching Rub' al-Khali desert. They decided to skip one of the five hot spots they'd identified. It was near a tiny town called Shisur. They thought it was an unlikely spot for a major trading center.

Questions

Key Idea and Details

3. What does the NASA scientist mean when he asks in **paragraph 8**, "What's science for, if not to find out what exists or doesn't?" Why does the author include this quotation?

Words and Phrases in Context

4. What is the meaning of the word *expedition* in the first sentence of **paragraph 12**? From the author's description, what can you infer about the members of the expedition team?

Questions

Text Structure

5. Explain the significance of Shisur. Why does the author mention it in **paragraph 13** and then discuss it again in **paragraphs 16–18**?

Key Ideas and Details

6. How did the team use both old and new methods to search for Ubar?

¶14 So where *was* Ubar? They left Oman without an answer. But they planned to return a few months later to resume the search. A short time later, though, war broke out in the region. The expedition had to postpone their return to Oman.

¶15 But as the war raged, the team received new images from NASA—and those images totally changed their strategy.

Like Spokes on a Wheel

¶16 The NASA images showed ancient roads buried beneath the Rub' al-Khali desert. They came from different directions and met at one center point, like spokes on a wheel. In 1991, the war in the area finally came to an end. This time, Clapp's team headed straight for the spot where the roads in the NASA images came together—Shisur. That was the tiny desert village that the team had decided not to visit on their first trip.

¶17 When Clapp arrived in Shisur, he asked an elder there if he knew where Ubar was. The man said he didn't. But he added, "maybe not far away." Then he pointed to a spot in the distance. There are some ruins there, he said, but they are not Ubar. They were the remains of a 500-year-old fort. Ubar, if it existed, disappeared around 300 C.E. It would be thousands of years old—not hundreds.

¶18 Still, the team decided to investigate the ruins. They had brought along a tool they called the "red sled." The red sled is a radar device designed to detect things underground. (Radar is a technology used to locate objects by bouncing radio waves off them.) By dragging the red sled across the ground, team members were able to get a rough picture of what lay beneath.

Amazing Finds

¶19 Thirty feet below the surface, the sled detected what looked like a stone well. That was interesting, but what did it mean? There was just one way to find out. Dig!

¶20 Within days, pieces of broken pottery had been found. They were thousands of years old. Some were from pots made in distant lands—like Syria and Greece.

This meant that the team had found the home of an ancient people who traded with foreigners—*like the people of Ubar*.

¶21 Next, the diggers uncovered a wall, then a tower. Soon, the outline of an eight-sided fortress was revealed. A 30-foot (9 meter) tower had stood at each corner. The fortress had enclosed a small city. Searching inside the walls, team members found unusual artifacts: tools used to turn tree sap into frankincense. *And Ubar was famous for frankincense*.

¶22 "The pieces were fitting," Clapp later stated. "But we didn't want to jump up and down and shout, 'Ubar! Ubar!' We were afraid we might break the spell."

Case Closed?

¶23 Had the team found Ubar? Almost certainly. The evidence is amazing. The layout of the walled city matches the legends. And the site dates from the time that Ubar would have existed.

¶24 The archeologists also found evidence of the trade caravans that traveled to and from Ubar. They discovered the buried remains of campfires at hundreds of sites around the city. These campfires marked the places where traders pitched their tents for a night of rest before heading back out across the desert.

¶25 Even the way the city disappeared echoes the ancient legends. It turned out that Ubar really had sunk into the earth. The excavation revealed a huge limestone cavern under the walled city. Scientists think the city was destroyed when it collapsed into the cavern.

¶26 After thousands of years, the legendary city had finally been found. NASA's technology had helped solved the ancient mystery. But the success of the mission was due to something much more basic, according to Professor Zarins: "Brains!" By putting their brains together to make sense of evidence from a huge variety of sources, the team members had made a historic discovery.

Questions

Text Structure

7. Why are the last sentences of **paragraphs 20–21** in italics? What does the author achieve with this effect?

Key Idea and Details

8. How does the author support the claim that the team had "almost certainly" found Ubar? Summarize the evidence.

Questions

Text Structure

9. How is the structure of **paragraphs 27–29** similar to and different from the first section of excerpt, **paragraphs 1–4**?

Key Idea and Details

10. How does Roggeveen know that "these few islanders" could not have carved the statues? Explain.

Easter Island: A Surprising Sight

¶27 On Easter morning in 1722, Admiral Jacob Roggeveen, a Dutch sea captain, stood at the helm of his ship and watched as a tiny island came into view. Roggeveen had been at sea for nearly eight months, exploring remote parts of the Pacific Ocean. He had not expected to run across this slip of land. And when Roggeveen saw the island up close, he was truly "struck with astonishment," he wrote in his journal.

¶28 The coast was lined with gigantic stone statues. They were human in form, and many of them stood on carefully carved platforms. Some had huge red blocks on their heads. Most of them had their backs to the sea. Their huge eyes gazed at the island's bare landscape.

¶29 These statues must have been built by an advanced society, Roggeveen thought. He expected to find a well-organized community when he landed on the island. But he was in for a shock.

The Mystery Deepens

¶30 When Roggeveen and his men went ashore, they found a community of about 2,000 people. They had a few leaky canoes, and not much else. Except for some chickens, there were no animals larger than insects. The island had no trees or bushes taller than 10 feet (3 meters). And nobody was carving statues.

¶31 "The island's wasted appearance could give no other impression than of a singular poverty and barrenness," Roggeveen wrote in his journal.

¶32 It was clear to Roggeveen that these few islanders could not have carved the statues, which they called *moai*. The smallest *moai* was about 4 feet (1.2 meters) high. The very largest was 72 feet (22 meters) high and weighed at least 145 tons. And there were almost 900 of the figures!

¶33 Roggeveen also wondered how these sculptures had been moved. The massive monuments were made of volcanic stone from quarries far from the coast. The islanders didn't have wheels or even strong vines to use as rope!

¶**34** Roggeveen wrote, "We could not comprehend how it was possible that these people, who [don't have] thick timber for making any machines, as well as strong ropes, had been able to erect such images."

¶**35** Roggeveen saw no signs that a society capable of building such massive sculptures had ever lived on the island. Were the statues the work of an earlier and more advanced civilization?

¶**36** Roggeveen left the island after five days with no answers to his questions. He called it Easter Island, in honor of the day he had arrived. It would be 200 years before scientists began to solve its mysteries.

Paradise Lost?

¶**37** In the early 1900s, scientists began looking for answers to the questions about Easter Island. Since then, they have learned a lot about the island and the people who once lived there. Their most surprising discovery was that the island hadn't always been a treeless wasteland. In fact, for most of its history, Easter Island was a leafy paradise.

¶**38** Scientists made this big discovery by studying something very tiny—pollen. Pollen is a powder produced by some plants. It's made up of tiny grains. Pollen makes it possible for some plants to reproduce.

¶**39** Plant scientists found fossils—or ancient remains—of pollen grains on the island. One plant's pollen does not look like the pollen from any other plant. So by examining the tiny pollen fossils, scientists were able to figure out what kind of plants had once grown on the island. They were also able to tell how many of those plants had grown there.

¶**40** Based on the pollen evidence, the scientists came to an amazing conclusion. For thousands of years, Easter Island had been a very green place. Many different plants and trees grew there. There were large forests of tall palm trees. Other areas were covered with grasses, ferns, and bushes.

Questions

Words and Phrases in Context

11. What is a *wasteland*? What effect does the author achieve by using the phrases "treeless wasteland" and "leafy paradise"?

Key Idea and Details

12. How did pollen fossils lead to the discovery of the leafy paradise?

Key Idea and Details

13. What is the "one thing" that "is certain"? Why is it certain? How is it important?

Text Structure

14. What does this subheading indicate about people who lived on Easter Island? What can you infer that you will learn in the last section of this text?

¶**41** All that plant life meant that Easter Island had been a place where a lot of people could live. There were enough natural resources to support a large population. Scientists figured out that the original settlers arrived between 700 and 800 C.E. They had sailed to Easter Island from other islands in the Pacific Ocean. After that, the population grew quickly. And as their numbers grew, the islanders developed a well-organized and advanced society.

¶**42** Archeologists believe that the islanders began building the mysterious statues after 1000 C.E. and continued through the 1500s. They don't know for sure why the islanders built them, but they have several theories. One is that the statues represented chiefs whom the islanders believed were descended directly from the gods.

¶**43** One thing is certain, however. There was enough food to go around, which meant that everyone didn't have to spend each day fishing or farming. The community could support a group of people whose job was to carve the giant statues.

¶**44** Scientists estimate that by the 1500s, more than 9,000 people were living on the island. But 200 years later, when Roggeveen arrived, the population had shrunk to less than 2,000. The trees had disappeared, and most of the birds were gone. Nobody was building statues.

¶**45** Something terrible had happened on Easter Island. It would take scientists a long time to figure out what that had been.

Spelling Their Own Doom

¶**46** Jared Diamond is an expert in history and biology who has studied Easter Island. He believes that "the pollen grains and [bird] bones yield a grim answer" to the question of what happened to the island.

¶**47** According to Diamond, the original settlers on the island began chopping down trees as soon as they arrived. They needed wood to build houses and canoes. They also needed firewood. And they probably used logs as rollers to move the statues that they carved from the island's volcanic stone.

¶48 Soon the islanders were chopping down the trees faster than they could grow back. What's more, there were rats that had come to the island on boats from other Polynesian islands. And these rats ran wild, feasting on palm seeds before they could sprout roots.

¶49 The pollen fossils show that by the 1400s, the Easter Island palm tree was extinct. Other trees also died out. Eventually, the forest was replaced by grass. With no trees to nest in, many of the native bird species were wiped out. That meant less food. And with no wood to build canoes, the islanders could only fish near shore. That also meant less food.

¶50 "As forests disappeared, the islanders ran out of timber and rope [made of vines] to transport and erect their statues," Diamond explains. So the statue building stopped, too. Eventually, a unique culture slowly faded away.

¶51 By the time Roggeveen arrived, the island had been treeless for a long time. The remaining islanders struggled to survive. They had little memory of their history—or of how the statues had been built and moved.

¶52 Scientists have worked hard to solve Easter Island's mysteries, and visitors today know a lot about its history. But the island still has many secrets. For instance, wooden tablets have been found with strange writing on them. The writing, which was carved into the wood using sharks' teeth, is called *rongorongo*.

¶53 Nobody has ever figured out how to read the tablets. But experts in ancient writing systems are trying to decipher them. If they succeed, will the tablets tell us more about how the islanders lived and what they believed? Or will they just add to the mystery of this tiny island?

Questions

Key Ideas and Details

15. Summarize the most important information in this text. What did you learn about Ubar and Easter Island? Why are the recent discoveries about these places important?

Literature Circle Leveled Novels

The House of Dies Drear by *Virginia Hamilton*
Thomas discovers secrets about his new home, which was once a stop on the Underground Railroad.
Lexile® measure: 670L

The Westing Game by *Ellen Raskin*
The mysterious death of an eccentric millionaire brings together an unlikely assortment of heirs who must uncover the circumstances of his death before they can claim their inheritance. **Lexile**® measure: 750L

The Wright 3 by *Blue Balliett*
Three friends must use their special abilities to piece together information about the tragic history of Frank Lloyd Wright's Robie House in order to save it. **Lexile**® measure: 870L

Fiction, Nonfiction, Poetry, and Novels

Frozen Man by *David Getz*. Read this fascinating account of the discovery and study of a mummified man who died more than 5,000 years ago in the Alps. **Lexile**® measure: 860L

The Bone Detectives by *Donna M. Jackson*. Learn about how forensic scientists use clues from human skeletons to solve mysteries of the past. **Lexile**® measure: 1100L

The Hero Schliemann by *Laura Amy Schlitz*. Read the true story of a man who searched for the lost city of Troy but didn't always want to find the truth. **Lexile**® measure: 910L

Angels of Pompeii by *Stephen Brigidi and Robert Bly*. Robert Bly's poems about the lost city of Pompeii are beautifully illustrated by Stephen Brigidi's photographs of the angels and other figures painted on the city's walls.

Mummies of the Pharaohs: Exploring the Valley of the Kings by *Melvin and Gilda Berger*. Explore the Valley of the Kings, where archeologists search for clues about the pharaohs of ancient Egypt. **Lexile**® measure: 1000L

Diving to the Past by *W. John Hackwell*. Learn how scientists use technology to locate, study, and preserve ancient shipwrecks.

Discovering the Inca Ice Maiden: My Adventures on Ampato by *Johan Reinhard*. Read about an anthropologist's amazing discovery of a mummy at the icy summit of a Peruvian volcano. **Lexile**® measure: 1030L

Frozen Girl by *David Getz*. Learn about the 1995 discovery of the frozen remains of an Inca girl and the steps taken to recover and study her clothes and other artifacts.

Films and TV

Ancient Mysteries—Pompeii: Buried Alive (A&E Home Video, 1998) Travel back to the first century to explore the city of Pompeii and re-create the events leading up to its burial under volcanic ash. (50 min.)

Beowulf (Paramount, 2007) Watch the epic battle between Beowulf and the monster Grendel, brought to life in this animated film. (114 min.)

Digging for the Truth—Giants of Easter Island (A&E Home Video, 2008) Explore Easter Island and its giant stone carvings, and try to solve the mystery of who carved them. (50 min.)

Dinosaurs Unearthed (National Geographic Video, 2008) Take an in-depth look at two ground-breaking discoveries of both mummified and fossilized dinosaurs. (100 min.)

In Search of History—Lost City of the Incas (A&E Home Video, 2005) Travel to the ruins of Machu Picchu and view footage of the earliest expeditions to find this incredible ancient city. (50 min.)

Lost Worlds (A&E Home Video, 2007) In this television series, historians and architects re-create ancient monuments and buildings to bring lost cities back to life. (39 min.)

Mummies and Pyramids: Egypt and Beyond (Image Entertainment, 2002) Join archeologists as they uncover mummies and artifacts from all over the world. (200 min.)

Raiders of the Lost Ark (Paramount, 1981) Share the adventures of archeologist Indiana Jones as he tries to find a powerful artifact before it falls into the wrong hands. (115 min.)

Websites

Archaeological Institute of America Education Pages Search for more information about the study of archeology.

Archaeology's Interactive Digs Follow the progress of archeological excavations and learn more about the scientists and their discoveries.

National Geographic Kids Follow links to learn about exciting archeological sites and explore virtual tombs in an interactive game.

Smithsonian Education Search the Web site to learn more about the Smithsonian's most interesting artifacts.

Magazines

Dig Stay up-to-date with the latest archeological discoveries and read firsthand accounts from people working at important excavations.

Discover Follow modern scientists and historians as they try to solve the mysteries of human evolution and learn more about ancient cultures.

History Search for articles that take a closer look at important historical discoveries and expeditions.

Natural History Use the articles, maps, photographs, and charts to learn more about modern discoveries in archeology and natural history.

THE BIG GIVE

What can one person do to make a difference?

Unit Introduction

In a folktale and a poem, read what motivates people to make sacrifices—or not! Study the techniques used to show how individuals relate to their world.

In the African folktale "Tale of a Wealthy Man," a rich farmer receives help from neighbors. He must decide what choices to make and how to accept the consequences. The reader learns an important lesson.

In the poem "If I Can Stop One Heart From Breaking" by Emily Dickinson, the speaker thinks about how to give her life meaning by helping others.

WRITING PERFORMANCE TASK

In these texts, what strategies are used to describe and explain relationships between individuals and the world?

FOLKTALE/POEM

"Tale of a Wealthy Man,"
a folktale of the Togo people, retold by Dianne Stewart

Language
- Academic Vocabulary
- Word Study: Context Clues

Reading Folktales
- Identify Evidence
- Key Ideas and Details
- Craft and Structure

"If I Can Stop One Heart From Breaking"
by Emily Dickinson

Language
- Academic Vocabulary
- Word Study: Precise Meaning

Reading Poetry
- Identify Evidence
- Key Ideas and Details
- Craft and Structure

SPEAKING AND LISTENING

Perform a Skit
- Collaborate and Present

Checklist: Skit
- Scoring Guide

WRITING

Writing: Informative Essay
- Read the Model
- Analyze the Model
- Gather Evidence
- Organize Ideas

- Language Study: Generalizations and Specifics
- Conventions Study: Correcting Vague Pronouns
- Revise, Edit, and Publish
- Performance Task Rubric

EXTENDED READINGS

Book Excerpt
from ***Ryan and Jimmy and the Well in Africa That Brought Them Together***
by Herb Shoveller

Book Excerpt
from ***Marina Silva: Defending Rainforest Communities in Brazil***
by Ziporah Hildebrandt

Academic Vocabulary

"Tale of a Wealthy Man,"
a folktale of the Togo people retold by Dianne Stewart

Rate your understanding of each word. Then write its meaning and a example sentence. If the example is given, write the meaning.

Word	Meaning	Example
agitate (v.) p. 278 ① ② ③ ④		The girl was agitated when she couldn't find her phone.
matter (n.) p. 278 ① ② ③ ④	a subject or situation that you have to think about or deal with	
proposal (n.) p. 278 ① ② ③ ④		The town's proposal to build a new school received a lot of support.
storm (v.) p. 279 ① ② ③ ④		Betsy stormed away after finding out that her friend had lied.
influential (adj.) p. 280 ① ② ③ ④	having the ability to influence or affect others	
lofty (adj.) p. 280 ① ② ③ ④	in a position of great height	

Rating Scale | ① I don't know the word. ② I've seen it or heard it.
③ I know its meaning. ④ I know it and use it.

Word Study

Use context clues to determine the meaning of the bold words in the sentences below.

1. He was very wealthy, and he took great pride in looking out at his gardens and the fields that **yielded** a great harvest year after year.

2. The weather was favorable, and Kaddo **reaped** such a good harvest that he built many **granaries** to store all his grain.

3. One villager suggested that Kaddo lend grain to those who did not have any to plant. When they **harvested** their **crop**, they would be able to repay him.

4. The sun had already started on its journey to the west when Kaddo finally announced that he would have the millet ground into **meal**.

Tale of a Wealthy Man

A Folktale of the Togo People, from Folktales From Africa
retold by Dianne Stewart

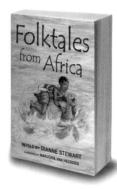

¶1 Long, long ago there was a man named Kaddo who lived in the village of Tendella, which was situated in the Seno kingdom. He was very wealthy, and he took great pride in looking out at his gardens and the fields that yielded a great harvest year after year.

The men who lived in the village helped clear the fields and turn the earth, while the women <u>sowed</u> seeds for Kaddo at planting time. The weather was favorable, and Kaddo reaped such a good harvest that he built many granaries to store all his grain.

¶3 People who met Kaddo when they passed through Seno on their travels could not believe that he owned so much food. Soon he became well known even beyond the borders of the kingdom.

Because Kaddo had so much grain in storage, he summoned the villagers together to discuss what he should do with all of the grain.

¶5 "As you can see, my granaries are filled to overflowing. My own relatives cannot eat all this food. What do you think should be done with it?"

The people thought deeply, and then a wise man said, "It is clear to me. You own so much <u>millet</u>, and more grain from your fields is added to it all the time. I think you should give some of your grain to families here in the village for whom life is difficult when they have nothing to eat."

Close Reading

Literary Analysis

1. How do the words and phrases "long, long ago," "gardens and fields," and "village" develop the setting?

Setting

The **setting** is the time, location, and environment where a story takes place.

Words and Phrases in Context

2. Why does the folktale use the word *summoned*? Looking at the dictionary definition, what is the folktale implying about Kaddo by using this word instead of the phrase "called for"?

Theme

Theme is the main message, lesson, or idea in a text.

Words to Know

<u>sowed</u>: *(v.)* to have planted seeds in the ground

<u>millet</u>: *(n.)* a type of grass that has a small seed that can be harvested for food

Close Reading

Literary Analysis

3. Describe Kaddo's character. Which words and phrases reveal his characteristics?

Words and Phrases in Context

4. Consider the meaning of the word *indignant* in **paragraph 12**. Why does the folktale describe Kaddo this way?

Literary Analysis

5. How do the villagers react to Kaddo's words? Cite examples from the text that support your answer.

Text Structure

6. Review **paragraphs 7–13**. Why does the folktale repeat the name *Kaddo* so often?

¶7 Kaddo looked **agitated** and replied in a loud voice, "No, I do not like that idea." He did not want to share his grain.

The villagers discussed the **matter** among themselves. Then one villager suggested that Kaddo lend grain to those who did not have any to plant. When they harvested their crop, they would be able to repay him.

¶9 "You would be highly <u>regarded</u> if you did that," said the villager, "and it would help to prevent poverty."

Kaddo considered the **proposal** but quickly said, "No, that is a bad suggestion." Kaddo was unwilling to share what he had with others.

¶11 Another villager spoke up from the crowd. "You could always sell some of your millet and buy cattle. Then your granaries would not be so full," he said.

Kaddo was <u>indignant</u>. "That would not be right," he said angrily.

¶13 Although many villagers made proposals, none were acceptable to Kaddo. Most of them required Kaddo to give away some of his <u>wealth</u>, which he did not want to do.

Words to Know

<u>indignant</u>: *(adj.)* filled with a strong feeling about something being offensive, unjust, or wrong

<u>regarded</u>: *(v.)* considered; thought of in a particular way

<u>wealth</u>: *(n.)* a large amount of money, property, goods, etc. that a person or country owns

The sun had already started on its journey to the west when Kaddo finally announced that he would have the millet ground into meal.

¶15 "Send all the girls of the village with their <u>mortars</u> and pestles tomorrow," said Kaddo. "At first light we will grind the millet."

The people went home dissatisfied, and although they were angry, they allowed their daughters to assist Kaddo in the hope that some of the ground grain would be passed on to the villagers.

¶17 As the sun lit up the eastern sky, the women walked eagerly to their place of work. They put grain into their mortars and began pounding it with all of their strength. They sang songs to help them complete the task. They worked like this for seven days, and each day the pile of grain grew higher and higher.

"Please fetch water from the spring," said Kaddo when all of the millet had been ground. The girls mixed the water with the grain as instructed, and millet bricks were made from the meal. They placed the bricks in the sun to dry out and harden.

¶19 Kaddo was very pleased with himself. "When the bricks are ready, I will build a magnificent wall around my house," he said proudly.

When the villagers heard of his plan, they **stormed** to his house to voice their disapproval.

¶21 "We have never heard of a man building a wall of millet around his home. Kaddo, you cannot use food in this way. So many people are hungry!"

Kaddo stared angrily at them and was very displeased.

¶23 "No one in our history has created a wall out of valuable food," they continued, trying to reason with him.

Close Reading

Text Structure
7. Reread **paragraphs 14–16**. Examine the sentences that talk about *sun* and *light*. How does the folktale use the sun? Why are these details included?

Literary Analysis
8. In **paragraphs 17 and 18**, why do the villagers help Kaddo even though they are angry? What does this suggest about the relationship between the people and Kaddo?

Academic Vocabulary
9. In **paragraph 20**, what does the word *stormed* indicate about the way the villagers felt?

Writing
10. What does Kaddo's wall symbolize? Why does the folktale use a wall rather than any other structure?

Symbol

A **symbol** is someone or something that represents a particular quality or idea.

Words to Know

<u>mortars</u>: *(n.)* bowls used for crushing ingredients, often used with pestles—crushing tools or sticks

Close Reading

Writing
11. How is Kaddo's character developed in **paragraphs 24–26**? Cite details to support your answer.

Academic Vocabulary
12. Reread **paragraph 27**. Why is Kaddo influential?

Literary Analysis
13. In **paragraph 28**, the folktale states that the news of Kaddo's wall "spread like the flames of a hot and hungry fire." How is the use of this simile ironic?

Text Structure
14. How is **paragraph 29** structured to create a turning point?

Turning Point

The **turning point** is the moment in a story where the fate of the main character becomes clear. The events of the plot begin to move toward an ending.

Rage grew in Kaddo. "This grain belongs to me, and I may do with it what I want. It is my right."

¶25 When the bricks were dry, Kaddo instructed the people to build the wall around his house. Brick by brick, it grew. Kaddo examined it when it was waist high and continued to do so until it was eye level and he could no longer see the countryside beyond it. When it was completed, the people decorated the wall with <u>cowrie</u> shells.

"I will become well known because of this amazing millet wall," observed Kaddo proudly.

¶27 The people of the village were shocked, and his actions did not help him to find <u>favor</u> with them. But he was a wealthy man and continued to be very **influential**. When visitors arrived, they had to stand by the gate in the wall and wait to be invited in to see him. When Kaddo gave the villagers instructions, he sat on the high wall so that they would have to look up at him as he addressed them from his **lofty** position.

News of Kaddo's wall spread like the flames of a hot and hungry fire, and he became even better known.

¶29 Life continued like that until one year <u>drought</u> held the kingdom of Seno in a tight grip. Day after day and night after night no rain clouds gathered in the sky to water the landscape below. The fierce sun baked the earth until it was iron hard and no grain grew from it. Despite having so many fields, Kaddo harvested no grain at all.

Words to Know

<u>cowrie</u>: *(n.)* a highly polished, small seashell often used to decorate objects or for making jewelry

<u>favor</u>: *(n.)* support or approval

<u>drought</u>: *(n.)* a period of dry weather severe enough to cause crops and/or animals to die

After a while, Kaddo and his family were forced to eat the grain they had set aside for planting. The drought continued into the next year and the next, and eventually Kaddo was forced to sell his fine horses and cattle to provide food for his family.

¶**31** So it was that year after year no grain grew in Tendella, and many of Kaddo's relations went to live in other parts of the kingdom of Seno. Kaddo could no longer keep any servants, as he could not afford to feed them. One by one the people left the village until only Kaddo, his daughter, and his donkey remained in that lonely place.

One day, when hunger roared loudly in his stomach, Kaddo peeled off a little millet meal from the wall and ate it hungrily. Every day he did the same until, after a while, the wall became lower and lower as brick by brick it was consumed. Eventually, there was no wall left at all, and the cowrie shells lay abandoned on the ground.

¶**33** Kaddo wondered where he would find food. Because of his selfish attitude when he had plenty, the people in the area wanted nothing to do with him.

Then one night, as Kaddo was lying anxiously awake, he thought of Sogole, the King of Ghana, who was a very kindhearted man.

¶**35** Because Kaddo and his daughter were desperate, they mounted their donkey and traveled for seven long, hot days until they reached the palace of Sogole. The king agreed to see Kaddo, and they sat on a skin on the ground drinking millet drinks. While Kaddo described the terrible drought to Sogole, he could only take small sips of the liquid, as his stomach was not used to drinking or eating anymore.

"I see that life has been difficult for you in Tendella," said Sogole. "We have plenty here, so I will give you what you <u>require</u>."

Words to Know

<u>require</u>: *(v.)* need

Close Reading

Words and Phrases in Context
15. Why does the folktale describe Kaddo's hunger as *roaring* in **paragraph 32**?

Literary Analysis
16. Why is it significant that Kaddo has to tear down the wall in **paragraph 32**? How is this action symbolic?

Text Structure
17. What character actions in **paragraphs 35 and 36** move the plot of the story forward?

Literary Analysis
18. Compare and contrast the characters of Kaddo and Sogole. Cite details from **paragraphs 34–36** to support your explanation.

Close Reading

Text Structure

19. Reread **paragraphs 38–46**. How does the text in this section indicate a change in Kaddo's personality?

Words and Phrases in Context

20. Why does the story point out that the king spoke *disbelievingly* in **paragraph 45**?

Literary Analysis

21. How is Kaddo's request for seeds in **paragraph 48** ironic?

Irony

Irony is a conflict between what might be expected to happen and what actually happens.

¶37 The king then asked Kaddo to tell him more about Tendella. "I know that the drought drove people away. But I did hear about a very wealthy man who lived in Tendella. I think he was called Kaddo. Is he still living?"

"Yes," replied Kaddo quietly.

¶39 "I heard that he built a wall of millet bricks around his house, and that he spoke to people from the top of the wall. Is this the truth?"

"Yes, he did build a wall of millet around his house."

¶41 "Is he still wealthy?" asked Sogole.

"No, he has lost everything, including the wall. Only his daughter remains."

¶43 "What a sad state of <u>affairs</u>," said the king. "Are you a relative of Kaddo?"

"Yes, I am a member of Kaddo's family. I had granaries full of grain and cattle, and I was very wealthy. In fact, I am Kaddo."

¶45 "You are Kaddo?" asked the king disbelievingly.

"Yes, I was a man of <u>means</u> and influence, but now I am a beggar asking for assistance."

¶47 "How can I be of assistance to you?"

"King of Ghana, please give me some seed so that I may return to my home in Tendella and replant my fields."

¶49 Sogole arranged bags and bags of millet seed for Kaddo, which were fastened to Kaddo's donkey. Kaddo was so grateful. He said farewell to the king, and he and his daughter began the long journey home.

Words to Know

<u>affairs:</u> *(n.)* things connected with your personal life, your financial situation, etc.

<u>means:</u> *(n.)* money or income

On the way home, Kaddo was nearly overcome with hunger. He was so <u>famished</u> that he could not continue with his travels. He took some of Sogole's seed from the sack to eat and shared it with his daughter. Because they were so hungry, they ate more and more, stopping all along the way to Tendella to eat.

¶51 When they arrived at their dusty home, they fell into an exhausted sleep. When they awoke, they ate again and again, and it did not matter to Kaddo that the millet grain was for planting. Eventually he became so ill that he lay on his bed, <u>writhing</u> with stomach cramps and—alas—he died.

The <u>descendants</u> of Kaddo still reside in the Seno kingdom, but they battle to make ends meet. They often refer to those who have experienced favor but refuse to share it in the following way: "What is the sense of building a wall of millet meal around one's home?"

Words to Know

<u>writhing</u>: *(v.)* twisting your body from side to side violently, especially because you are in pain

<u>famished</u>: *(adj.)* extremely hungry

<u>descendants</u>: *(n.)* people who are related to a person who lived a long time ago

Close Reading

Literary Analysis

22. Evaluate Kaddo's behavior in **paragraph 51**. How does his choice affect the final outcome of the folktale?

Text Structure

23. How is the structure of the last paragraph different from the rest of the folktale? Why is it written differently?

Writing

24. What lesson is the folktale supposed to teach? How does the folktale's final line in **paragraph 52** support the theme?

Identify Evidence | Analyze Individuals, Events, and Ideas

Reread **"Tale of a Wealthy Man"** identifying the values that the folktale describes and explains.

How does the folktale include details to support a theme?

- In the Value column, name a value that individuals use to relate to the world.
- In the Individual(s) column, name the individual or group who demonstrates or conveys that value.
- In the Text Support column, record details from the folktale that show how that particular value is conveyed.

Value	Individual(s)	Text Support
1. Wealth	Kaddo	"He took great pride in looking out at his gardens and the fields that yielded a great harvest year after year." (¶1)
2. Compassion	the "wise man" in paragraph 6 and Sogole, the King of Ghana	
3. Admiration and Respect from Others		

Value	Individual(s)	Text Support

Key Ideas and Details

Determining the Central Idea

1. Use the evidence you collected to summarize the key idea of this folktale.

Character Analysis

2. List four character traits that describe Kaddo. For each trait, provide a quotation as support.

Character Trait	Quote
angry	"Kaddo looked agitated and replied in a loud voice, 'No.'"

3. List two character traits that describe Sogole. For each trait, provide a quote.

Character Trait	Quote

Internal Traits

Internal character traits are adjectives that describe what a person is like *on the inside*. A character's feelings, thoughts, and words often reveal their internal traits.

External Traits

External character traits are adjectives that describe what a person is like *on the outside*. External traits include a character's looks, voice, and outward behavior.

Craft and Structure

Structure and Purpose of a Folktale

1. Except for Kaddo, why doesn't the folktale give specific names to the villagers?

2. What is the central conflict in the folktale? What is the turning point?

3. What emotions are created by these two contrasting descriptions of setting?

"As the sun lit up the eastern sky, the women walked eagerly to their place of work. They put grain into their mortars and began pounding it with all of their strength. They sang songs to help them complete the task."

"Day after day and night after night no rain clouds gathered in the sky to water the landscape below. The fierce sun baked the earth until it was iron hard and no grain grew from it. . . . Kaddo had no grain at all."

4. How does Kaddo's death support the purpose of the folktale?

Academic Vocabulary

"If I Can Stop One Heart From Breaking"
by Emily Dickinson

Rate your understanding of each word. Then read the examples. Use the Word Study on the right to select the most accurate meaning.

Word	Meaning	Example
vain *(adj.)* p. 289 ① ② ③ ④		The man tried in vain to push his car out of the mud.
ease *(v.)* p. 289 ① ② ③ ④		The child eased his thirst with a big, cold glass of water.
faint *(v.)* p. 289 ① ② ③ ④		I ran so hard at the beginning of the race that I fainted before the finish line.

Word Study

Precise Meaning

- Many words have definitions that contain multiple variations on one idea.
- A reader can use the dictionary and context clues together to determine the precise meaning of a word.

Read the words and meanings below. Choose the correct meaning to record in the chart, based on the example.

vain *(adj.)* 1. excessively proud of one's own looks, abilities, or position 2. without success, in spite of effort 3. without real significance

ease *(n.)* 1. if you do something *with ease*, it is very easy for you to do it, [as in: *they won with ease = easily*]
ease *(v.)* 1. to make a pain or hardship gradually become less 2. to make a process happen more easily 3. to move slowly, carefully into another position

faint *(adj.)* 1. difficult to see, hear, etc. 2. very small or slight 3. weak or ill
faint *(v.)* 1. to suddenly become unconscious for a short period of time

Rating Scale | ① I don't know the word. ② I've seen it or heard it. ③ I know its meaning. ④ I know it and use it.

"If I Can Stop One Heart From Breaking"

by Emily Dickinson

1   If I can stop one heart from breaking,

    I shall not live in **vain**;

    If I can **ease** one life the aching,

    Or cool one pain,

5   Or help one **fainting** <u>robin</u>

    Unto his nest again,

    I shall not live in vain.

Close Reading

Literary Analysis

1. Analyze the author's choice to begin the poem with the word *if*. What are the implications?

Words and Phrases in Context

2. How can a person "cool" a pain?

Writing

3. What is the author's perspective about how people should relate to others? How does she convey her perspective?

Repetition

Repetition is doing or saying the same thing many times. Authors and poets often use repetition to emphasize the meaning of a central idea.

Words to Know

<u>robin</u>: *(n.)* a common brown or reddish brown bird found in every state in the United States

Identify Evidence | Analyze Individuals, Events, and Ideas

Reread **"If I Can Stop One Heart From Breaking,"** identifying all the uses of the word *one*.

- In the Evidence column, record each phrase that contains the word *one*.
- In the Explanation column, explain what the author wants when she uses this line.

Evidence	Line	Explanation
1. "one heart from breaking"	1	She wants to save one person from losing love, from having their heart broken.
2.		
3.		
4.		

Reread **"If I Can Stop One Heart From Breaking,"** identifying all the uses of the word *I*.

- In the Evidence column, record each phrase that contains the word *I*.
- In the Explanation column, explain what the author wants when she writes this line.

Evidence	Line	Explanation
5.		
6.		
7.		

Key Ideas and Details

Determining the Central Idea

1. Use the evidence you collected to summarize the key idea of Emily Dickinson's poem.

Analyzing Details

2. List four people/things that the speaker in the poem would like to help. Record the line from the poem that supports your answer.

Who does she want to help	What line supports this
a person hurt by love	

3. What do these people and things have in common? How are they different?

Similarities	Differences

Craft and Structure

Structure of the Poem

1. What one line does Dickinson repeat as a refrain?

2. What does that line imply?

3. What ideas are emphasized through the rhyming words in the poem?

Narrative Perspective

4. Why does the speaker focus on saving people or animals from small troubles instead of wanting to solve big problems?

5. Going back to the very first question, why does the speaker say "if"? What does this suggest about how she sees herself?

6. What message is the speaker of the poem sharing about the relationships between herself and the larger world?

Collaborate and Present

Write and Perform a Skit

Assignment: Choose a scene from "Tale of a Wealthy Man" and work in a group to create a short skit exaggerating and dramatizing the relationships between the characters. Include a brief introduction explaining the context and purpose.

Analyze the Content

1. With your group, **reread the folktale** and choose a scene to dramatize.

   Consider the following questions:
   • Which scenes best show how people relate to each other?
   • Which characters do you need in order to create your skit?
   • Is any dialogue missing? Will you have to write additional lines for some members of the group to say as they play villagers or other parts?
   • What multimedia elements will you include in your skit? Props? Sounds?
   • How will you emphasize the main point and increase the level of drama?
   • What message do you want to communicate to your audience?

Write the Script

2. **Organize ideas** by charting out the details needed to act out the scene.

Characters	Dialogue From the Text	Physical Details

3. Work with your group to **write the script** for your skit, including the introduction and any stage directions. Now is also the time to collect or create multimedia.

Practice and Present

4. As a group, **practice** performing your skit. Be sure every person in your group has a chance to practice their role.

5. Introduce your skit, and then **present your performance** to the class.

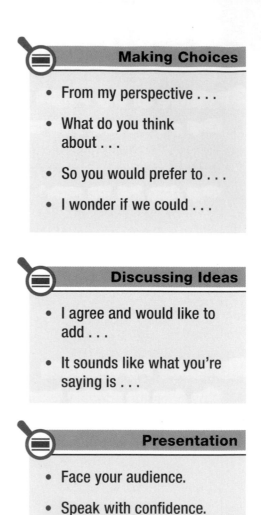

Making Choices

• From my perspective . . .
• What do you think about . . .
• So you would prefer to . . .
• I wonder if we could . . .

Discussing Ideas

• I agree and would like to add . . .
• It sounds like what you're saying is . . .

Presentation

• Face your audience.
• Speak with confidence.
• Avoid fidgeting.

Skit Checklist

Use the checklist below to evaluate your collaboration skills, reasoning, and final presentation.
Think carefully about your work. If you know you completed an item thoroughly, give yourself a check (✓).

COLLABORATE AND PRESENT CHECKLIST		
Comprehension & Collaboration	**Evidence and Reasoning**	**Presentation of Knowledge & Ideas**
☐ Come to discussions prepared, having read and studied the folktale.	☐ Explain the context and purpose of the skit.	☐ Adapt language to fit the context of the skit while demonstrating knowledge of formal English.
☐ Refer to evidence when contributing to the discussion of which scene to choose.	☐ Focus the skit on one clear message about how people relate to each other.	☐ Include multimedia components in the skit (e.g., props, images, music, sounds).
☐ Follow rules for discussions and lead by example.	☐ Explain why the group chose this particular scene.	☐ Use appropriate volume/tone (clear, not too fast, too slow, or too loud) and avoid diversions from the script.
☐ Ask and answer specific questions.	☐ Perform only relevant material.	
☐ Make comments that contribute to the topic under discussion.	☐ Effectively emphasize character relationships.	☐ Have strong posture, a confident stance, and make frequent eye contact.
☐ Review the key ideas under discussion and demonstrate understanding of multiple perspectives through reflection and paraphrasing.	☐ Draw explicitly from the folktale and use both dialogue and setting from the story.	☐ Occasionally move from one spot to another without fidgeting.
		☐ Smile and act relaxed.
Number of ✓s in this category: ___	**Number of ✓s in this category:** ___	**Number of ✓s in this category:** ___
	Total # of ✓s: __	

Add up the total number of checks (✓) in each category. Then use the scoring guide below to calculate your final score.

Scoring Guide			
16 to 18 ✓s	13 to 15 ✓s	11 to 12 ✓s	10 or less ✓s
④ Exemplary	③ Meets Standards	② Needs Work	① Does Not Meet Standards

Read the Model

In a literary analysis essay, the writer interprets how elements of a literary text contribute to the overall meaning. Read and discuss the model literary analysis essay below.

Fiction Techniques for Facts   By Kiana Thompson

Informative Essay

- The **introduction** states the title and author of the text that the writer will analyze, and includes the thesis statement.

- The two **body paragraphs** express the writer's main points about the text.

- The **conclusion** sums up or restates the thesis. It also explains why the information in the essay matters.

- Find two examples of the author's use of formal, academic language.

Like fiction writers, authors of literary nonfiction use narrative strategies to develop the individuals, experiences, and events in their writing. In the excerpt from *Marina Silva: Defending Rainforest Communities in Brazil,* author Ziporah Hildebrandt uses a non-chronological structure and descriptive details to convey the strength, determination, and bravery of Marina Silva.

Hildebrandt writes about Silva's life and work in a non-chronological way. She begins the excerpt in the middle of Silva's story, during a dramatic event in her life. Hildebrandt introduces Silva to readers when she is a "thin young woman" protesting the destruction of a rainforest (312). This scene is full of action and drama, as Silva and "a dozen others" stand in front of a bulldozer in order to save "their whole way of life" from being destroyed along with the forest (312). This scene immediately establishes Silva's bravery and commitment and gets readers interested in her story.

One strategy that makes this scene and the rest of the excerpt effective is the use of descriptive details. These details help readers vividly imagine Silva and understand the passion she demonstrates trying to save the rainforests. First, the author describes Silva's "dark, flashing eyes" and the protestors' "strong, brown arms" as they stand before the bulldozers and chain saws that "whine angrily" (312). Later, she describes Silva's journey "from illiterate poverty to the doors of a top university" as "more spectacular than Cinderella's dance from rags to riches" (314). These details emphasize that Silva is a unique, hard-working individual.

Hildebrandt vividly develops Silva as a strong, fearless subject in her excerpt through the use of a non-chronological structure and vivid description. As a result, readers are left with respect and appreciation for this remarkable activist and senator.

Analyze the Model

Use the outline below to analyze the model essay. Your notes can be written using shorthand and phrases.

Introduction	
¶1 Thesis Statement	
Body Paragraphs	
¶2 Topic Sentence/Key Idea	**Relevant Evidence**
¶3 Topic Sentence/Key Idea	**Relevant Evidence**
Conclusion	
¶4 Restatement + Why it Matters	

Literary Analysis

- A thesis statement in the introduction presents the focus of the essay.

- In the two topic sentences, the writer states the key idea of each paragraph.

- Relevant evidence supports each paragraph's topic sentence and the essay's thesis statement.

- The writer includes citations for all direct quotations from the text.

Step 1 | Gather Evidence

[**In these texts, what techniques are used to describe and explain relationships between individuals and the world?**]

What You Need to Know | The techniques these texts use to convey ideas about relationships between individuals and the world

What You Need to Write | Evidence that is most relevant to the performance task

"Tale of a Wealthy Man"

Technique: *descriptive details*

Evidence: *"He took great pride in looking out at his gardens and the fields that yielded a great harvest year after year."*

Significance: *shows that Kaddo valued his wealth*   Page and ¶: *p. 1, ¶1*

Technique:

Evidence:

Significance:

Page and ¶ _____

Technique:

Evidence:

Significance:

Page and ¶ _____

"If I Can Stop One Heart From Breaking"

Technique:

Evidence:

Significance:

Page and Line # _____

Technique:

Evidence:

Significance:

Page and Line # _____

Technique:

Evidence:

Significance:

Page and Line # _____

Step 2 | Organize Ideas

What You Need to Know | The ideas expressed in the texts about how individuals relate to the world; clear examples of the techniques used to express these ideas

What You Need to Write | An outline of your literary analysis essay

Introduction
¶1 Thesis Statement

Body Paragraphs	
¶2 Topic Sentence/Key Idea	Relevant Evidence
¶3 Topic Sentence/Key Idea	Relevant Evidence

Conclusion
¶4 Restatement + Why it Matters

Step 3 | Draft

Write a draft of your essay on the computer or on paper.

Language Study | Generalization and Specifics

See It

When writers make a general statement, they support it with specific evidence. Choose the specific detail that best supports the underlined generalization.

The examples below are based on the excerpt from *Ryan and Jimmy and the Well in Africa That Brought Them Together* by Herb Shoveller.

1. Jimmy's life had been shaped by <u>unimaginable difficulties</u>.

    a. Jimmy was a bright young boy who loved going to school.

    b. Jimmy lived in the village of Agweo with his Aunt Sofia.

    c. Both of Jimmy's parents disappeared when he was young.

Try It

Choose the specific detail that best supports, proves, or explains the underlined generalization.

2. Ryan and Jimmy lived <u>such different lives</u>.

    a. They were connected by Ryan's well.

    b. Ryan lived in Canada and Jimmy lived in Africa.

    c. Jimmy attended Angolo Primary School.

3. Ryan <u>inspired people</u> with his big ideas.

    a. Newspapers ran stories about Ryan's project.

    b. Ryan and Jimmy exchanged many letters.

    c. The well had changed Ryan's life too.

4. Ryan and Jimmy <u>hit it off</u> like long-lost friends.

    a. Ryan spent the day with Jimmy in school.

    b. Ryan traveled for two days to reach Uganda.

    c. A camera crew filmed the trip for a television documentary.

Apply It

Think about the topic you wrote about in your essay. Which sentences should be general? Which should be specific?

Create a chart that explains which sentences should be general and which should be specific.

General Sentences	Specific Sentences

Now, **go back to your draft** and revise any sentences that should be more general or more specific.

Conventions Study | Correcting Vague Pronouns

See It | Vague, or unclear, pronoun reference makes writing confusing. Read the three examples below, paying close attention to the unclear pronouns.

- Jimmy arrived on time to class. <u>It</u> made his teacher happy.
- Jimmy arrived on time to class. <u>This</u> made his teacher happy.
- Jimmy arrived on time to class, <u>which</u> made his teacher happy.

To correct vague pronouns, you can:

1. Combine the sentences: *Jimmy's on-time arrival to class made his teacher happy.*

2. Replace *it* with a noun: *Jimmy arrived on time to class, and <u>his attitude</u> made his teacher happy.*

3. Add a noun where *this* is used: *Jimmy arrived on time to class, and <u>this punctuality</u> made his teacher happy.*

4. Add a noun before *which*: *Jimmy arrived on time to class, <u>a change which</u> made his teacher happy.*

Try It | Use these strategies to clarify the pronouns in the sentences below. You can correct each sentence in more than one way.

1. Luisa has three big projects to complete tomorrow which she doesn't have time for.

2. The coach doesn't appear to care if players cheat, and it really bothers me.

3. Jackie decided to play baseball, and it came as a surprise to all his friends.

4. Doctors recommend drinking eight glasses of water each day; they find that this gives them more energy.

5. Alanna promised to volunteer at the event with me, which I didn't believe for a minute was a disaster.

Apply It | Now, go back to your draft. Analyze each sentence, editing and making sure you use pronouns clearly and correctly in number and person.

Step 4 | Revise and Edit   Revise your draft with a partner.

Organization and Clarity

Clearly introduce the topic in the introduction.	Self	1	2	3	4
	Partner	1	2	3	4
Include a thesis statement that tells the main point of the literary analysis.	Self	1	2	3	4
	Partner	1	2	3	4
Include general, controlling ideas in the topic sentences of each body paragraph.	Self	1	2	3	4
	Partner	1	2	3	4
Wrap up ideas in a concluding paragraph.	Self	1	2	3	4
	Partner	1	2	3	4
Include a final thought about why this information is important.	Self	1	2	3	4
	Partner	1	2	3	4

Evidence and Reasoning

Include three or more pieces of specific evidence in each body paragraph.	Self	1	2	3	4
	Partner	1	2	3	4
Cite the author and page number for each piece of evidence.	Self	1	2	3	4
	Partner	1	2	3	4

Language and Conventions

Use appropriate academic vocabulary and precise language to discuss the topic.	Self	1	2	3	4
	Partner	1	2	3	4
Establish and maintain a formal, objective tone throughout the essay.	Self	1	2	3	4
	Partner	1	2	3	4
Use correct capitalization, punctuation, spelling, and grammar.	Self	1	2	3	4
	Partner	1	2	3	4

Scoring Guide | ① needs improvement   ② average   ③ good   ④ excellent

Step 5 | Publish   Publish your essay either in print or digital form.

Publish

Publish your literary analysis essay either in print or digital form. Use the rubric below to consider the success of your final performance task.

PERFORMANCE TASK RUBRIC

Score Point	Organization and Clarity	Evidence and Reasoning	Language and Conventions
Exemplary ④	• introductory paragraph introduces the **topic clearly** and includes a thesis statement that tells the main point of the literary analysis • body paragraphs are **logically organized and provide a thoughtful and focused analysis** of the techniques the writers use • includes **well-chosen** text evidence, precise language, and pronouns • concluding statement **wraps up the ideas** in the essay effectively	• **accurately explains and convincingly analyzes** the techniques writers use to describe relationships between an individual and their world • includes **several examples of relevant** factual evidence from the poem and folktale that illustrate the techniques the writers use and support the writer's generalization	• demonstrates a **strong command** of the conventions of standard English grammar and usage, as well as of standard English capitalization, punctuation, and spelling • vocabulary is **appropriate** to the topic (vocabulary to analyze character and conflict; accurate terms for referring to writer's technique; effective use of pronouns for variety)
Meets Standards ③	• introductory paragraph introduces the **topic clearly** • body paragraphs are **logically organized** and **analyze** the techniques the writers use with examples that support the thesis statement • includes **some** text evidence, precise language, and pronouns • concluding statement **wraps up the ideas** in the essay	• **accurately explains and generally analyzes** the techniques writers use to describe relationships between an individual and their world • includes **some relevant** factual evidence from the poem and folktale that illustrate the techniques the writers use and support the writer's generalization	• demonstrates **a near command** of the conventions of standard English grammar and usage, as well as of standard English capitalization, punctuation, and spelling **with some errors** • vocabulary is **appropriate** to the topic (vocabulary to analyze character and conflict; accurate terms for referring to writer's technique; effective use of pronouns for variety)

PERFORMANCE TASK RUBRIC

Score Point	Organization and Clarity	Evidence and Reasoning	Language and Conventions
Needs Work ②	• introductory paragraph introduces the **topic** • body paragraphs are **somewhat logically organized** and **attempt to analyze** the techniques the writers use, though some examples do not support the thesis statement • includes **a limited amount** of text evidence, precise language, and pronouns • concluding statement **refers to some of the ideas** in the essay	• **accurately explains** the techniques writers use to describe relationships between an individual and the world with **limited analysis** • includes **some textual evidence** from the poem and folktale support analysis; some examples do not support the writer's generalization	• demonstrates a **marginal command of** the conventions of English grammar and usage, as well as of standard English capitalization, punctuation, and spelling • there **are many errors; however, the text is still understandable** • includes only **one or two examples** of vocabulary that is appropriate to the topic (vocabulary to analyze character and conflict; accurate terms for referring to writer's technique; effective use of pronouns for variety)
Does Not Meet Standards ①	• introductory paragraph is **unclear** • body paragraphs are **not organized logically** and/or **do not analyze** the techniques the author uses • essay includes **little text evidence** and few pronouns • concluding statement is **unclear or does not wrap up** the ideas in the essay	• response is **partial or inaccurate analysis** of the techniques writers use to describe relationships between an individual and the world • includes **no textual evidence** from the poem and folktale	• demonstrates **almost no command** of the conventions of standard English grammar and usage, as well as of standard English capitalization, punctuation, and spelling • there **are many errors that disrupt** the reader's understanding of the text • **does not include** vocabulary that is appropriate to the topic (vocabulary about each challenge; terms for referring to text structure and language; vocabulary for writing complex sentences, including *because* and *since*)

Questions

Words and Phrases in Context

1. What is the meaning of the word *lack* in **paragraph 1**? What context clues helped you determine its meaning?

Text Structure

2. What is the effect of setting off one word as its own paragraph for **paragraph 2**?

from *Ryan and Jimmy and the Well in Africa That Brought Them Together*

by Herb Shoveller

¶**1** Ryan Hreljac (Herl-*JACK*) couldn't believe what his first grade teacher was saying. She had been talking to the class about problems faced by people around the world. One of the most serious problems, she explained, was the lack of safe drinking water. Every year, thousands and thousands of people, many of them children, got sick and died because they didn't have clean water to drink.

¶**2** Water?

¶**3** Ryan thought about his own house in Canada, which he shared with his parents, two brothers, and a dog named Riley. All they had to do was turn on a tap, and out came all the clean water they could possibly want. Yet his teacher was saying that millions of people had to spend hours each day searching for water. And when they found it, it was often dirty and dangerous to drink. The more Ryan thought about it, the more upset he became. Couldn't something be done to help these people?

¶**4** Ryan's teacher explained that in Africa it cost $70 to build a <u>well</u> that could supply a village and its surrounding area with safe, clean water. That was it! Ryan would find a way to raise the $70 it would take to build a well.

¶**5** It was a small idea in the mind of a small boy. But in the coming months and years, Ryan's idea would grow. It would grow so big that it would eventually change the lives of hundreds of thousands of people. It would certainly change Ryan's life. And it would change the life of a boy Ryan had never met, a boy named Akana Jimmy who lived in a small village in the African country of Uganda. (It is customary in some African countries for surnames to be written first.)

Words to Know

<u>well:</u> *(n.)* a deep hole in the ground from which people take water

Jimmy's Story

¶6 Like Ryan, Jimmy was a bright young boy who loved going to school and playing soccer. But Jimmy's life had been shaped by unimaginable difficulties. Both of his parents disappeared when he was young, and are thought to be dead. The details are not known, but it is almost certain that their disappearance is connected to a <u>civil war</u> that has raged in Uganda since before Jimmy was born. Thousands have been killed. Thousands more are terrorized each year by <u>bands</u> of violent rebels.

¶7 When his parents disappeared, Jimmy moved to the village of Agweo to live with his Aunt Sofia. Aunt Sofia's home consisted of three huts made of mud and grass. One hut served as the kitchen and the other two were bedrooms, one for adults and one for children. Each hut, because it is separate, is called a "house," and when Jimmy was ten Aunt Sofia built him a house (which was Jimmy's bedroom).

¶8 It takes experience and skill to build a house with mud and grass that can withstand the rains when they come, but these houses were sturdy. There was only one tiny window, about the size of a small book. Too many windows would let in too much heat. There was no electricity or plumbing.

¶9 Going to school was not possible for Jimmy at first. There was no money for school fees, and even if there had been, living with his aunt meant he had to help pay his way by doing chores. Tending her garden was one task, as was gathering water, which is a major responsibility, especially for a child aged five, six, or seven.

¶10 There is some water around Jimmy's village during the rainy season, but there are long periods in the year when water is scarce. Then children, including Jimmy, would have to walk up to 5 kilometers (3 miles) each way to get water. Jimmy sometimes made that walk four or five times a day. And it was not as if you could always go to a specific spot for the water. You had to look for it. When you found it you had to carry it back.

Words to Know

<u>civil war:</u> *(n.)* a war in which opposing groups of people from the same country fight each other in order to gain control

<u>bands:</u> *(n.)* groups

Questions

Text Structure

3. What does the subhead before **paragraph 6** signal?

Key Ideas and Details

4. What details does the author include in **paragraphs 6–9** to show how different Jimmy's life is from Ryan's life?

Questions

Key Ideas and Details

5. What details does the author include in **paragraphs 14–15** to explain how the well changed Jimmy's and Ryan's lives?

Words and Phrases in Context

6. What does the author mean in **paragraph 15** when he writes that more money "poured in"?

A New Friend

¶**11** As the news of Ryan's work spread, his classmates in Kemptville were anxious to get involved. His teacher, Lynn Dillabaugh, wanted to help too, and decided to bring her students and the children of Angolo Primary School in Uganda together as pen pals. In 1999, Ryan and his friends at school wrote to their new pen pals. The letters were packaged up and shipped to Uganda, half a world away. And they waited. And waited.

¶**12** Finally, in June, letters from Uganda arrived. Ryan was overjoyed as he unfolded the letter from the pen pal who had been chosen for him.

¶**13** Over the next year, Ryan and Jimmy exchanged many letters. Though they lived such different lives, they shared a curiosity about each other and the world. And they were connected by Ryan's well.

¶**14** The well had changed everything for Jimmy and the other students at Angolo Primary School. For the first time in their lives, they didn't have to worry about water. It came right from the ground—beautiful, clear water.

¶**15** The well had changed Ryan's life too. More newspapers ran stories about his project, and more money poured in. His new goal was $25,000—enough to buy a power drill for mining water that could be carried from village to village on the back of a truck. He was invited to speak at conferences all over Canada, where he inspired people with his big ideas.

¶**16** Then, in the summer of 2000 came the chance of a lifetime: CPAR arranged for Ryan and his parents to visit Uganda. Ryan would see his well. And he would get to meet Jimmy.

¶**17** He and his family traveled for two days by air and jeep to reach the CPAR camp in northern Uganda. Ryan knew the trip was important. A camera crew had come along to film the trip for a television documentary. But nothing in his life could have prepared him or his parents for what awaited him. As their jeep approached Agweo village, a sound like distant thunder filled the air. Ryan could see people—

adults, students, and young children—standing along the road, as far as he could see. They were all clapping. Thousands of pairs of hands clapping to welcome Ryan and express gratitude for all that he had done.

¶18 There were speeches by village leaders, dance performances, and songs. There was a feast of African food. And there was Jimmy, who welcomed Ryan in a speech in English that he had practiced over and over. Ryan and Jimmy hit it off like long-lost friends. Ryan spent the next day with Jimmy in school. And that night Jimmy was able to sleep over with Ryan at the CPAR camp. It felt as if they had known each other forever.

¶19 And then, too soon, it was time to say goodbye. Ryan didn't cry, but his face was glum. He wanted to spend more time with Jimmy, and so did his parents.

¶20 "I had this terrible feeling in my stomach that we were never going to see this kid again," Ryan's dad said of Jimmy. "I felt so awful."

¶21 Mark Hreljac's premonition wasn't far off. After such a happy time, life was going to take a serious turn for the worse for Jimmy. The civil war that had claimed Jimmy's parents was still raging, the rebel army still wreaking terror on the village.

Screams and Gunpowder

¶22 One night after Ryan's departure, Jimmy woke up to the sound of screams and the smell of gunpowder. Like everyone in his village, he knew what this meant. Soldiers with the Lord's Resistance Army (LRA) were back. The LRA raided villages at night, kidnapped children and forced them to become soldiers. Jimmy knew the LRA had something to do with his parents' disappearance. He also knew if you were captured and managed to escape, the LRA would come after you again. The second time, you wouldn't be so lucky—they would kill you. Jimmy had already managed to avoid the rebels once during an earlier raid. The rebels knew it. This time if he was captured . . .

Words to Know

raid: *(n.)* a short attack on a place by soldiers, planes, or ships, intended to cause damage

Questions

Words and Phrases in Context

7. What is the meaning of the word *premonition* in **paragraph 21**? Which context clues helped you determine its meaning?

Text Structure

8. What is the effect of ending **paragraph 22** with an ellipsis?

Questions

Key Ideas and Details

9. What details does the author include to bring the scene to life for the reader in **paragraph 24**?

Words and Phrases in Context

10. What does the author mean in **paragraph 25** when he writes that Jimmy "gathered his courage"?

¶23 Flashlight beams probed the inside of the hut.

¶24 "Get up! Get up!" the soldiers shouted. There was nowhere to run. The soldiers tied Jimmy's hands together and bound him to his cousin, Isaac. As they marched through the middle of the village, Jimmy noticed that his rope was a bit loose. He snuck the knot up to his mouth and pulled to loosen it. He looked at his cousin, Isaac, who seemed to understand. But then Isaac looked away. He had given up! In minutes, the rebels would lead the captives out of the village and on a long trek deep into the wilds of northern Uganda. This was Jimmy's only chance to escape. He worked on his ropes and finally freed his hands. He glanced once more at Isaac, who made it clear he wasn't coming along. Jimmy would have to go it alone.

¶25 Jimmy was in the middle of the group, far enough away from the soldiers at the front and back to make his break. He estimated there was a distance of about half a soccer field when he would be in the open before he reached the tall grass and bush. With luck and the <u>element</u> of surprise, he could be halfway there before anyone noticed. It would take all of his running and dodging skills to save his life. This was it. Jimmy closed his eyes and gathered his courage, then, feeling like he was going to throw up, he took off.

¶26 He made his break. One step. Two steps. Top speed. Sweat poured off his forehead. Then came a shout, and within seconds a bullet whizzed by his head. He heard soldiers running, but he'd made it to the edge of dense grass. He ran until he was certain the rebels couldn't track him. Then he collapsed.

¶27 Jimmy had never felt so helpless. Or alone.

¶28 But he was not alone.

Words to Know

element: *(n.)* one part or feature of a whole system or plan

One Safe Place

¶**29** The Hreljacs were worried. Reports from Uganda were telling a frightening story. They were eager for news about Jimmy. Then came a chilling email from a close friend, Tom Omach, a Ugandan who worked for CPAR. He had heard about the rebel attack and had gone searching for Jimmy. He told the Hreljacs that Jimmy had been <u>abducted</u> but had managed to escape.

Finding a New Home

¶**30** Then, miraculously, Tom found Jimmy. He had lost everything, but he was alive. Tom found a spot for Jimmy at a boarding school in the Ugandan town of Lira. But it soon became obvious that Jimmy would never be safe in Uganda; the rebels were still looking for him. Luckily, there was a place where Jimmy could be truly safe: in Canada, with Ryan and his family.

¶**31** But was it possible? The challenge seemed enormous.

¶**32** Against all odds, Tom was able to secure the <u>papers</u> necessary for Jimmy to leave Uganda and legally go to Canada. Through a <u>refugee hearing</u>, the Hreljacs were able to convince the Canadian government that Jimmy must stay in Canada for his own protection. After such a long road, Jimmy could call Canada his new home and settle into a life with Ryan's family—his family now.

¶**33** Who could have imagined, when Ryan and Jimmy met in Uganda, that one day they would be brothers?

Questions

Text Structure

11. What is the effect of ending the selection with a question?

Words to Know

<u>abducted</u>: *(v.)* taken away by force

<u>papers</u>: *(n.)* legal documents

<u>refugee hearing</u>: *(n.)* a special meeting to decide if someone who has been forced to leave their country (especially during a war) can enter and live in another country

Questions

Key Ideas and Details

1. Who are the two groups in conflict, as described in **paragraph 1**?

Words and Phrases in Context

2. What does the author mean when she writes that Brazil has an "unjust society" in **paragraph 4**? What details help you understand what the author means?

from ***Marina Silva: Defending Rainforest Communities in Brazil***

by Ziporah Hildebrandt

¶1 A thin young woman with dark, flashing eyes stood—fierce and <u>determined</u>—with a dozen others. Their strong, brown arms linked them together as their voices rang out in an inspiring song. But the roar of bulldozers and chain saws blasted their harmonies.

¶2 A work crew had been ordered to clear the rain forest. Giant trees, plants, and animals would die to make a <u>cattle pasture</u>. The families living on the land would lose everything: homes, gardens, the rubber trees that sustained their <u>meager</u> living—their whole way of life.

¶3 The young woman, Marina Silva, tightened her arms with the men beside her as a worker came close. Marina looked him in the eyes as he made his chain saw whine angrily. He brought it within inches of their linked arms.

¶4 Marina didn't flinch, though she and others were all that stood between the saws and the rain forest. She and her neighbors lived by harvesting, or tapping, rubber from the trees. Although they were poor and had little power in Brazil's unjust society, the rubber tappers had found a way to fight for their forest life. One demonstration at a time, they worked to save their rubber trees from rich cattle ranchers.

¶5 *Don't cut these trees*, Marina prayed silently.

Words to Know

<u>determined</u>: *(adj.)* having a strong desire to do something, so that you will not let anyone stop you:

<u>cattle pasture</u>: *(n.)* land covered with grass, used for cows to feed on

<u>meager</u>: *(adj.)* small, much less than is needed

¶6 The voice of their group's leader, Chico Mendes, rang out. "Why help the rich boss take away our homes?" he said to the workers. "We should stand together, help each other—that's the way we both can live."

¶7 The worker was young, in his twenties—Marina's age. His eyes met hers doubtfully, then slid away. "I need the money," he mumbled.

¶8 "Of course," Marina answered. "We all do. But is it right that you make a little cash by taking away our rubber trees? You'll have money in your pocket for a few days, a few weeks, and then what? When the trees are cut, the boss will fire you. You'll be hungry again, and so will we because we won't have anything. It's the boss who gets rich from our work and our land."

¶9 The worker nodded in agreement. A shot rang out, but Marina kept her <u>gaze</u> locked on the young man. "The boss thinks nothing of killing us," Chico Mendes shouted. "You and your family could be next. We have to stand together."

¶10 But more shots were fired, and someone cried out. At the other end of the line, the work crew was beating the unarmed demonstrators with clubs. The young man Marina was talking to put down his saw and disappeared into the forest. Then Marina covered her head as the clubs crashed down.

¶11 The *seringueiros*, or rubber tappers, did not strike back. They retreated into the forest, carrying hurt friends. One young man had been shot and would probably die. Marina heard the man's mother and sister crying.

¶12 This <u>demonstration</u> had failed, but the *seringueiros* would try again and again. They knew that by fighting for the rain forest, they were fighting for their lives.

Questions

Text Structure

3. What purpose do the quotations serve in **paragraphs 6–9**?

Words and Phrases in Context

4. What descriptive words and phrases does the author use to develop the conflict between the *seringueiros* and the workers in **paragraph 10**?

Words to Know

<u>gaze:</u> *(n.)* a long steady look

<u>demonstration:</u> *(n.)* an event at which a large group of people meet to protest or to support something

Questions

Text Structure

5. How does **paragraph 13** differ from the previous paragraphs?

Words and Phrases in Context

6. What is the meaning of the word *fate* in **paragraph 15**? What context clues helped you determine its meaning?

First the Dream

¶**13** Marina had grown up in the *seringal*, the rubber-tapping region of Amazonia. The rain forest was her people's life. They loved their trees as friends and relatives. Marina dreamed that her people would be recognized for their character and their knowledge of the forest, rather than scorned for their poverty and <u>illiteracy</u>. She dreamed of a day when all forest people would be safe in their homes and earn a decent living from their traditional ways. Forest people and communities would control their own lives instead of suffering under the <u>brutal</u> power of wealthy ranchers, businesspeople, and politicians.

¶**14** Most people shook their heads at Marina's dreams. Things had always been this way. How could they change? But that didn't stop her. "First the dream, then the fight," she later said. Already her impossible dreams had brought her from illiterate poverty to the doors of a top university—in Brazil, a journey more spectacular than Cinderella's dance from rags to riches. No magic was involved: Marina had come every step of the way on determination, intelligence, and dreams.

¶**15** If her dream of getting an education could come true, why not her dream for forest people? She did not know then that her dream would bring her to the highest chamber of Brazil's government. As senator for her state of Acre, she was one of only five women in the senate. In years to come, Marina, who couldn't read until she was 16 years old, would fly to the world's most powerful countries and discuss the fate of the rain forest and its people with presidents, prime ministers, and the pope. The *seringueiros'* peaceful demonstrations would lead to a totally new way to save millions of acres of forest.

Words to Know

<u>illiteracy:</u> *(n.)* lack of education; not being able to read or write

<u>brutal:</u> *(adj.)* cruel and violent

From Rain Forest to Desert

¶**16** Marina's state of Acre is in Amazonia, the largest remaining rain forest on Earth. When Brazil's government decided to build in Amazonia, settlers and cattle ranchers burned thousands of miles of forest to make farms and pastures. But the <u>soil</u> was thin and poor. Crops failed. Farmers gave up and moved west, to freshly cleared land.

¶**17** They left behind a desert. The rain forest acts like a sponge: It soaks up rain, uses it to grow, and releases moisture back into the atmosphere to make more rain. Dense layers of leaves protect the thin soil. Without trees, the soil washed away, then baked hard in the tropical heat.

¶**18** Brazil's government didn't know how people could make a living from this land. Yet people have lived for tens of thousands of years in the forest. By growing food, fishing, and gathering the natural products of the forest, <u>indigenous</u> people and *seringueiros* have lived well and brought valuable goods to market. They understand what the government does not: how to take from the forest without destroying it.

¶**19** Senator Marina Silva hopes to teach Brazil and the rich countries of the world how to do the same. Otherwise the rain forest and its peoples will vanish from the earth forever.

Questions

Key Ideas and Details

7. What details in **paragraphs 16–18** help you understand the author's attitude toward Marina and deforestation of the rain forest? What is the author's attitude?

Words to Know

<u>soil</u>: *(n.)* the top layer of the earth in which plants grow

<u>indigenous</u>: *(adj.)* native; having always been in the place where they are

Literature Circle Leveled Novels

Number the Stars *By Lois Lowry*
Ten-year-old Anne Marie and her family smuggle her Jewish friend's family out of Denmark to Sweden during World War II. A suspenseful account of bravery and near-misses, this book is difficult to put down. **Lexile**® measure: 670L

Carlos Is Gonna Get It *by Kevin Emerson*
Trina and her friends are out to "get Carlos" because he's so strange, but when Trina is assigned to work with Carlos on a project, she discovers how troubled and special he is. **Lexile**® measure: 870L

Elijah of Buxton *by Christopher Paul Curtis*
This is the story of Elijah, the first black child born into freedom in Buxton, Canada. He travels to the United States at age 11 and gets involved in a plot to free a group of slaves. **Lexile**® measure: 1070L

Fiction, Nonfiction, and Novels

One Hen—How One Small Loan Made a Big Difference *by Katie Smith Milway.* Inspired by true events, this is the story of Kojo, who uses a small loan to change his community for the better. **Lexile**® measure: 810L

Banker to the Poor: Micro-Lending and the Battle Against World Poverty *by Muhammad Yunus.* Yunus pioneered a program that grants small loans to empower poverty-stricken people around the world. **Lexile**® measure: 1090L

Be the Change! Change the World. Change Yourself *edited by Michelle Nunn.* Read the personal stories of people who have found their own way of making a difference in the world.

The Difference a Day Makes: 365 Ways to Change Your World in Just 24 Hours *by Karen M. Jones.* Change the world one day at a time.

How to Change the World: Social Entrepreneurs and the Power of New Ideas *by David Bornstein.* Men and women are finding creative solutions to social and economic problems around the world.

It's Your World—If You Don't Like It, Change It: Activism for Teenagers *by Mikki Halpin.* Learn how to get involved and become activists at home, at school, and in the community.

The Kid's Guide to Social Action: How to Solve the Social Problems You Choose *by Barbara A. Lewis.* Projects to help students make a difference.

What Do You Stand For? For Teens: A Guide to Building Character *by Barbara A. Lewis.* Students can discover who they are and what positive traits shape their personality.

Films and TV

A Powerful Noise (Unify Films, 2009) Three women struggle with poverty and oppression, and manage significant victories, illustrating the ability of women to make a difference in the world. (90 min.)

Beatrice's Goat (CBS, 2005) This 60 Minutes episode examines how Heifer International helped Beatrice, who grew up in poverty in Uganda, attend college in the United States. (10 min.)

Beat the Drum (Z Productions, 2003) A young orphaned boy in Africa shows how one small voice can start big changes and make a difference in the nation. (114 min.)

Biography: Nelson Mandela: Journey to Freedom (A&E Home Video, 2004) Follow the story of this iconic leader as he fights against apartheid in South Africa. (60 min.)

Compassion in Exile (Festival Media, 2005) Follow the story of the fourteenth Dalai Lama and his lifelong mission to save the unique culture and religion of the people of Tibet. (62 min.)

Gandhi (Sony, 1982) Mohandas K. Gandhi brings the idea of nonviolent resistance to India, which leads to India's independence. (191 min.)

Life Below the Line: The World Poverty Crisis (Associated Television International, 2007) Examine the hardships faced by impoverished people around the world and learn how you can help.

Pay It Forward (Warner, 2000) Junior high school student Trevor sets out on a project to change the world and sets in motion a chain reaction of good deeds. (123 min.)

Websites

Central Asia Institute Explore this site for Greg Mortenson's organization, whose mission is to provide education for girls in Pakistan and Afghanistan.

Do Something This site gives students information on how to get involved in causes from animal welfare to poverty to human rights.

Pennies for Peace Start a campaign in your class and community to raise funds to provide education to children in Pakistan and Afghanistan. Use the program's toolkit to incorporate cultural education in the classroom.

Magazines

Need: The Humanitarian Magazine Read about people who are working to help other people around the world.

National Geographic Take a look at the people around us and their involvement in how our world is changing.

Wildlife Conservation Learn about rare and endangered animals, and the people who are fighting for them.

The Environmental Magazine Find tips and advice for living responsibly and improving our environment.

COURSE I | Table of Contents

p. 3t: © Matt Vincent; p. 4t: © CLEO Freelance Photography, b: © Ray Wise/Getty Images; p. 5t: © Brad Yeo via The iSpot, b: © Franck Reporter/iStockphoto; p. 6tl: © Floriano Rescigno/iStockphoto, tc: © Kenneth Garrett, tr: © David Boyer/National Geographic Stock, b: © Kamigami/Dreamstime

UNIT 1 | Stories of Survival

pp. 8–9: © Matt Vincent; p. 13br: © Matt Vincent; p. 31: © Colin M. Lenton

UNIT 2 | Live Your Dream

p. 59tl: CLEO Freelance Photography; p. 63: © Elsa/Getty Images; p. 74br: © Ho New/Reuters

UNIT 3 | World Wonders

pp. 98–99: © Ray Wise/Getty Images; p. 99tl inset: © Richard I'Anson/Getty Images; p. 101t: © Intrepix/Dreamstime; p. 102br: © Sebastien Cote/iStockphoto; p. 111b: © Bob Krist/eStock Photo; p. 118br: © Horizons WWP/Alamy; p. 119bl: © Jim Keir/Alamy

UNIT 4 | Coming to America

pp. 146–147: © Brad Yeo via The iSpot; p. 149t: © Dinesan Pudussery/Shutterstock; p. 151l: © Drive Images/Alamy; p. 152br: © Michael Goulding/KRT/Newscom; p. 161br: by permission of the author, Mawi Asgedom

UNIT 5 | Cities of Gold

pp. 188–189: © Franck Reporter/iStockphoto; p. 191: © SpiralDelight/Getty Images; p. 192r: © Arthur Gerlach/Getty Images; p. 193: © Howard Kingsnorth/Getty Images; p. 200r: Library of Congress; p. 204br: Library of Congress

UNIT 6 | History Lost and Found

p. 230l: © Floriano Rescigno/iStockphoto, r: © Kenneth Garrett; p. 231: © David Boyer/National Geographic Stock; p. 234br: © Taylor S. Kennedy/National Geographic Stock; p. 246br: © Kenneth Garrett

UNIT 7 | The Big Give

pp. 274–275: © Kamigami/Dreamstime; p. 278r: © Chris King; p. 283bl: © Chris King; p. 289: © Bea Kraus/Thinkstock

NOVEL STUDY COVER CREDITS

I Thought My Soul Would Rise and Fly: The Diary of Patsy, A Freed Girl by Joyce Hansen. Copyright © 1997 by Joyce Hansen. Published by Scholastic Inc. All rights reserved. Cover: (background) Historic New Orleans Collection, (inset) tim O'Brien.

Tuck Everlasting by Natalie Babbitt. Copyright © 1975 by Natalie Babbitt. Published by Scholastic Inc. by arrangement with Farrar, Straus and Giroux, LLC. All rights reserved.

Grateful acknowledgment is made to the following sources for permission to reprint from previously published material. The publisher has made diligent efforts to trace the ownership of all copyrighted material in this volume and believes that all necessary permissions have been secured. If any errors or omissions have inadvertently been made, proper corrections will gladly be made in future editions.

UNIT 1 | Stories of Survival

"Tuesday of the Other June" by Norma Fox Mazer. Copyright © 1986 by Norma Fox Mazer. Reprinted by permission of the Elaine Markson Literary Agency.

"Life Doesn't Frighten Me" from *And Still I Rise* by Maya Angelou. Copyright © 1978 by Maya Angelou. Reprinted by permission of Random House, Inc.

"Dirk the Protector" from *My Life in Dog Years* by Gary Paulsen. Copyright © 1998 by Gary Paulsen. Published by Bantam Doubleday Dell, a division of Random House, Inc. Reprinted by permission of Flannery Literary Agency. All rights reserved.

UNIT 2 | Live Your Dream

From *The Life You Imagine: Life Lessons For Achieving Your Dreams* by Derek Jeter with Jack Curry. Copyright © 2000 by Turn 2, Inc. Reprinted by permission of Random House, Inc. All rights reserved.

From *Dreams From My Father* by Barack Obama. Copyright © 1995, 2004 by Barack Obama. Reprinted by permission of Random House, Inc. All rights reserved.

"Peak Performance" by Samantha Larson from *Teen Vogue* magazine, October 2007. Copyright © 2007 by Condé Nast Publications. Reprinted by permission of Condé Nast Publications.

UNIT 3 | World Wonders

"World's Wonders, Worn Down?" by Cody Crane from *Science World* magazine, February 19, 2007. Copyright © 2007 by Scholastic Inc. All rights reserved.

From "How to Save the Taj Mahal?" by Jeffrey Bartholet from *Smithsonian* magazine, September 2011. Copyright © 2011 by Jeffrey Bartholet. Reprinted by permission of the author.

"The Rise and Fall of China's Great Wall: The Race to Save a World Treasure" from *Current Events* magazine, September 27, 2002. Copyright © 2002 by Scholastic Inc. All rights reserved.

UNIT 4 | Coming to America

From *Funny in Farsi: A Memoir of Growing Up Iranian in America* by Firoozeh Dumas. Copyright © 2003 by Firoozeh Dumas. Reprinted by permission of Villard, an imprint of The Random House Publishing Group, a division of Random House, Inc. All rights reserved.

From *Of Beetles & Angels: A Boy's Remarkable Journey from a Refugee Camp to Harvard* by Mawi Asgedom. Copyright © 2001, 2002 by Mawi Asgedom. Reprinted by permission of Little, Brown & Company.

From "1905: Einstein's Miracle Year" by John Schwartz from *The New York Times Upfront* magazine, April 18, 2005. Copyright © 2005 by Scholastic Inc. All rights reserved.

From *Shutting Out the Sky: Life in the Tenements of New York 1880-1924* by Deborah Hopkinson. Copyright © 2003 by Deborah Hopkinson. Reprinted by permission of Orchard Books, an imprint of Scholastic Inc. All rights reserved.

UNIT 5 | Cities of Gold

"City" by Langston Hughes from *The Collected Poems of Langston Hughes.* Copyright © 1994 by The Estate of Langston Hughes. Reprinted by permission of Alfred A. Knopf, a division of Random House, Inc. All rights reserved.

"Song of the Builders" by Jessie Wilmore Murton from *Celebrate America in Poetry and Art* edited by Nora Panzer. Copyright © by Jessie Wilmore Murton. Published by Hyperion Books for Children, an imprint of Disney Children's Book Group, LLC. All rights reserved.

"Our City" from *Angels Ride Bikes and Other Fall Poems* by Francisco X. Alarcón. Copyright © 1999 by Francisco X. Alarcón. Reprinted by permission of Children's Book Press, an imprint of Lee & Low Books Inc.

From *The Wonderful Wizard of Oz* by L. Frank Baum.

From *Here Is New York* by E. B. White. Copyright © 1949, 1976 by E. B. White. Reprinted by permission of ICM on behalf of the Estate of E. B. White.

From *Reading Lolita in Tehran: A Memoir in Books* by Azar Nafisi. Copyright © 2003 by Azar Nafisi. Reprinted by permission of Random House, Inc. All rights reserved.

UNIT 6 | History Lost and Found

From "New Discoveries in Ancient Egypt" by Bryan Brown from *Junior Scholastic* magazine, September 6, 2004. Copyright © 2004 by Bryan Brown. Reprinted by permission of Scholastic Inc. All rights reserved.

From *Curse of the Pharaohs: My Adventures With Mummies* by Zahi Hawass. Copyright © 2004 by Zahi Hawass. Reprinted by permission of National Geographic Society.

Adapted from *Cities of the Dead: Finding Lost Civilizations* (24/7: Science Behind the Scenes) by Denise Rinaldo. Copyright © 2007 by Scholastic Inc. Reprinted by permission of Scholastic Inc.

UNIT 7 | The Big Give

"Tale of a Wealthy Man" from *Folktales from Africa* retold by Dianne Stewart. Copyright © 2006 by Dianne Stewart. Reprinted by permission of Random House Struik.

"If I Can Stop One Heart from Breaking" by Emily Dickinson.

From *Ryan and Jimmy and the Well in Africa That Brought Them Together* by Herb Shoveller. Text copyright © 2006 by Herb Shoveller. Reprinted by permission of Kids Can Press, Ltd.

From *Marina Silva: Defending Rainforest Communities in Brazil* by Ziporah Hildebrandt. Copyright © 2001 by Ziporah Hildebrandt. Reprinted by permission of the Permissions Company, Inc. on behalf of The Feminist Press.